IMAGES
of America

INDEPENDENCE COUNTY
ARKANSAS

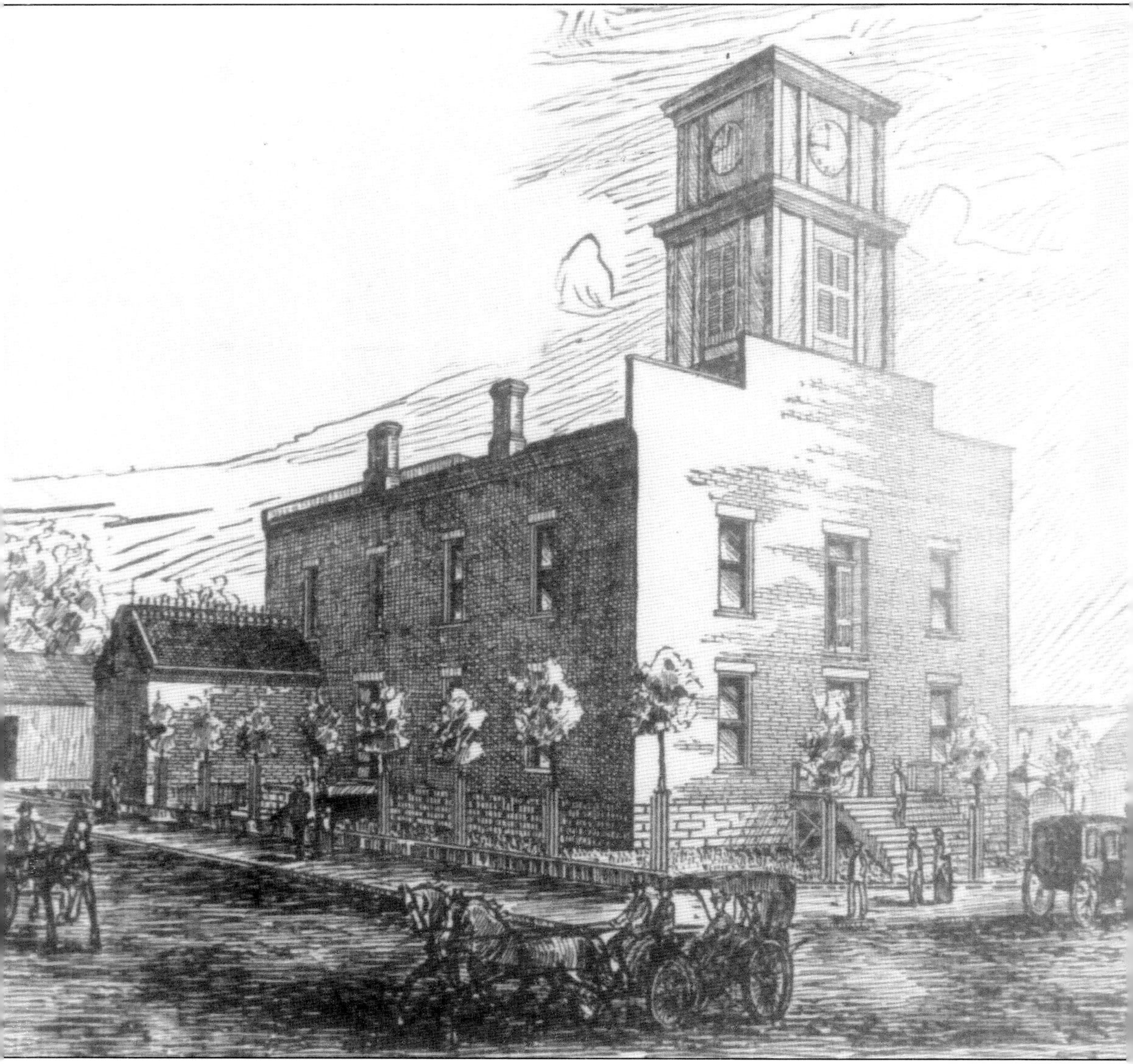

No photograph remains of the first Independence County courthouse, a small brick structure located on the original Public Square on lower Main Street, but this second one was constructed in 1859. It was built farther up Main Street on the site of the present courthouse. The projecting room on the side of the building at the rear was a vault. (Hempstead's *Pictorial History of Arkansas*)

IMAGES
of America

Independence County Arkansas

Brian K. Robertson and Nancy Britton

ARCADIA PUBLISHING

ISBN 978-0-7385-1884-8

Published by Arcadia Publishing
Charleston, South Carolina

Printed in the United States of America

Library of Congress Catalog Card Number: 2001090725

For all general information contact Arcadia Publishing at:
Telephone 843-853-2070
Fax 843-853-0044
E-mail sales@arcadiapublishing.com
For customer service and orders:
Toll-Free 1-888-313-2665

Visit us on the Internet at www.arcadiapublishing.com

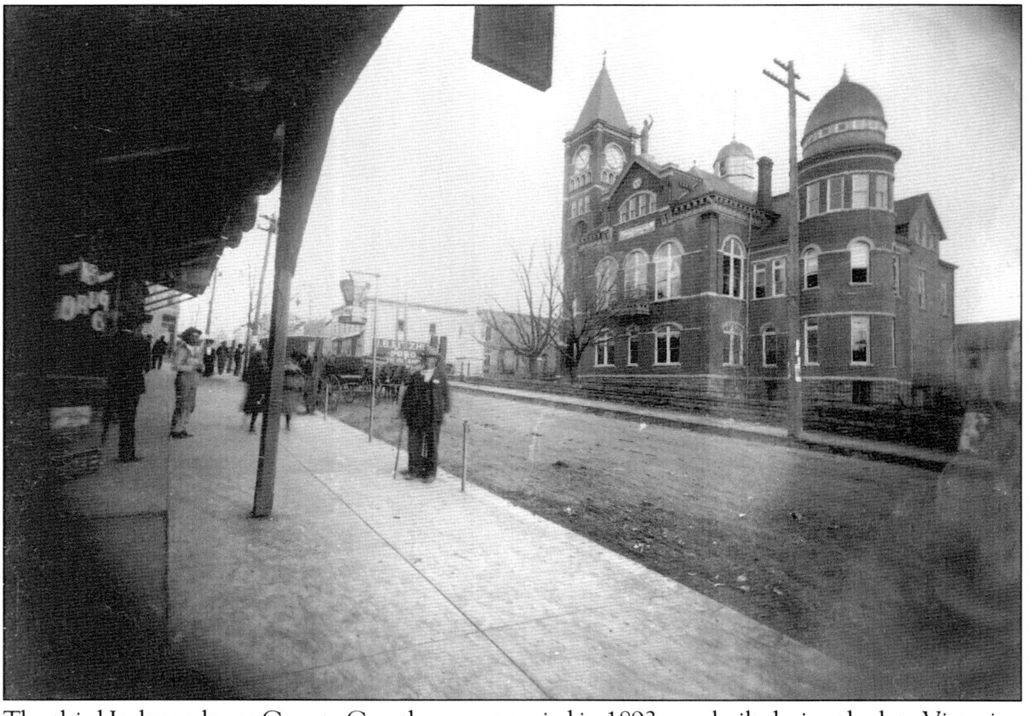

The third Independence County Courthouse, occupied in 1893, was built during the late Victorian era and boasted the ornamental towers, dormers, and cupolas of that style. (Wilson Powell)

Contents

ACKNOWLEDGMENTS

We would like to thank all of the individuals who have provided images for this book. Without their assistance this project would not have been possible. A special thanks goes to Wilson Powell, Robert D. Craig, Brooks Blevins, Gene Hyde, Twyla Gill Wright, Jo Blatti, Becky Wood, Sandra Cox, Kenny Gerhardt, Mary Crow Shields, and Bubba Burks for their extraordinary support.

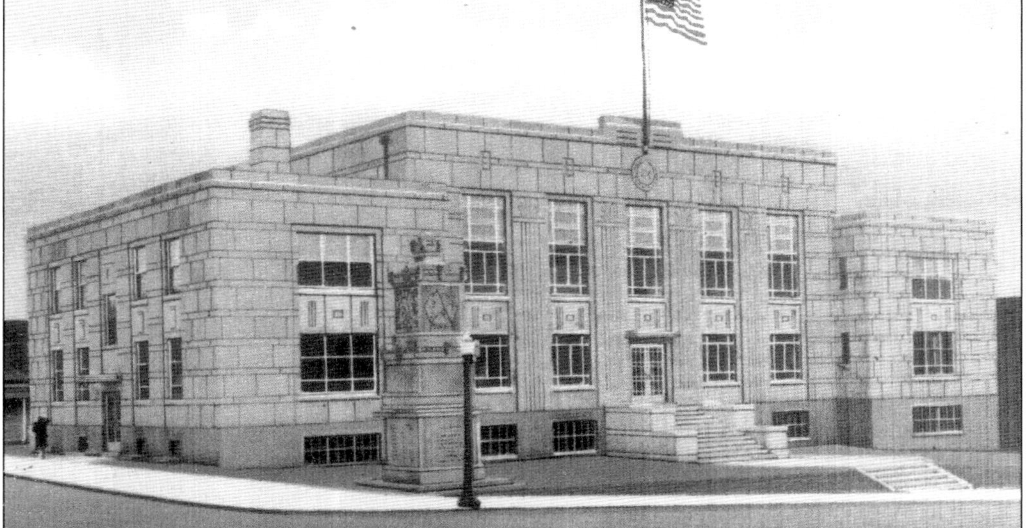

The third Independence County Courthouse was torn down in 1939 and replaced by the present Art Deco courthouse, a WPA building project. (Wilson Powell)

INTRODUCTION

Independence County, Arkansas, the only county in the United States to bear the name, was carved from Lawrence County in October 1820. It was the ninth county created in the new Arkansas Territory, set apart from Missouri the previous year. Over the next 50 years, the original county would be reduced in size as parts of its territory were carved away to be included in eleven new counties.

Permanent settlement of the county can be documented from the years 1810–1815. An early rendezvous for hunters and trappers was established at the mouth of Poke Bayou where it flowed into White River. A man named James Reed was operating a store there in 1812 and St. Louis merchant John C. Luttig opened another trading post in 1814. The town which grew up around these posts was first called Poke Bayou. Some early families in the county before 1820 were the Beans, Gills, Hardins, Laffertys, Magnesses, Millers, Moores, Musicks, Ruddells, and Wyatts. Henry Rowe Schoolcraft paddled a canoe down White River in 1819 and wrote in his journal that Poke Bayou was "a village of a dozen houses . . . pleasant and advantageous as a commercial and agricultural depot." Flatboats could be poled up the White as far as the town, and the prize farm land of the Greenbrier and Oil Trough Bottoms was being cleared and planted. Numerous rapid streams made milling possible, and there was still game in the woods and fish in the rivers. Poke Creek, or Poke Bayou, post office opened on November 7, 1820, but since the town was usually referred to as Batesville after 1821, the name of the post office was officially changed in 1824. The name honored Judge James Woodson Bates, first territorial delegate to Congress. Batesville is the oldest post office in Arkansas with continuous service. The earliest population count for Independence County is the sheriff's taxlist of 1824. It enumerated 388 male heads of households. The federal census of 1830 indicated a total population, excluding slaves and Indians, of 2,031.

The steamer *Waverly* docked at Batesville in January 1831, opening a new era of commerce and expansion. For the next fifty years, steamboats provided transportation for people, for farm products, merchandise, and other freight up and down the White River, thence up and down the Mississippi from St. Louis to New Orleans.

The first official military organization from Independence County was a company of Arkansas Mounted Rangers under the command of Captain Jesse Bean. The company was recruited for one year in 1832 and was sent to Fort Gibson on the Arkansas River above Fort Smith to patrol the Indian frontier. This troop was immortalized by Washington Irving in his book *A Tour of the Prairies*, published in 1835. Other Batesville men took part in the Mexican War a decade later.

Schools were being founded in Batesville by the 1830s. Aaron Lyon opened an academy for boys in 1834, and Reverend and Mrs. H.W. Hunt opened a "Seminary for the Instruction of Young Ladies" in 1839. Free public schools were not established in the region until after the Civil War.

Religion came early to Independence County. Methodist, Baptist, and Cumberland Presbyterian preachers on horseback brought preaching to scattered settlements, holding services in brush arbors, homes, or outdoors. Reverend Eli Lindsey, a Methodist, is known to have preached in and around Batesville as early as 1816. The first Arkansas Conference of the Methodist Episcopal Church was hosted by the Batesville Methodist Society in 1836; Baptist and Presbyterian churches followed in the 1840s. Methodists and Presbyterians also contributed a religious flavor to higher education in the town. In 1849 the Methodists established Soulesbury Institute, which did not survive the Civil War. The Presbyterians founded Arkansas College in 1872, still functioning today as Lyon College. Other secular academies were established with varying success at Jamestown, Sulphur Rock, Bethesda, and Pleasant Plains during the 19th century.

When secession came, Arkansas joined the Confederacy, and 23 companies were organized for the South in Independence County. Batesville was occupied by Federal troops in May 1862 and again in December 1863. No major action took place in the county except for skirmishes at Waugh's Farm in Washington Township and at Saffolds' near Oil Trough. There are, of course, recorded accounts of bushwhacking and guerrilla warfare both during and after the war.

County residents with Union sentiments generally laid low during the early enthusiasm for the Confederacy. During General Samuel Curtis's occupation in 1862, however, some 365 local men left with his forces. In 1864, Batesville lawyer and future governor Elisha Baxter, a former slave owner, recruited a company of 450 men for the Union. A number of local freedmen also joined the United States Army.

The railroad came to Independence County in 1883, stimulating the economy much as the steamboats had done some 50 years earlier. One important industry that resulted was the Handford Cedar Yard, where thousands of cedar logs were converted into railroad ties and telephone poles. The railroad also contributed to development of manganese mining in the Cushman area. The growth of business and industry brought payrolls and an increased need for banks.

By 1910, the population of Independence County was 24,776, including 1,264 African Americans. The latter number had begun a long, slow decline, as blacks moved north and west to find better jobs and opportunities after the turn of the century. Overall population showed a loss by 1920, when only 23,976 residents were enumerated.

Like most counties across the South, Independence County has suffered from tornadoes, flooding, fires, and the Great Depression of the 1930s. In spite of tough times, the county reached a peak population in 1940, recording 26,643 residents. Still, many left the county during World War II, moving to war industry jobs in California, Washington State, and Wichita, Kansas. Cotton declined as a staple crop, to be replaced eventually by soybeans and rice.

Today, in 2001, Batesville enjoys financial stability as a center of light industry such as poultry processing, banking, and health care for the whole county.

One

PEOPLE

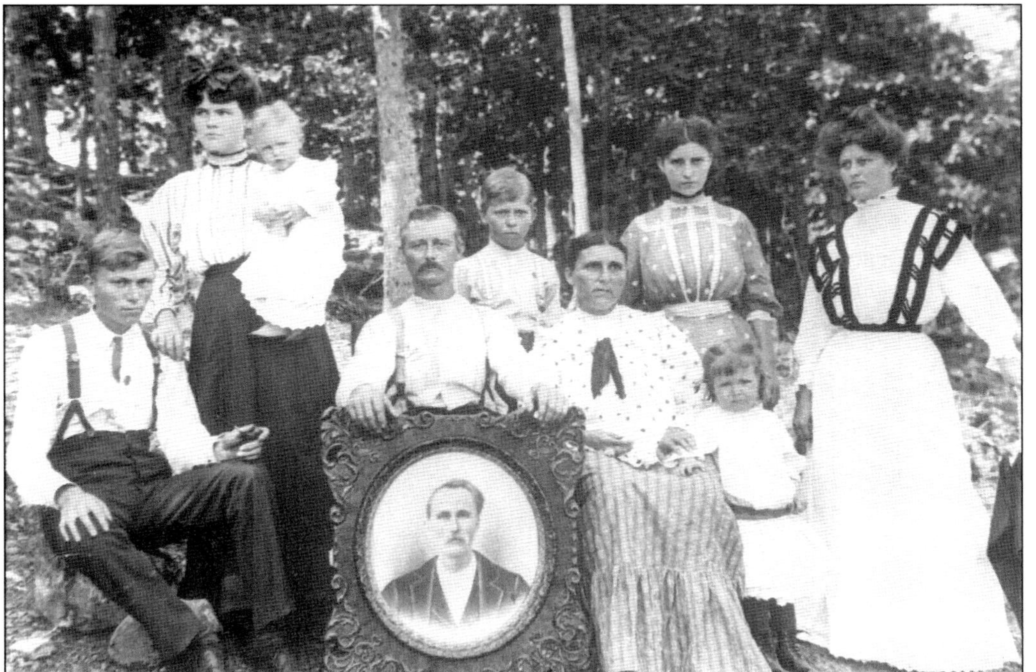

The Bufford family posed for this picture on Jamestown Mountain about 1906. Father Benjamin Franklin Bufford is holding a large framed photograph of his father, William Christopher Allison Bufford. Others in the family are, from left to right, as follows: Walter Bufford, his wife Henrietta Manuel Bufford holding baby Mary Katherine Bufford (Plaster), Adolph Lonnie Osborn Bufford, mother May Malinda Uhles Bufford, her sister Lydia Uhles Pulley, little girl Bessie Bufford (Sexton), and Mayna Malinda Bufford (Heston). The Uhles sisters were granddaughters of Daniel James, early settler of Jamestown. (Independence County Historical Society)

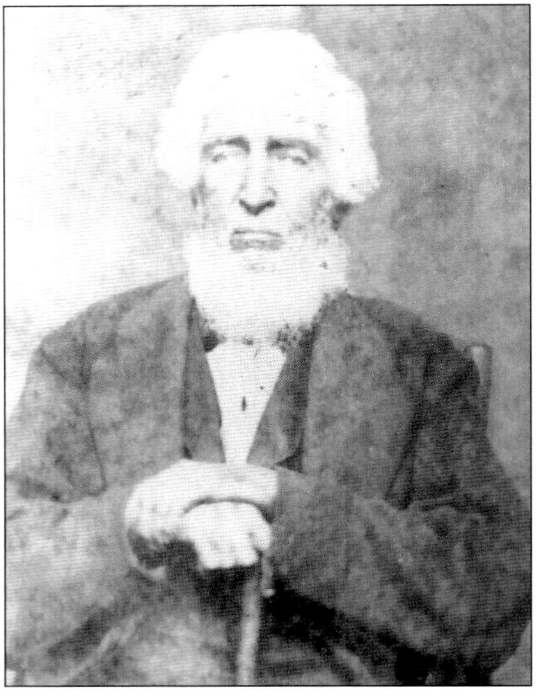

Robert "Bobby" Bates (1793–c. 1875) was an Irishman who arrived in Batesville in the early 1820s. He has been described as a tailor, hotel or innkeeper, farmer, and real estate developer. Bates Tavern, which stood on lower Main Street, was a leading hostelry and meeting place in early Batesville history. (Nancy Britton)

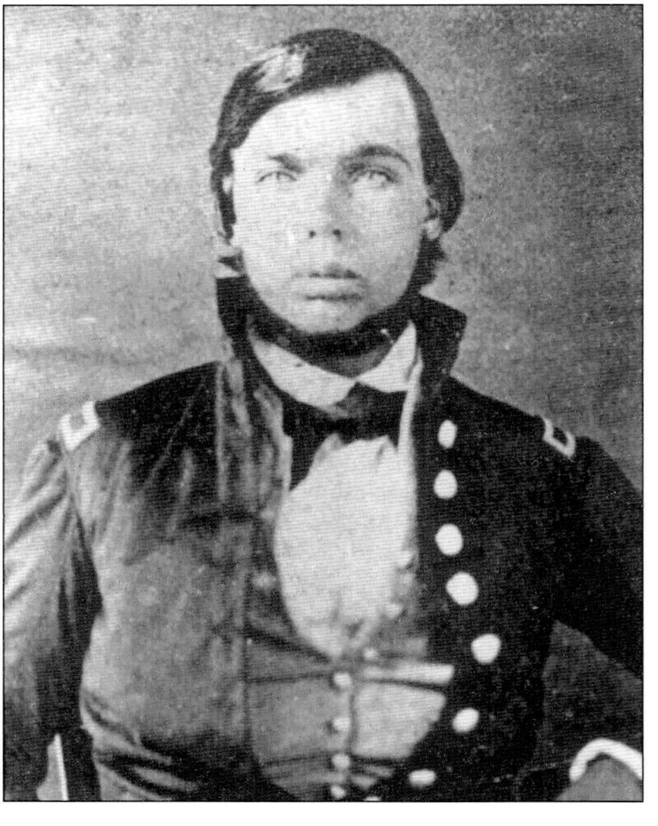

Descendants claim this picture of Lloyd Magruder (1825–1863) in his Mexican War uniform may have been taken in Batesville. He came here from Virginia in 1845 and joined the Arkansas Volunteer Cavalry when war with Mexico broke out the following year. After being wounded in the Battle of Buena Vista in February 1847, he enlisted in the Regular Army and returned to Batesville on recruitment duty. Soon, however, he left for California with the "Golden Army" of 49ers. He was robbed and murdered near Virginia City, Montana (then part of Idaho Territory) in 1863. (Nancy Britton)

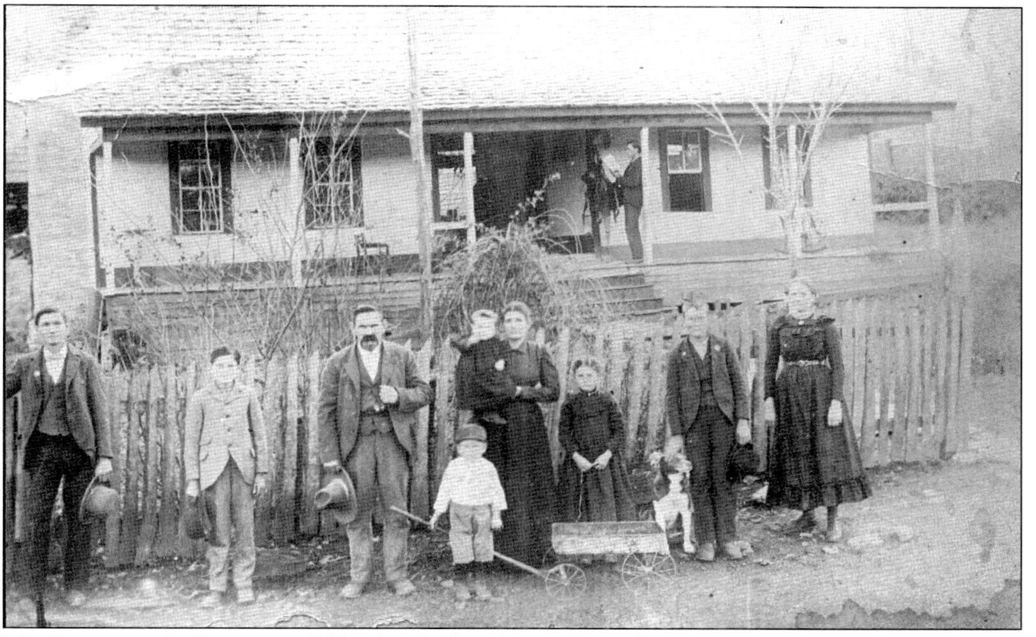

Mr. Benjamin Ball, a son of Elbridge Ball and grandson of Benjamin F. Ball, is pictured here with his family in front of his home in the Hickory Valley community. They are, left to right, as follows: J. Wesley Ball, Phenander Ball, father Benjamin Ball (born *c.* 1859), little boy in white shirt with wagon is William N. "Nels" Ball, mother Talitha Mariah Hardin Ball (holding baby Frank Ball), Julie Ball, Commodore Ball, and Letha Ball. On the porch is Walter Burr, a cousin. (Independence County Historical Society)

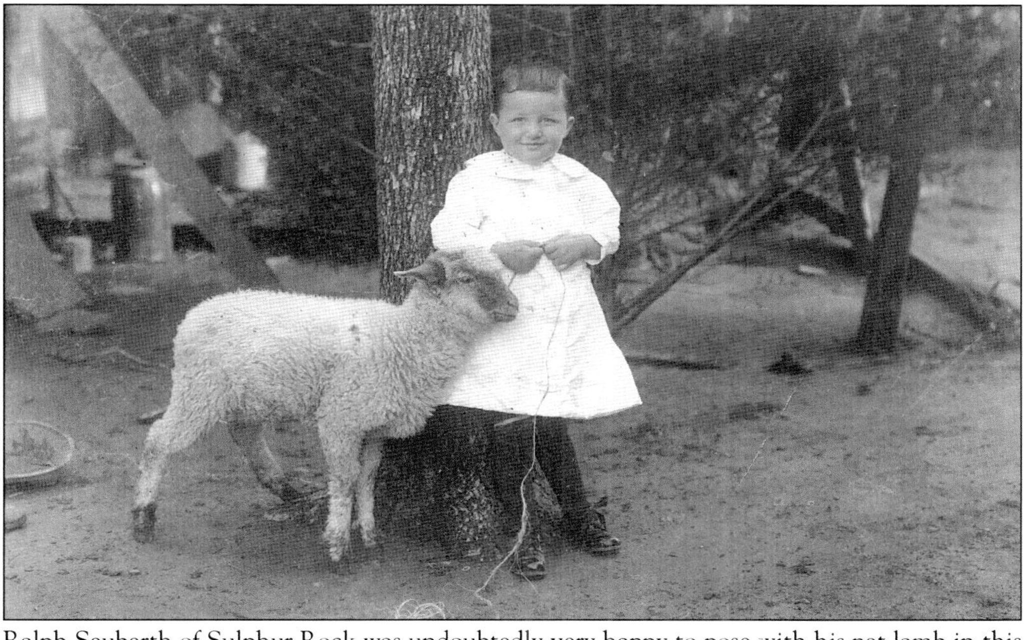

Ralph Seuberth of Sulphur Rock was undoubtedly very happy to pose with his pet lamb in this vintage photograph. (Wilson Powell)

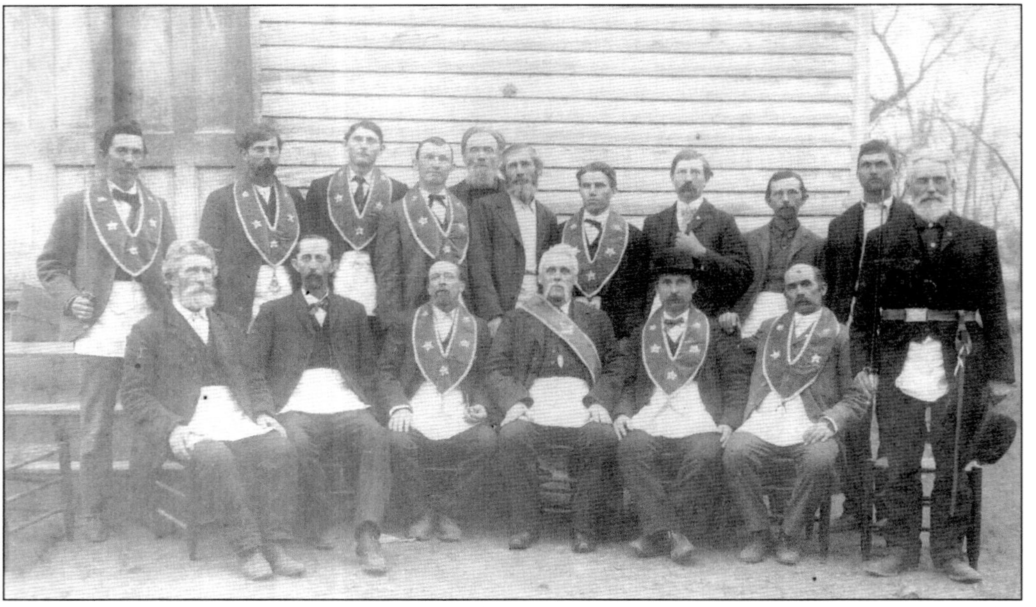

Members of the Bayou Dota Lodge No. 126, F.&A.M. posed for this picture on March 5, 1904. The members pictured, from left to right, are as follows: (seated) Jim Best, Will Ward, Tom Herrington, Bill Kent, Dr. Long, and P.L. Lane; (standing) E.L. Jernigan, Jim Long, Frank Conner, J.C. McGill, Bob Williamson, Tom Best, Ira Pickens, Bob Long, A.E. Fallis, Cal Williamson, and Jim Huddleston. (Independence County Historical Society)

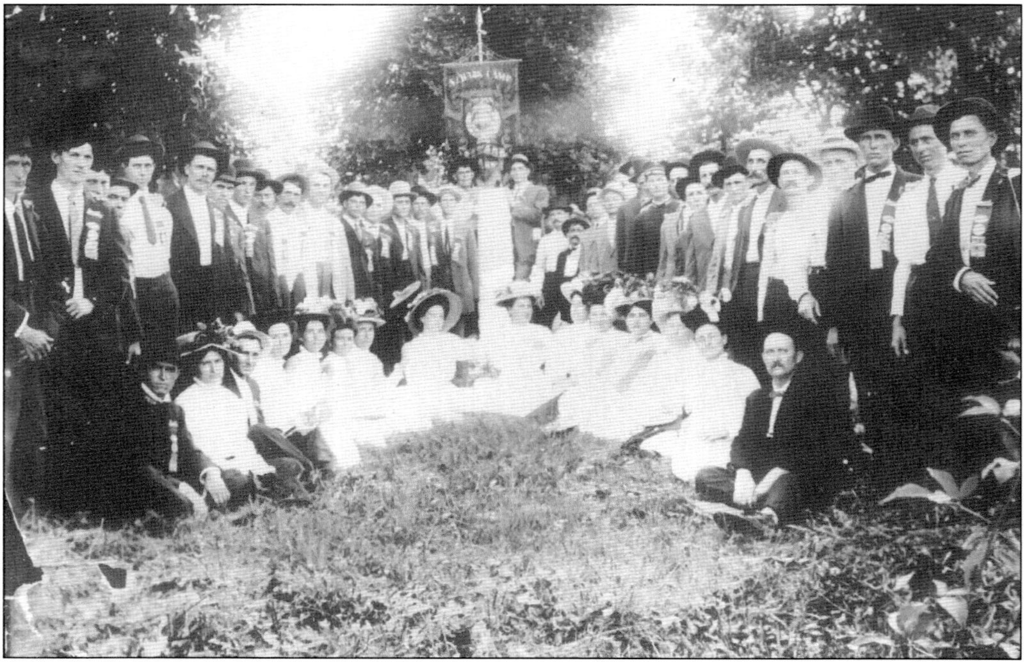

The Newark Camp of the Woodmen of the World gathered for this photo about 1902. (Marietta Postier)

Thomas Jefferson James of Cedar Grove joined the Union Army in 1862. He died the following year as a Confederate prisoner of war. (Independence County Historical Society)

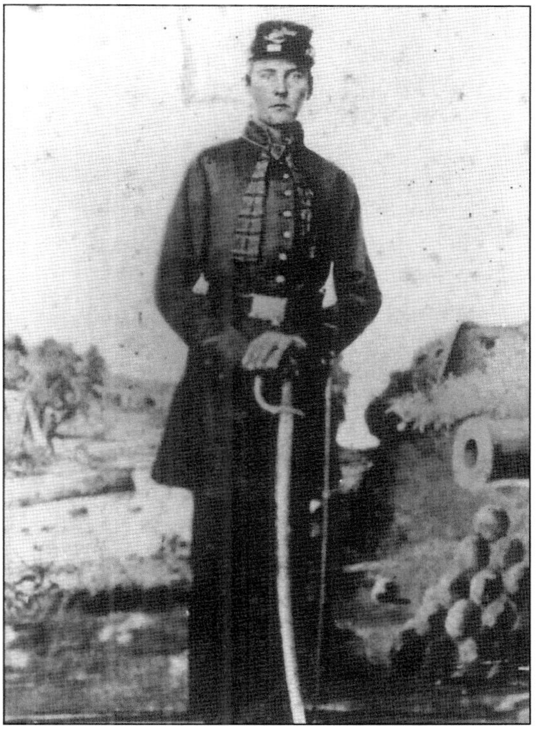

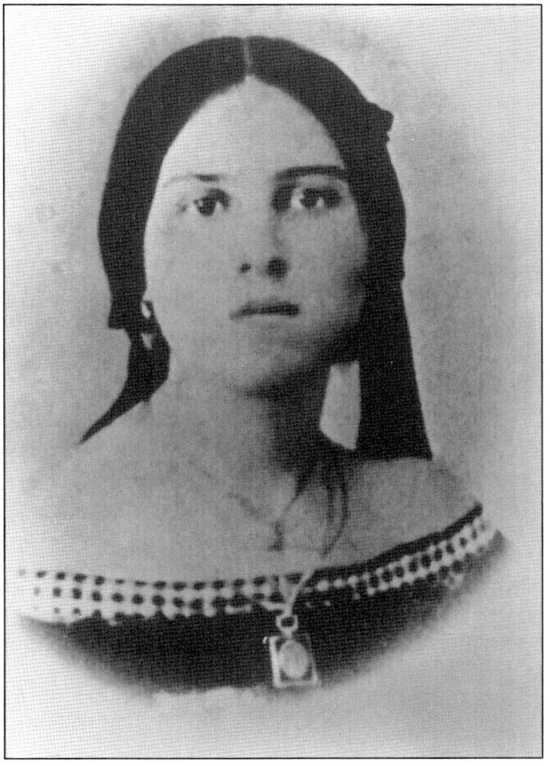

Nannie Wilson Wood was one of Batesville's "Confederate Belles." She was the stepdaughter of William Byers and was residing at the magnificent Catalpa Hall north of Batesville during the war. Confederate troops under General Jo Shelby named their nearby Camp Nannie Wilson in her honor in 1863; shortly thereafter, in a romantic wartime wedding, she was married to Captain Carroll Wood of Shelby's staff. (Independence County Historical Society)

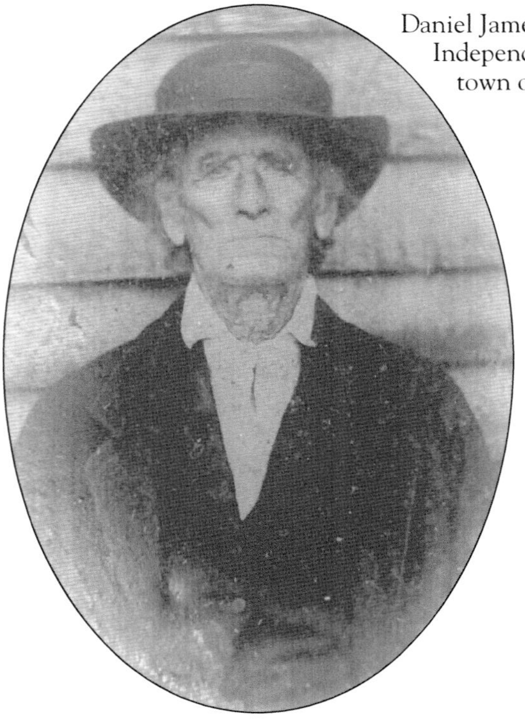

Daniel James was an early settler of southern Independence County and the man for whom the town of Jamestown was named. (Nancy Britton)

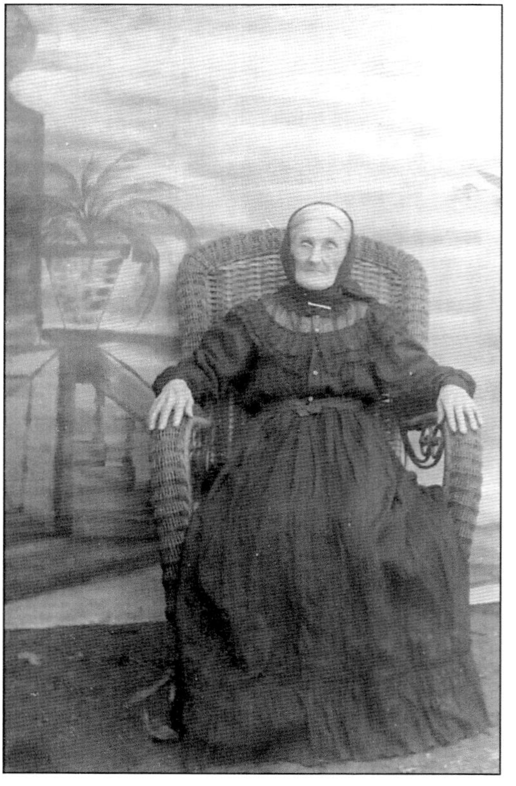

Susan Sewell Trotter of Oil Trough bore witness to many things in her lifetime, and most likely told a good story to any eager listener. (Sandra Cox)

"Two Little Confederates" was hand-written under this picture of James Conway Hail (1882–1964) and Fairfax Stuart Hail (1884–1911), sons of Stevadson A. Hail of Batesville, a Confederate veteran. (Independence County Historical Society)

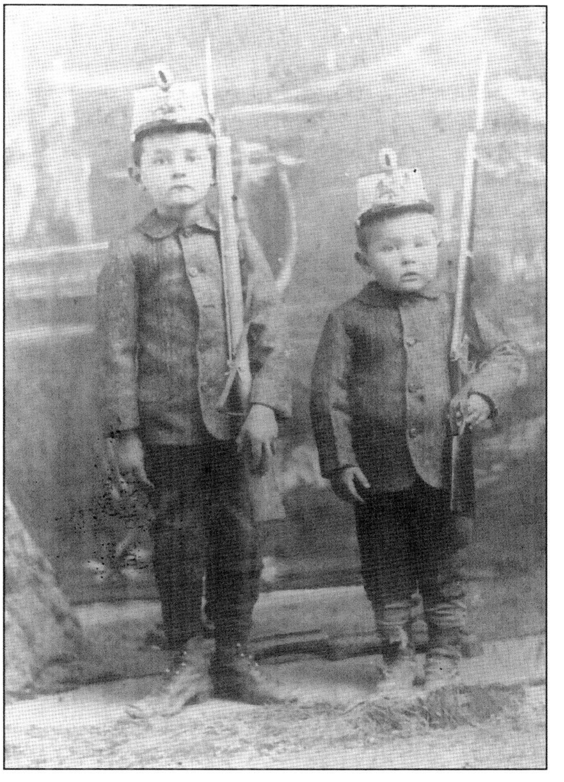

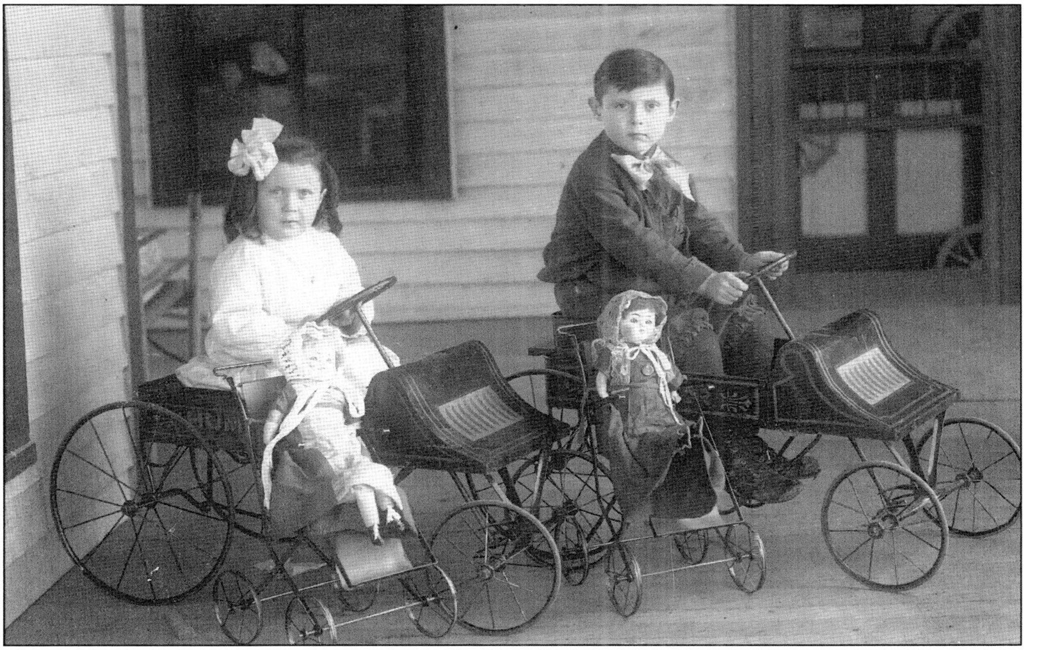

The Jemmerson children of Sulphur Rock are showing off their new toys in this *c.* 1912 image. (Wilson Powell)

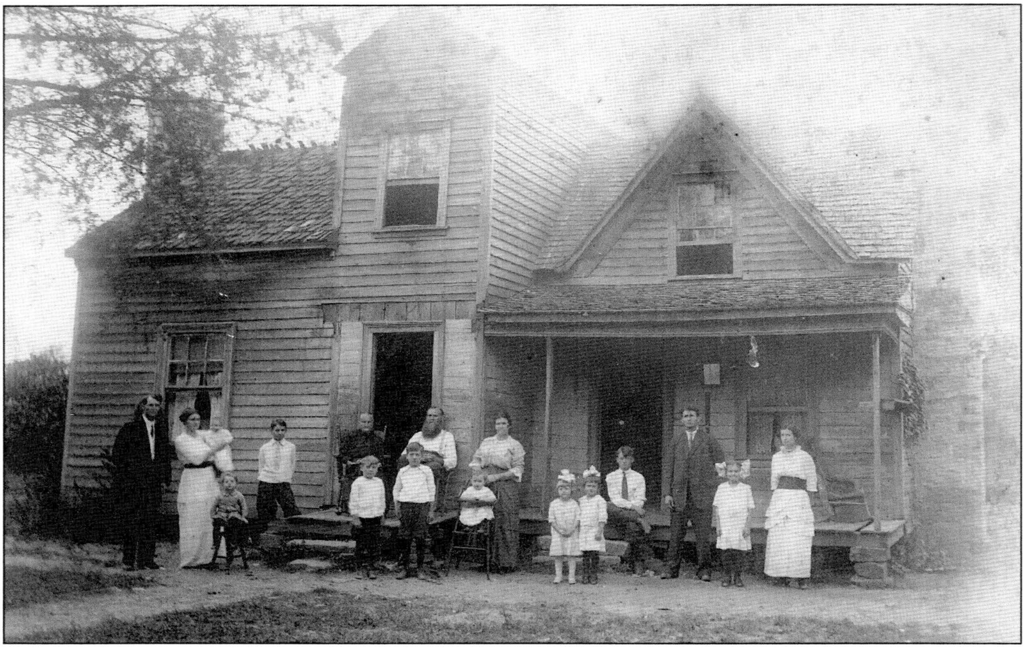

Family members gathered at the Hutchinson Mountain home of Bill Graddy for this *c.* 1890 photo. (Sandra Cox)

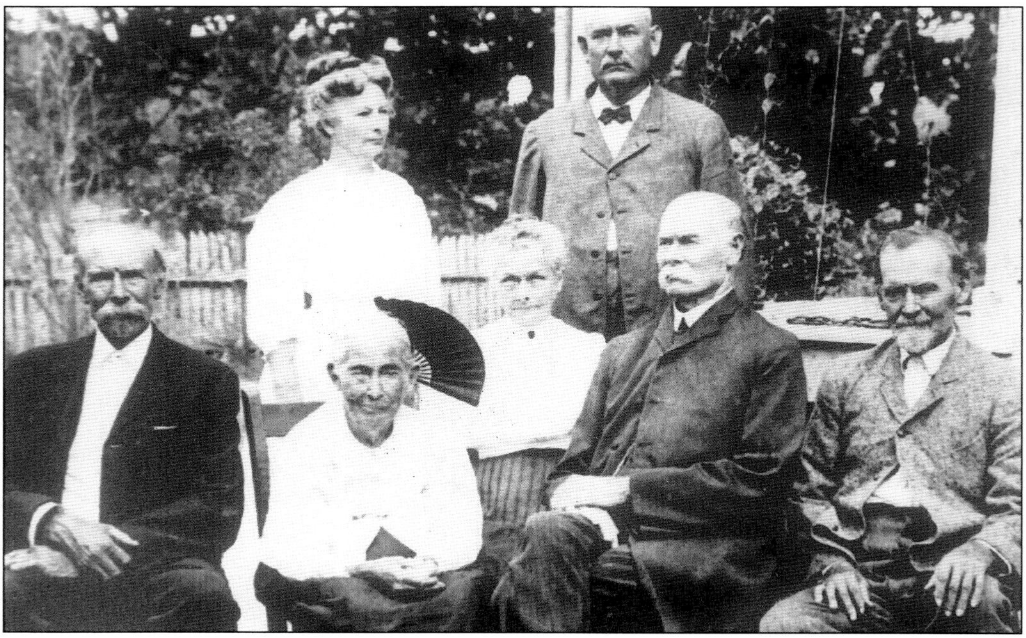

Margaret Ann Hardin (Mrs. John L.) celebrated her 90th birthday in August 1907 with six of her eight children. The celebrants, from left to right, are as follows: (seated) James Levi Craig, Margaret Ann Hardin Craig, Elizabeth Craig Tucker, County Judge Andrew J. Craig, and Joseph Hardin Craig; (standing) Laura Craig Dunaway and Mark R. Craig. Mrs. Craig's grandfather had fought in the Revolutionary War. (Independence County Historical Society)

William Read Miller was the first native-born governor of Arkansas, serving from 1877 to 1881. His Miller family had been among the earliest settlers of Independence County. Two other Independence County men have served as governor—Thomas S. Drew (1844–49), and Elisha Baxter (1873–74). (Independence County Historical Society)

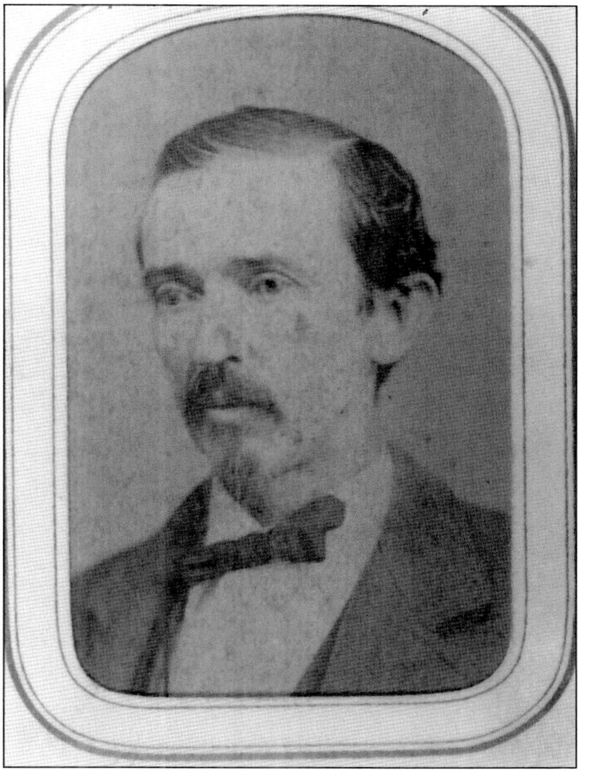

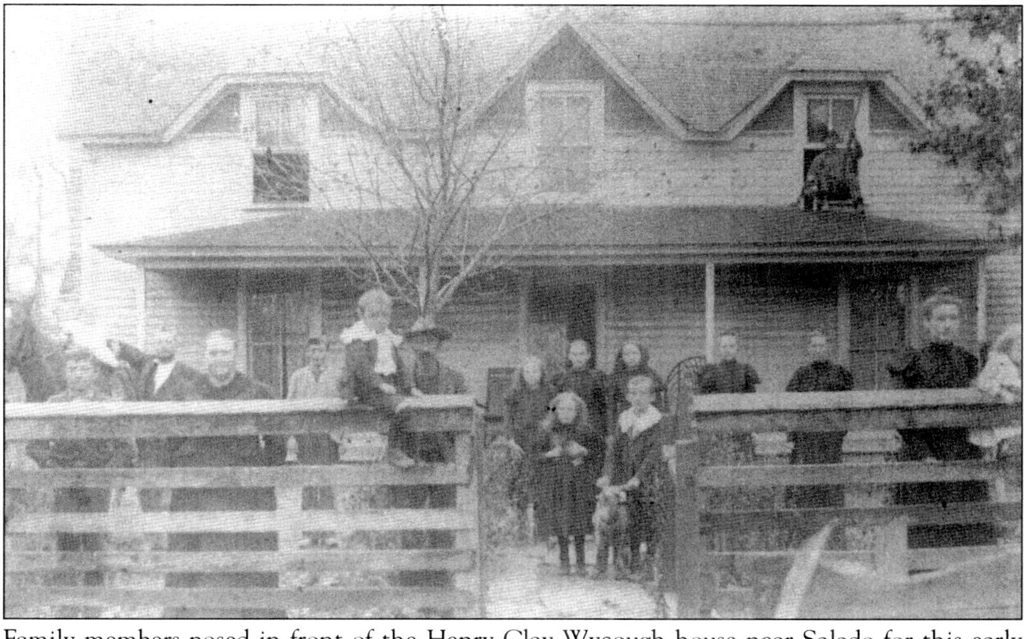

Family members posed in front of the Henry Clay Wycough house near Salado for this early photograph. (Independence County Historical Society)

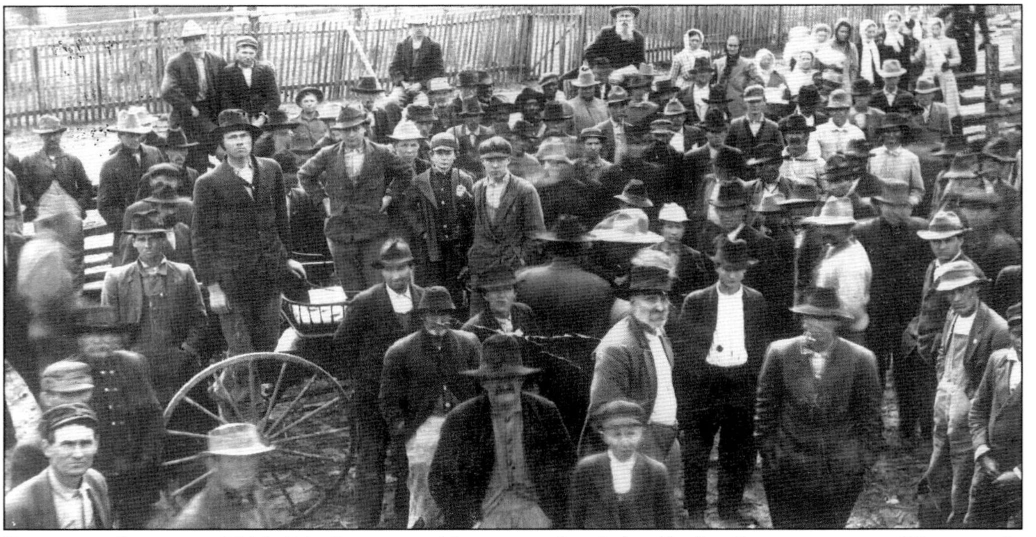

Sometime between 1915–17, the venerable patriarch of the Bethesda community, Thomas A. McSpadden, sold his belongings and went to live with one of his children. Thomas (1837–1924) is the white-bearded man standing top, center, by the gate. McSpadden had 21 children and over 100 grandchildren. One story relates that he was riding through the community on horseback one day and spotted a little girl playing by the road. "Which one of my grandchildren are you?" he asked. She replied that she wasn't his grandchild, but some years later she grew up and married one of his grandsons! It was also told that McSpadden had so many children living in the area that he could "halloo" from a field in the bottomland and ask that something be brought down to him from his house, and a chain of McSpaddens could relay the message for miles. (Lynn McSpadden)

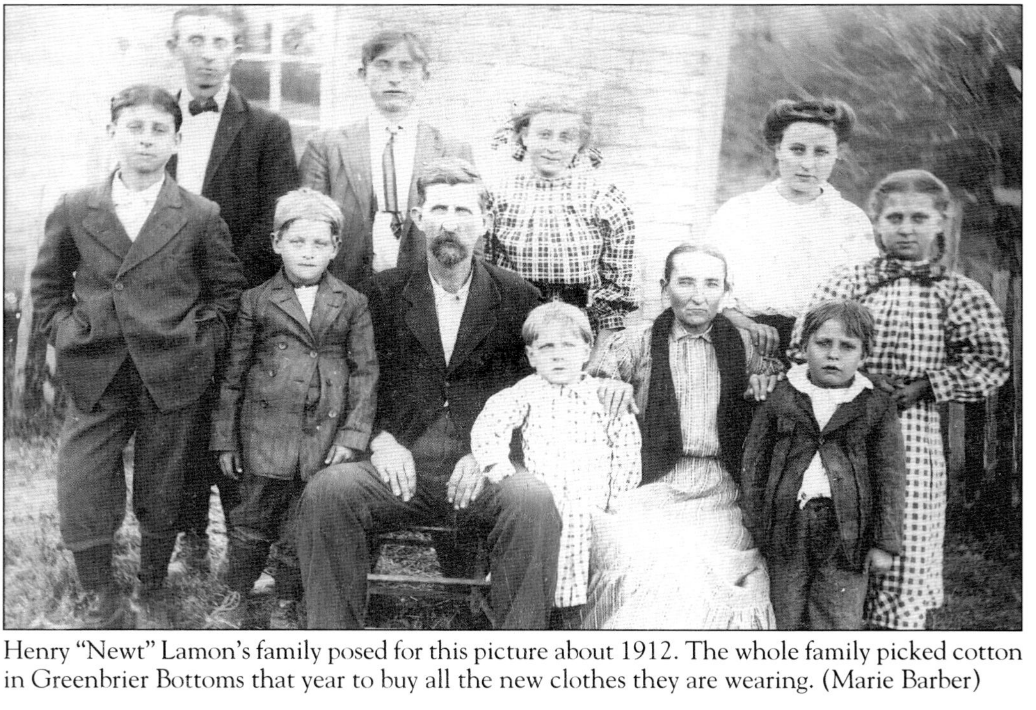

Henry "Newt" Lamon's family posed for this picture about 1912. The whole family picked cotton in Greenbrier Bottoms that year to buy all the new clothes they are wearing. (Marie Barber)

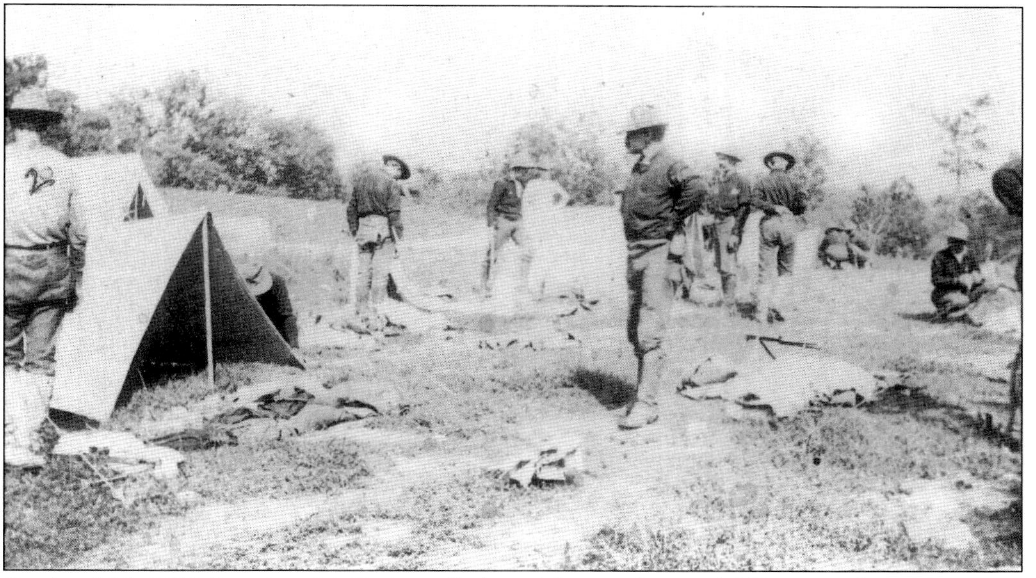

On April 25, 1898, President McKinley called on Arkansas for two 1,000 men infantry regiments to quell Spanish intervention in Cuba. In May the Second Arkansas Infantry, U.S. Volunteers, was mustered into service. Co. B of the unit was known as the V.Y. Cook Rifles and was composed of a number of local men. Members of Co. B are engaged in outpost duty in this photo taken at Camp Thomas, Chickamauga, Georgia. (Regional Studies Center, Lyon College)

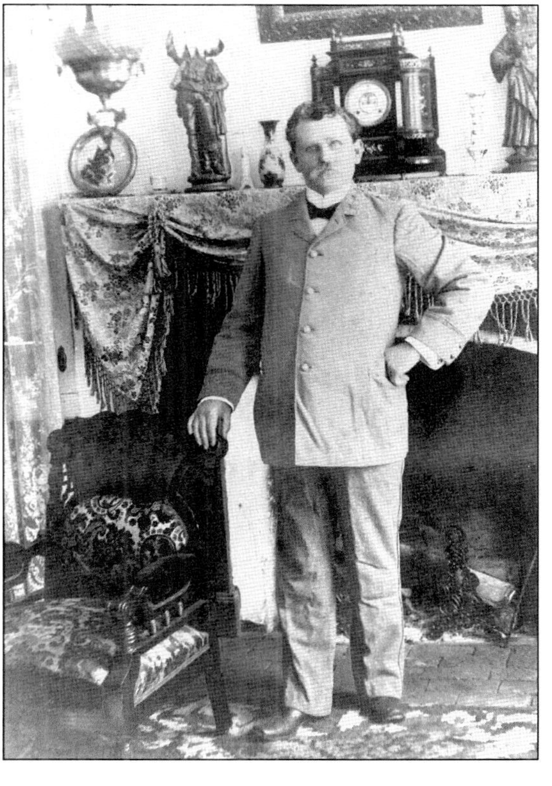

Col. V.Y. Cook of Independence County was the commander of the Second Arkansas Infantry Regiment. He had fought for the Confederacy during the Civil War but was now eager to serve his country against the Spanish. In 1897, Cook had been appointed brigadier general in the Arkansas Militia. When the Second Arkansas Volunteer Infantry was mustered into federal service he was commissioned as a colonel and given command. After the war Cook moved from Elmo, east of Oil Trough, to Batesville and lived there until his death in 1922. He was actively involved with the United Confederate Veterans organization and also served a term as president of the Arkansas Historical Association. (Regional Studies Center, Lyon College)

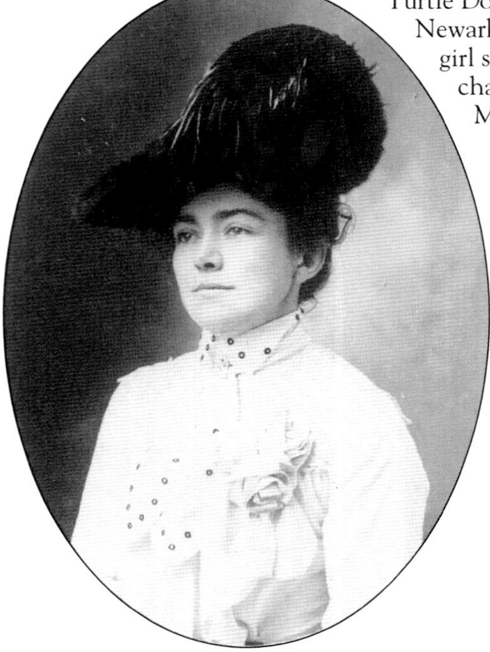

Turtle Dove Tomlinson Edwards was the daughter of Newark town founder John N. Tomlinson. As a young girl she helped her father by carrying the surveyor's chain as the new town was laid out. (William Perry Magness)

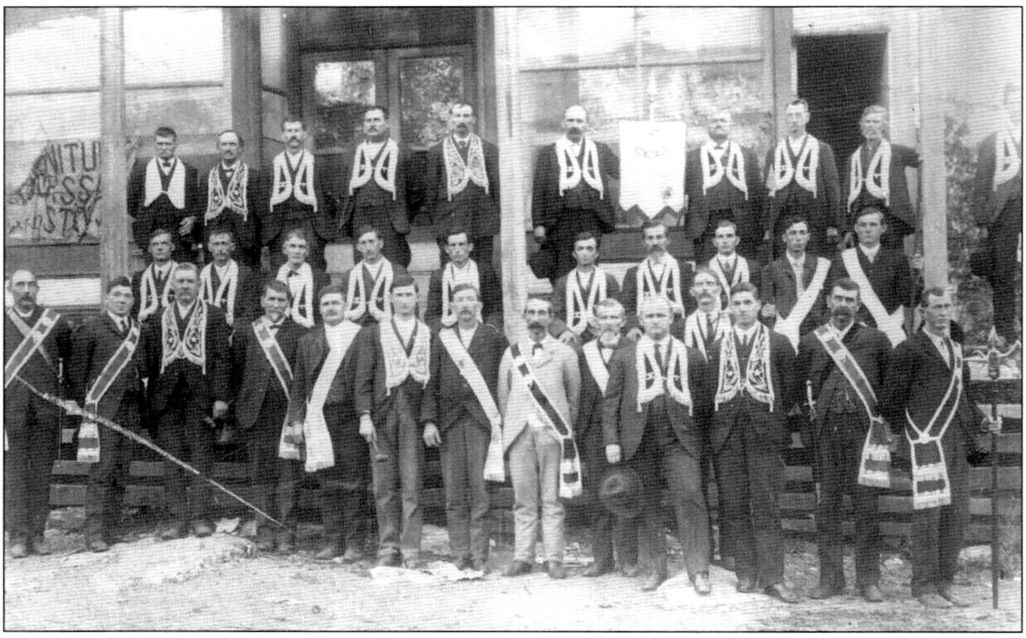

This group of men is standing in front of the Columbus Long building in Jamestown. The following groups used the second story of the building for meetings: Masons, Odd Fellows, Woodmen of the World, Odd-Man's Circle, and the Yeoman's Insurance Organization. Judging by the variety of regalia worn here, these men seem to be representatives from all of these groups. The building once housed a barber shop on the ground floor, was used for a time as a movie theater, and during World War I for Red Cross work. It burned in the Jamestown fire of 1922. (Bubba Burks)

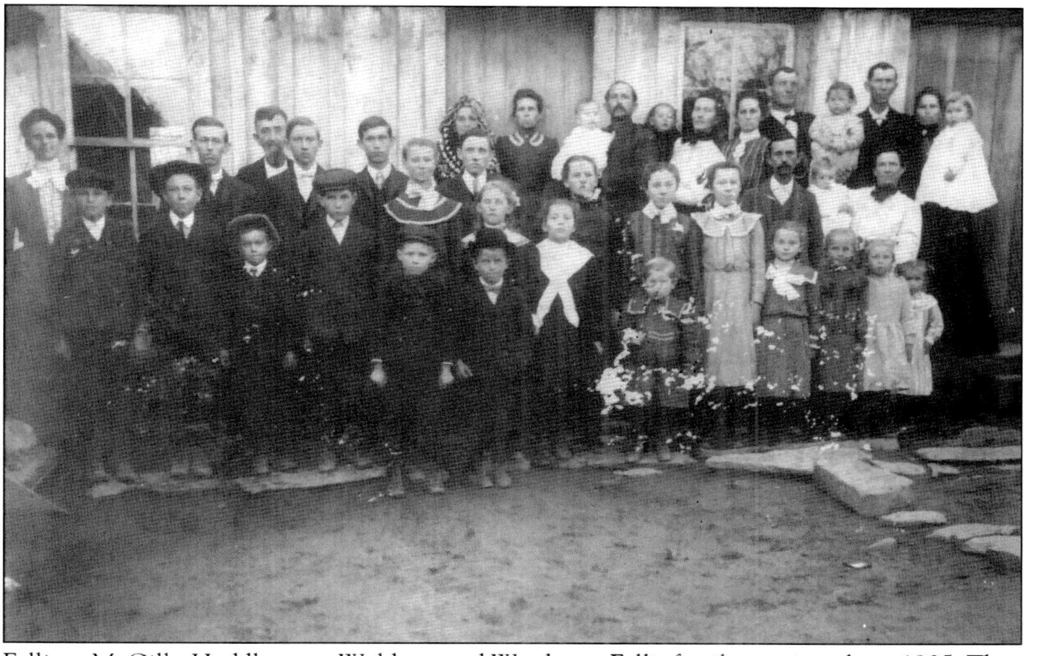

Fallises, McGills, Huddlestons, Waldens, and Wards at a Fallis family reunion about 1905. They are standing in front of the Fallis homeplace near Charlotte. (Nancy Britton)

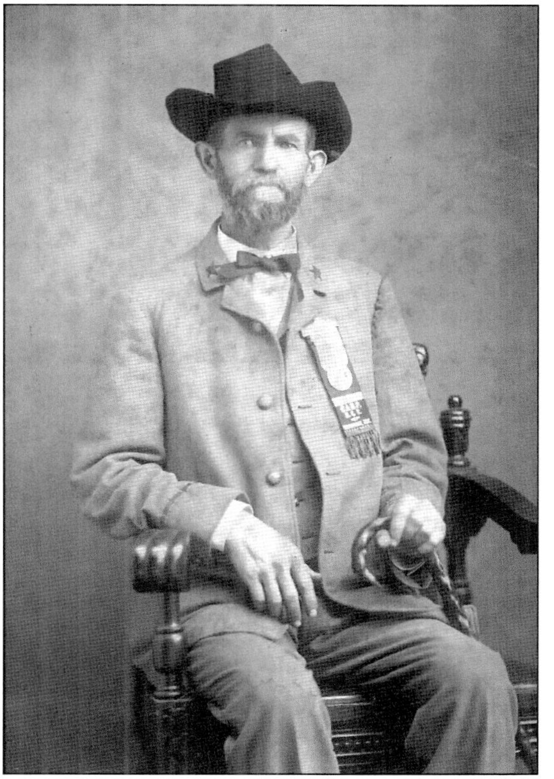

S.A. Hail was a native of Tennessee and came to Arkansas with his parents at age five. Hail served in the Confederate Army and after the war came to Batesville and entered the business profession. He founded S.A. Hail & Company in 1879. The company operated as a bookstore, but also sold a variety of light housewares. Hail later served as county judge. He was also a leader in Confederate Veterans activities and is pictured here in his United Confederate Veterans uniform. (Regional Studies Center, Lyon College)

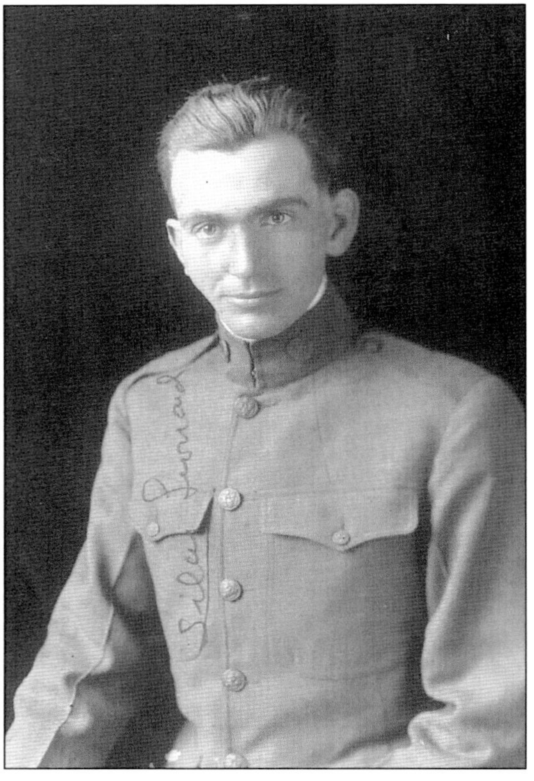

Silas Leonard of Bethesda heeded his country's call when the United States entered World War I in 1917. (Brian Robertson)

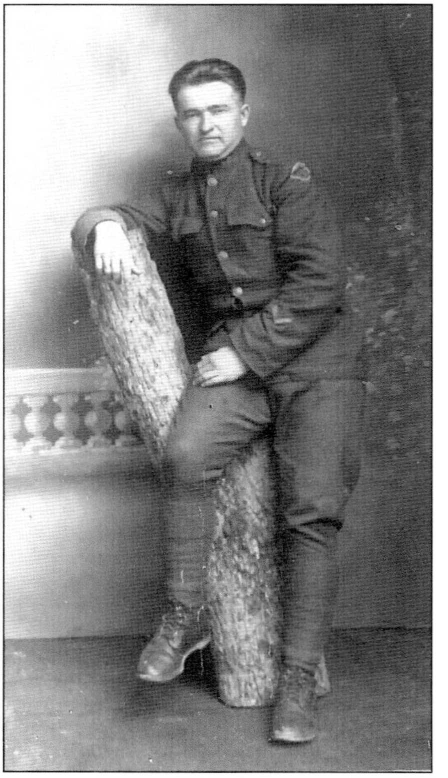

Private D.L. Barber of Hutchinson Mountain sent this photo of himself home to his family while he was stationed in France during World War I. (Marie Barber)

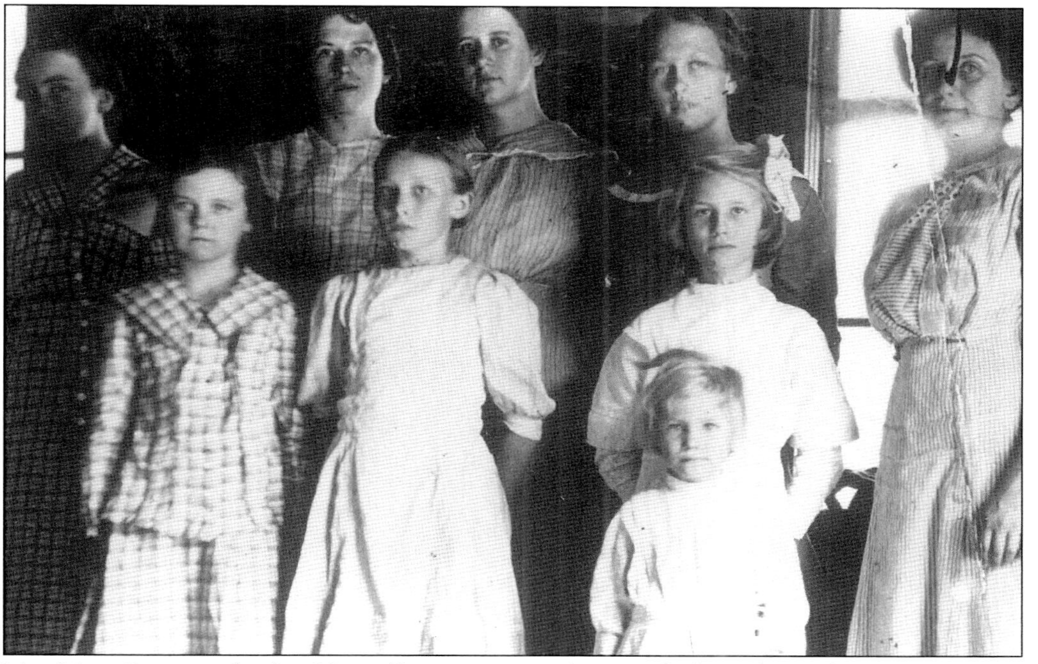

Miss Mary Case was the first Home Demonstration Agent in Independence County, serving in 1913–1914. She is pictured here with some members of a local unit. Miss Case later married Dr. M.S. Craig. (Regional Studies Center, Lyon College)

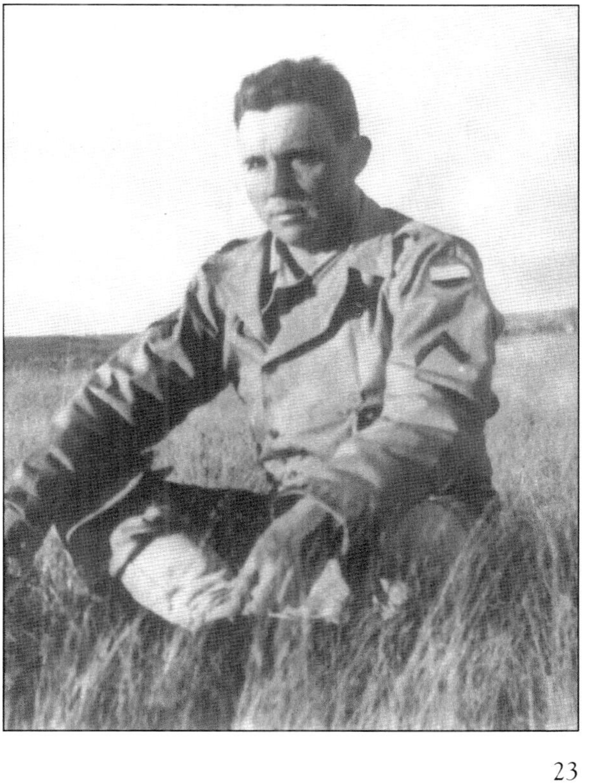

The dean of Independence County historians, Wilson Powell, is pictured here at Camp Wolters, Texas. He later went on to serve in the Pacific Theater during World War II. From his office at the *Batesville Guard*, Powell has helped literally thousands of people with research in local history and genealogy for nearly 50 years. (Wilson Powell)

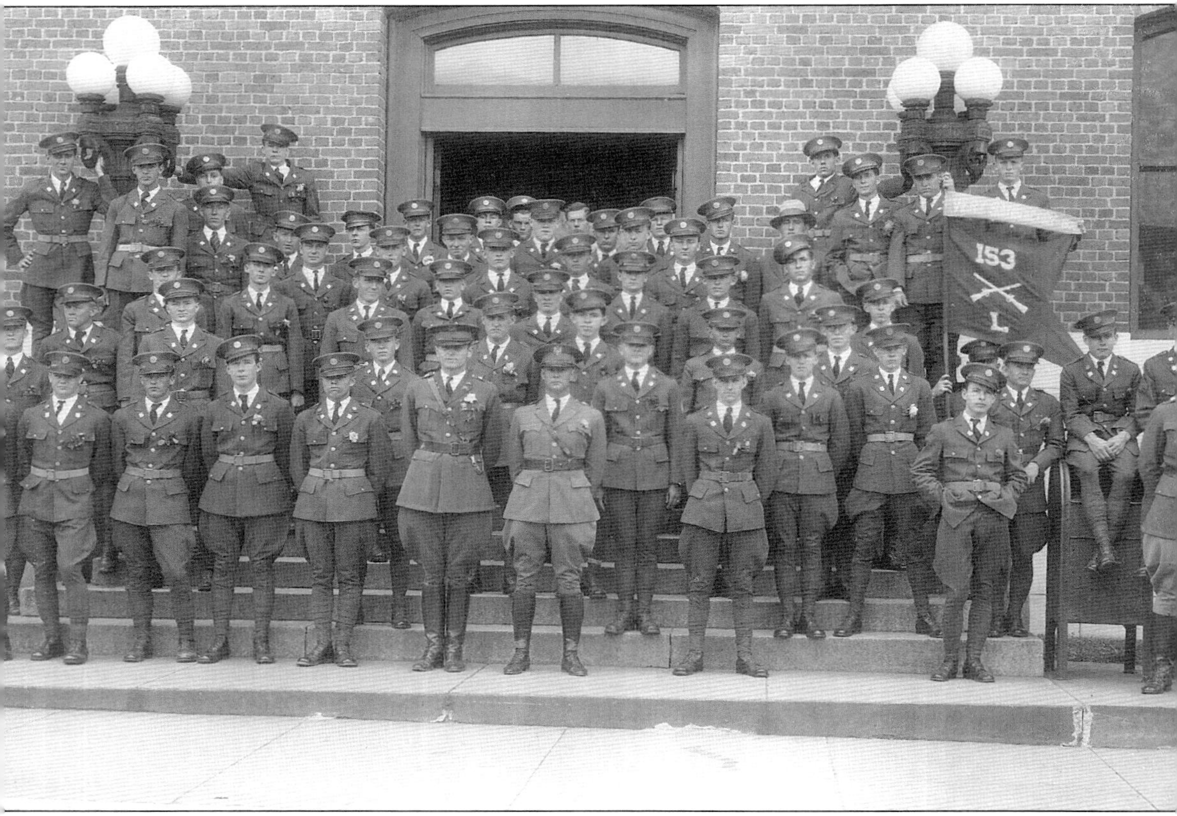

Members of National Guard unit, Company L, 3rd Battalion, 153rd Infantry, posed on the post office steps in Batesville for this image taken May 10, 1932. From left to right are as follows: (front row) unidentified, George C. Roberson, James P. Evans, Oscar N. Brooks, Robert E. Browning, Capt. Lucien Abraham, 1st Lt. Edward C. Linebarger, Rollin Barnett, Walter C. Ivy, and 2nd Lt. George M. Evans; (second row) unidentified, John W. Meachum, Lindley G. Ginn, Merida F. Kibbee, Jessie C. Fowler, Robert J. Earnheart, unidentified, William T. Collins, Thomas L. Shaver, and William D. Landreth; (third row) unidentified , unidentified, Carlton L. Johnson, John A. Hix, Herbert C. Durham, Jack L. Evans, Luther Gossett, Ardith S. Sullivan, Flynn G. Atkins, Evans Yeager, and unidentified; (fourth row) unidentified, unidentified, Wilber D. Lewis, Ernest D. Shirley, James R. Kirkland, Boyce L. Evans, John W. Jackson, Thomas R. King, Archie C. Bales, unidentified, and unidentified; (fifth row) George P. Bone, Sam Compton, James W. Headstream, Coy L. Spicer, Charles P. Buchanan, James P. Johnson, William Kibbee, Edwin D. Huddleston, Warren D. Simpson, and unidentified; and (sixth row) unidentified, unidentified, Thomas B. Padgett, Norman B. Gray, Ernest Jones, unidentified, Oscar W. Allen, Frank N. Carter, Conway J. Huddleston, and Lee E. Seery. (Old Independence Regional Museum)

Two

Homes and Buildings

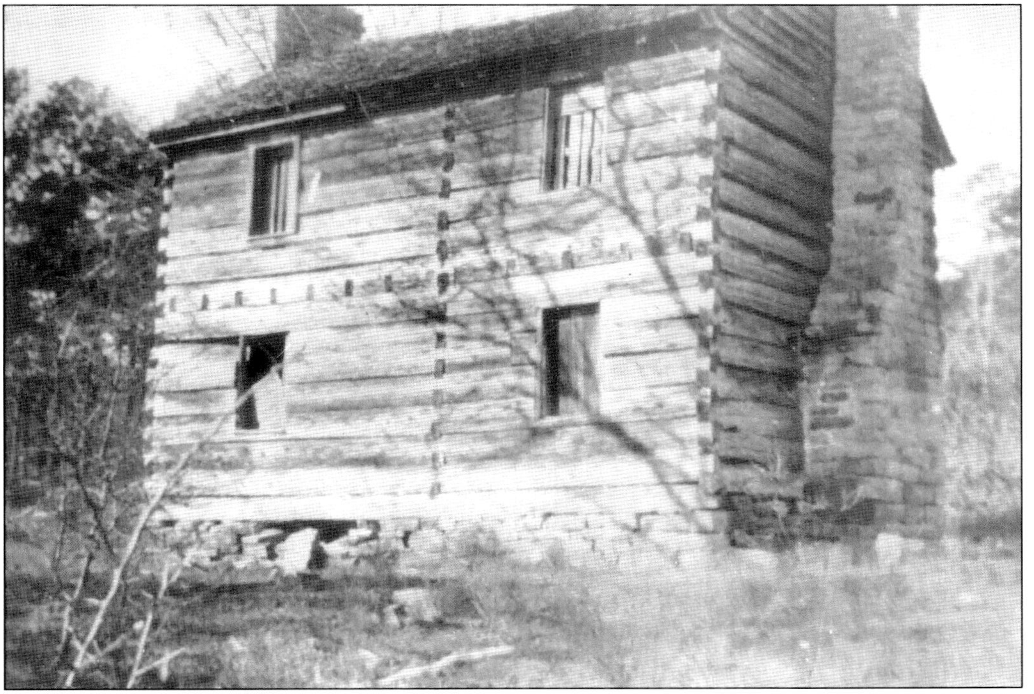

One of the earliest homes built in Independence County was this two-story log house built by George Gill in the late 1820s. It stood facing the White River near the present community of Bethesda. (Twyla Gill Wright)

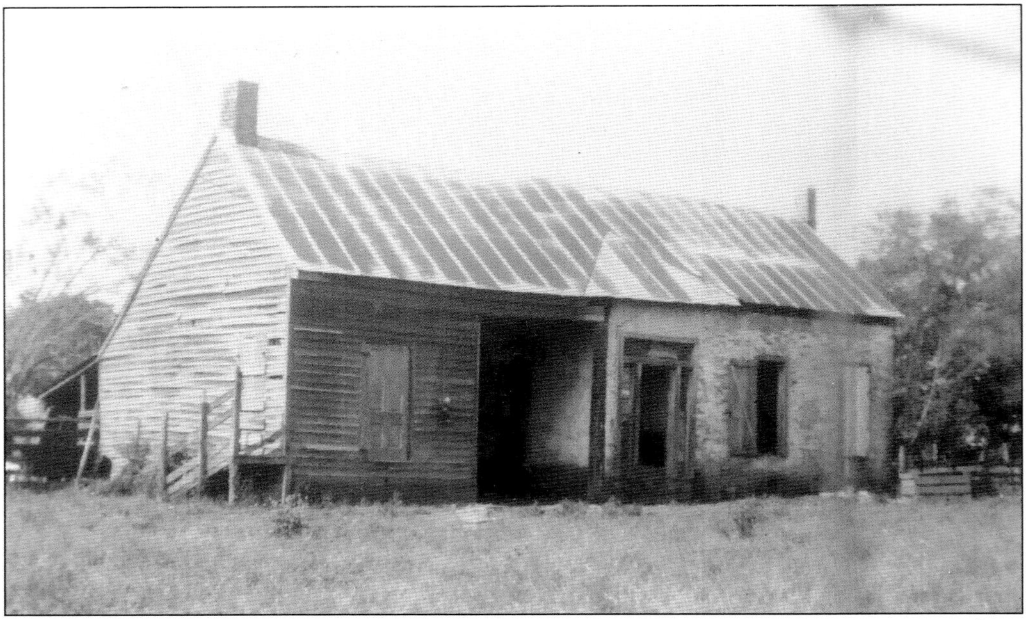

Hartwell Boswell's home and law office was located on the lower end of what became College Street in Batesville. This part pink brick, part frame structure was possibly built, at least in part, as early as 1830. It stood for over a century, ending its existence as a stable and hay barn. (Independence County Historical Society)

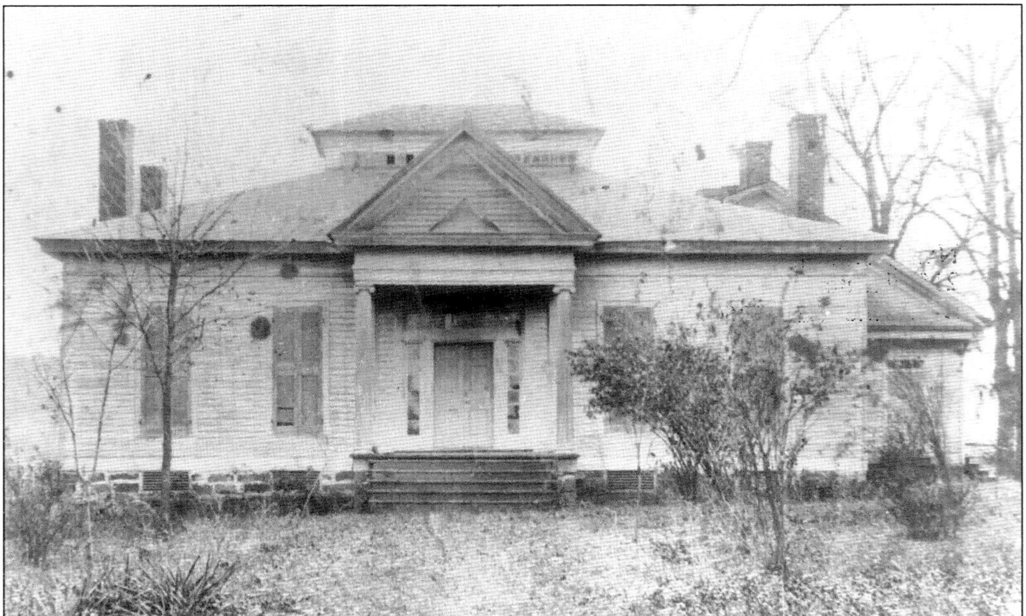

One of the finest homes in 19th century Independence County was "Catalpa Hall," built a few miles north of Batesville by William Byers in 1846. After the Civil War, the house was purchased by Gov. Elisha Baxter and later by the Glenn family. It was razed in 1952. (Nancy Britton)

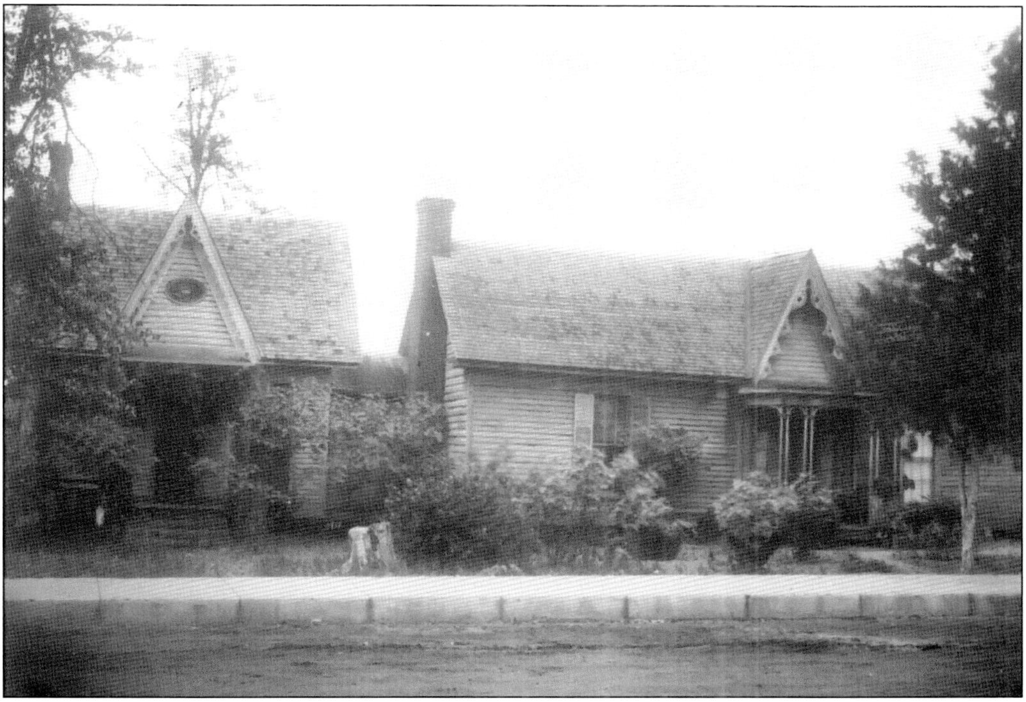

U.M. Rose came to Batesville from Kentucky in 1853. He built this house with the detached office building for his law practice on Main Street and remained here until he was appointed chancellor in 1860. His wife and family lived here throughout the Civil War, eventually joining him in Little Rock, where he established the well-known Rose Law Firm. (Arkansas History Commission)

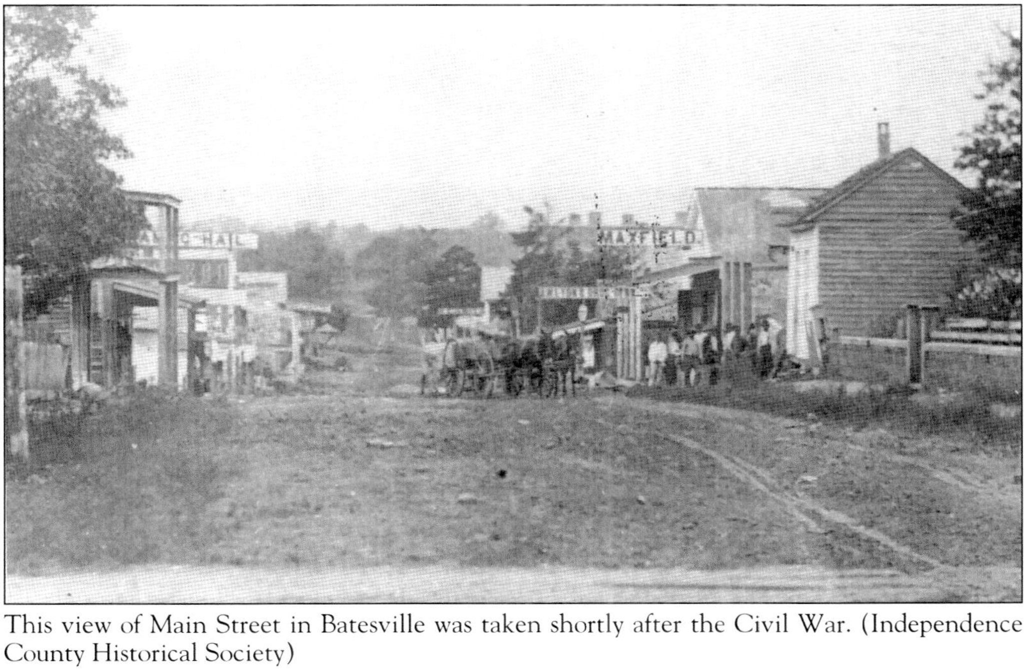

This view of Main Street in Batesville was taken shortly after the Civil War. (Independence County Historical Society)

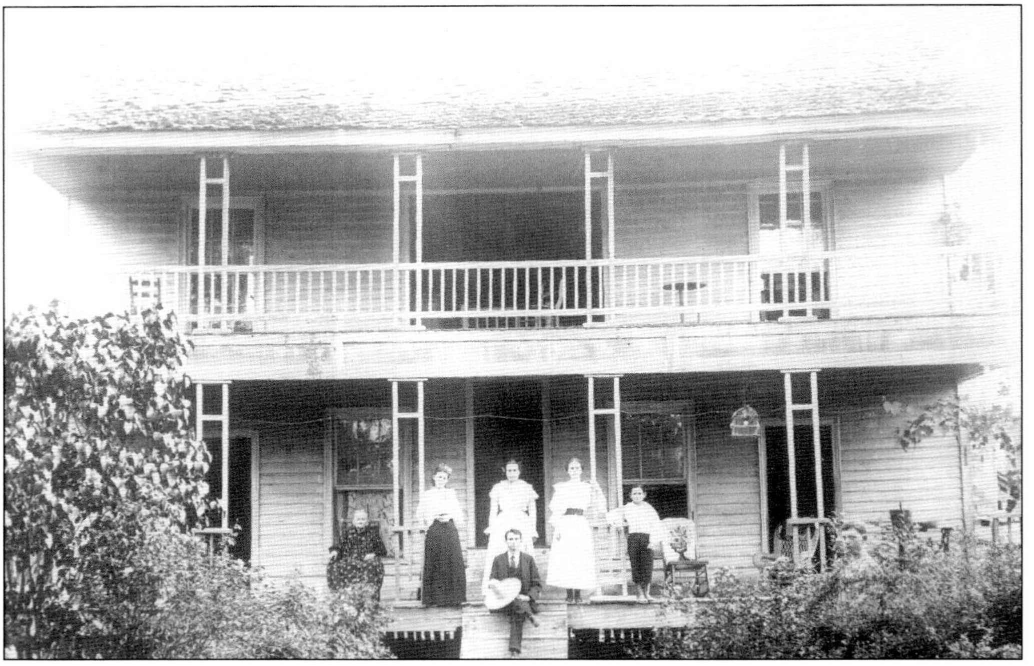

This image of Dr. Alfred W. Williamson's home was taken *c.* 1895. From left to right are as follows: (back row) Caroline Virginia Sanders Williamson, Imogene Williamson, Lucy Margaret Williamson, Jessie Williamson, and Basil Williamson; (seated on the steps in front) Cliff Williamson; and (in the bushes at right) Hamblin Williamson. (Mary Crow Shields)

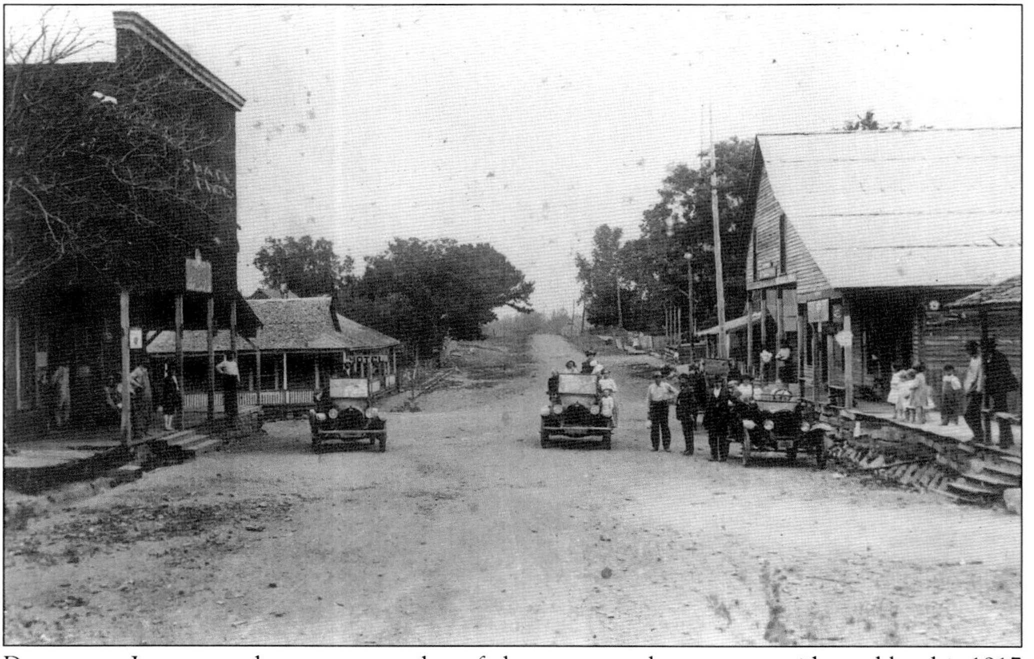

Downtown Jamestown has seen a number of changes over the years as evidenced by this 1917 photograph of Main Street. (Bubba Burks)

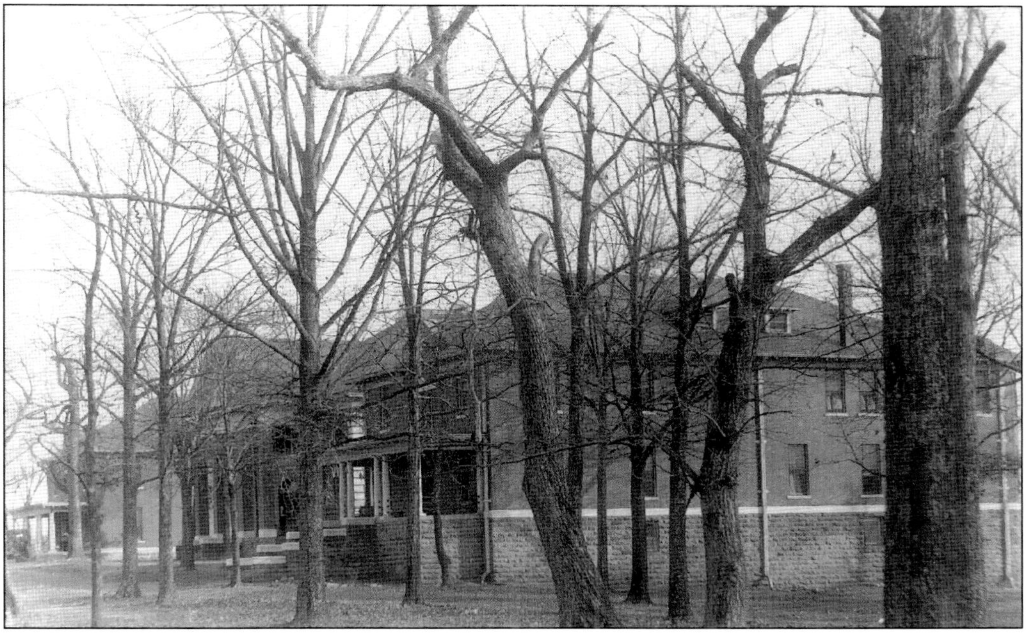

The Masonic Lodge opened a home for orphans in Batesville in 1907. The Home closed in 1947, and three of the original buildings became part of the new campus for Arkansas (now Lyon) College. (Brian Robertson)

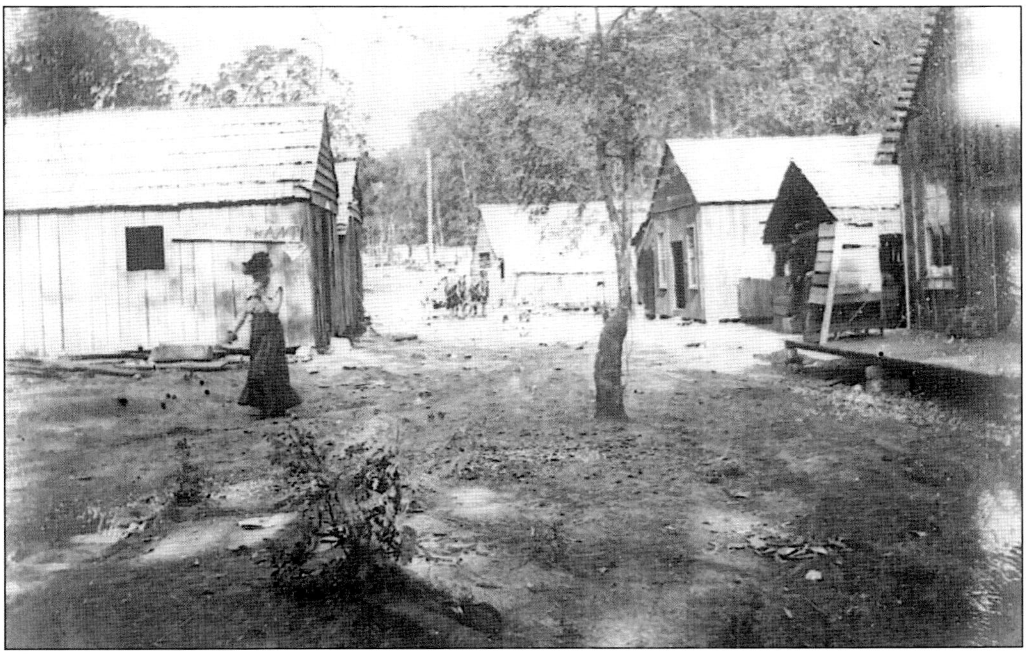

This rare photograph was made around the turn of the century by Dora Weaver Baker. It depicts a small African-American neighborhood which once stood along Poke Bayou below Elm Street and the school bus parking lot behind the Batesville Intermediate School. Close examination indicates that the building at left bears a sign identifying it as a restaurant. (Dora Le Ferguson)

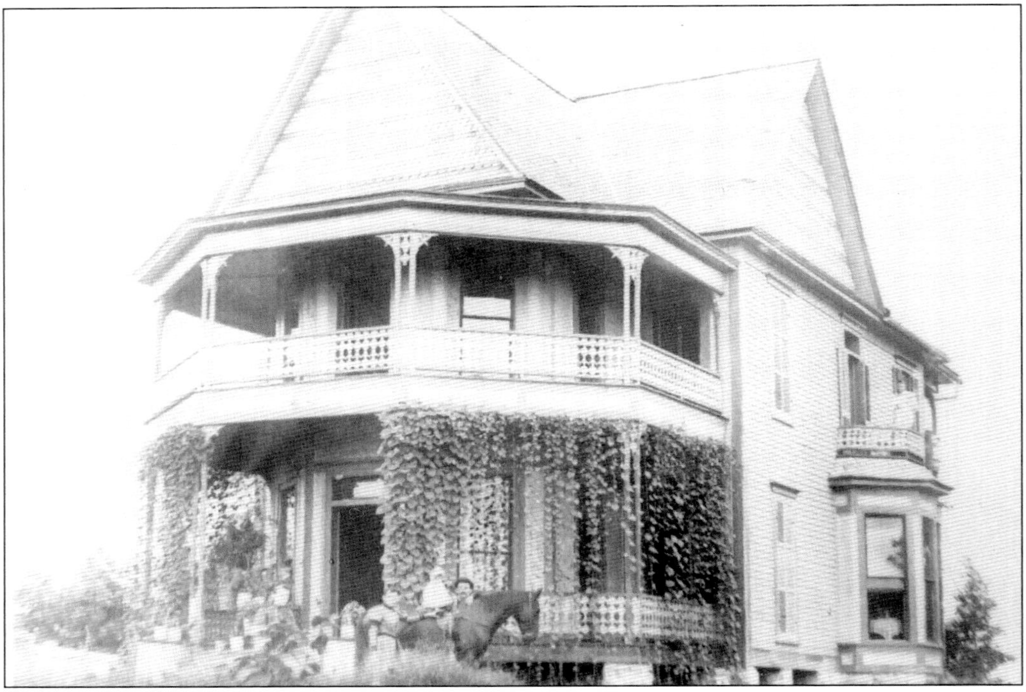

C.W. Maxfield's unusual home with its hexagonal front rooms and wraparound porches was said to resemble a steamboat. It was built in the 1880s, but stood empty for many years before in was torn down in 1972. (Independence County Historical Society)

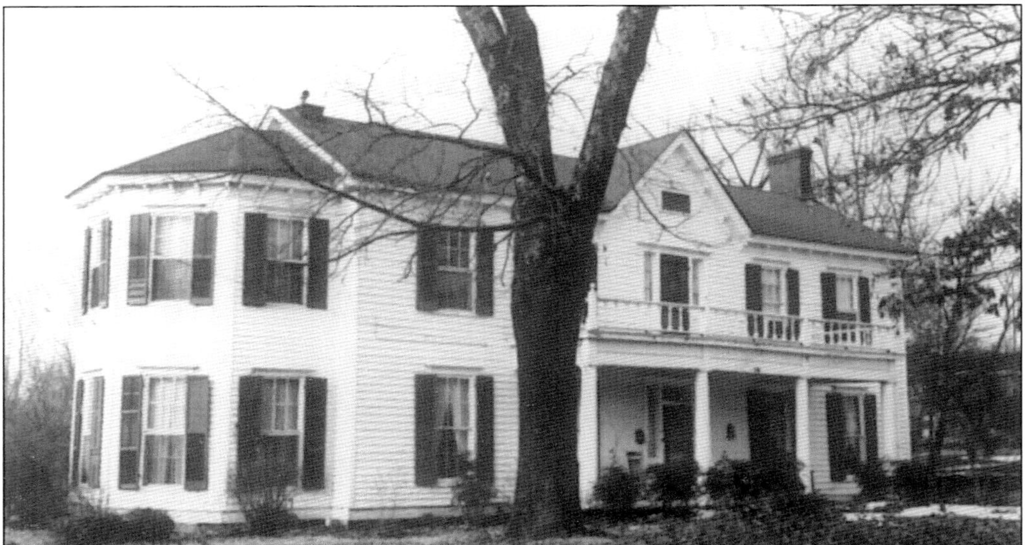

The original part of the Soulesbury Institute/Glenn House was built as a Methodist school in 1849. It was closed in 1861, and according to local tradition was used as a hospital during the Civil War. There was an unsuccessful attempt to reopen the school after the war, but the building was sold to the Glenn family in 1872. Remodeled several times from its original appearance, it remains in the Glenn family. (Independence County Historical Society)

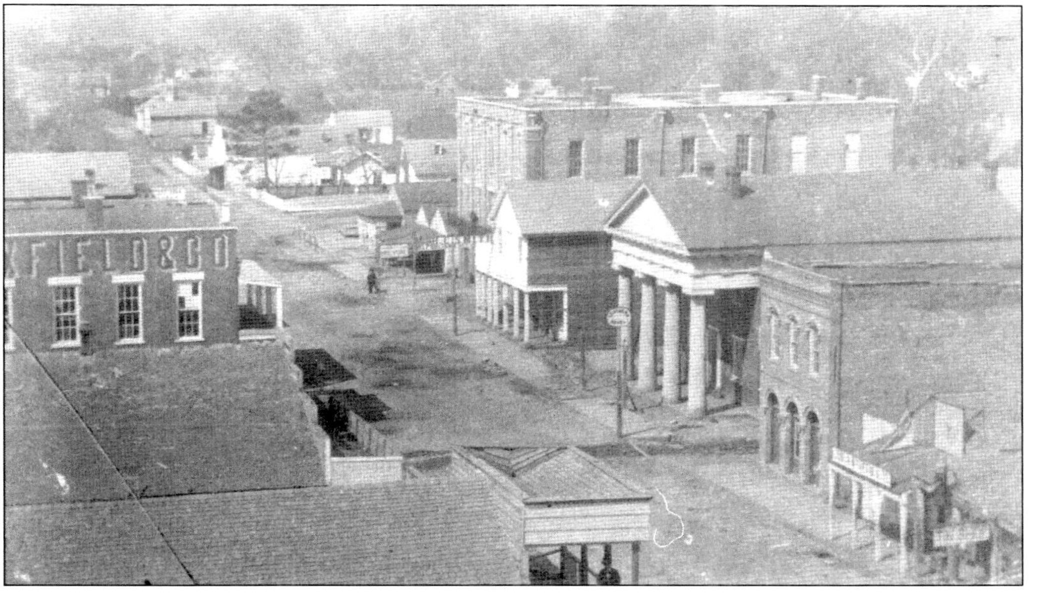

This image of lower Main Street in Batesville is believed to date from the 1870s. (Independence County Historical Society)

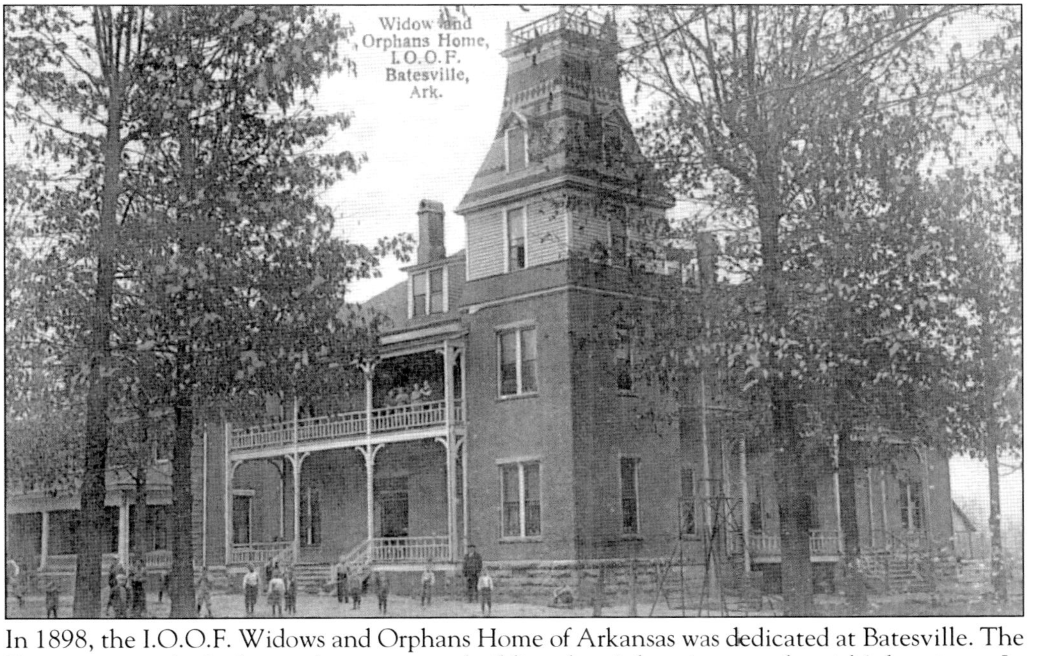

In 1898, the I.O.O.F. Widows and Orphans Home of Arkansas was dedicated at Batesville. The Home consisted of a large administration building, boys' dormitory, and a girls' dormitory. In addition to receiving a literary education, the children were also taught more practical living skills. The home was located on the present site of West Side School. (Brian Robertson)

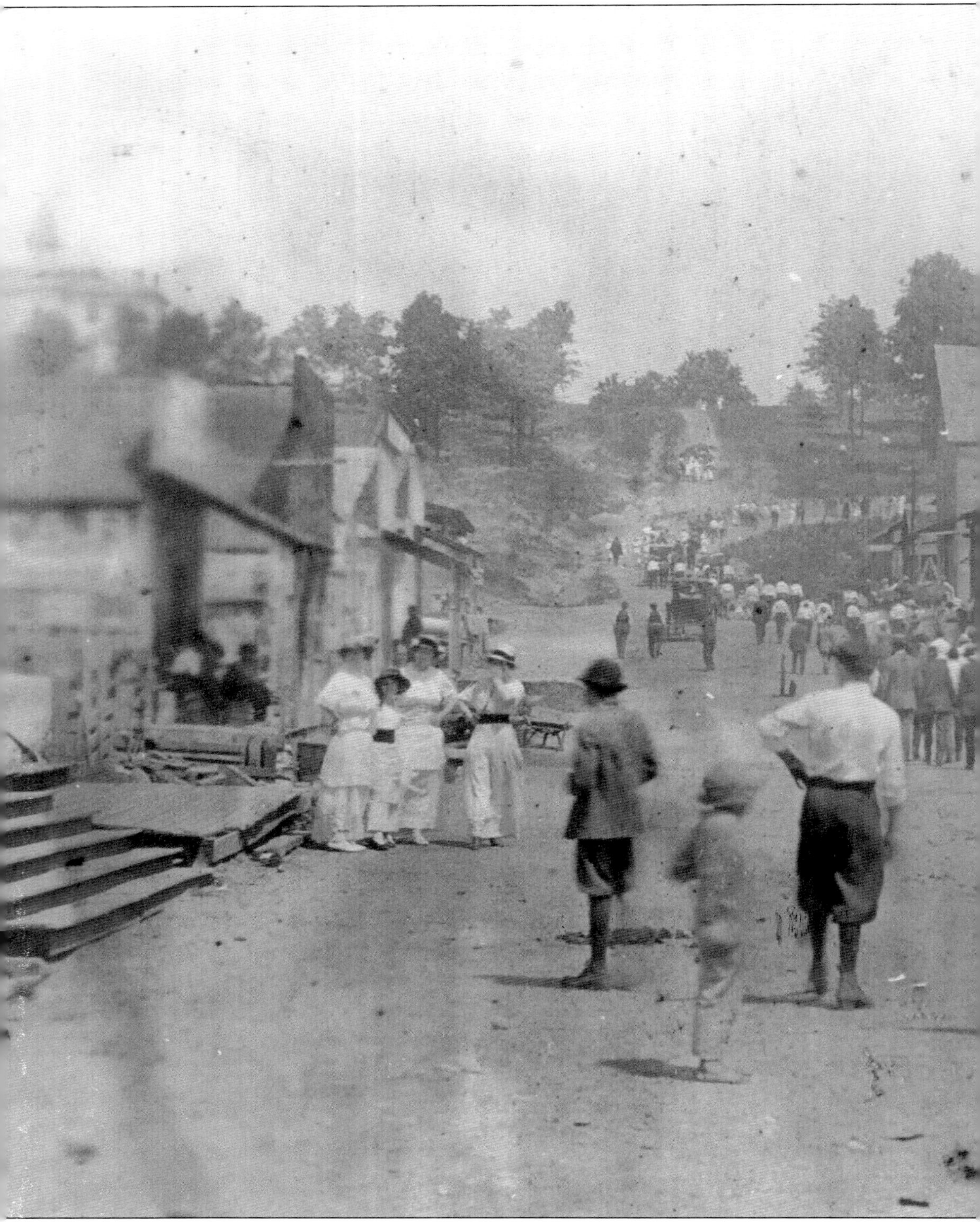

This scene shows Main Street Cushman, *c*. 1907. (W.C. Blankenship/Independence County

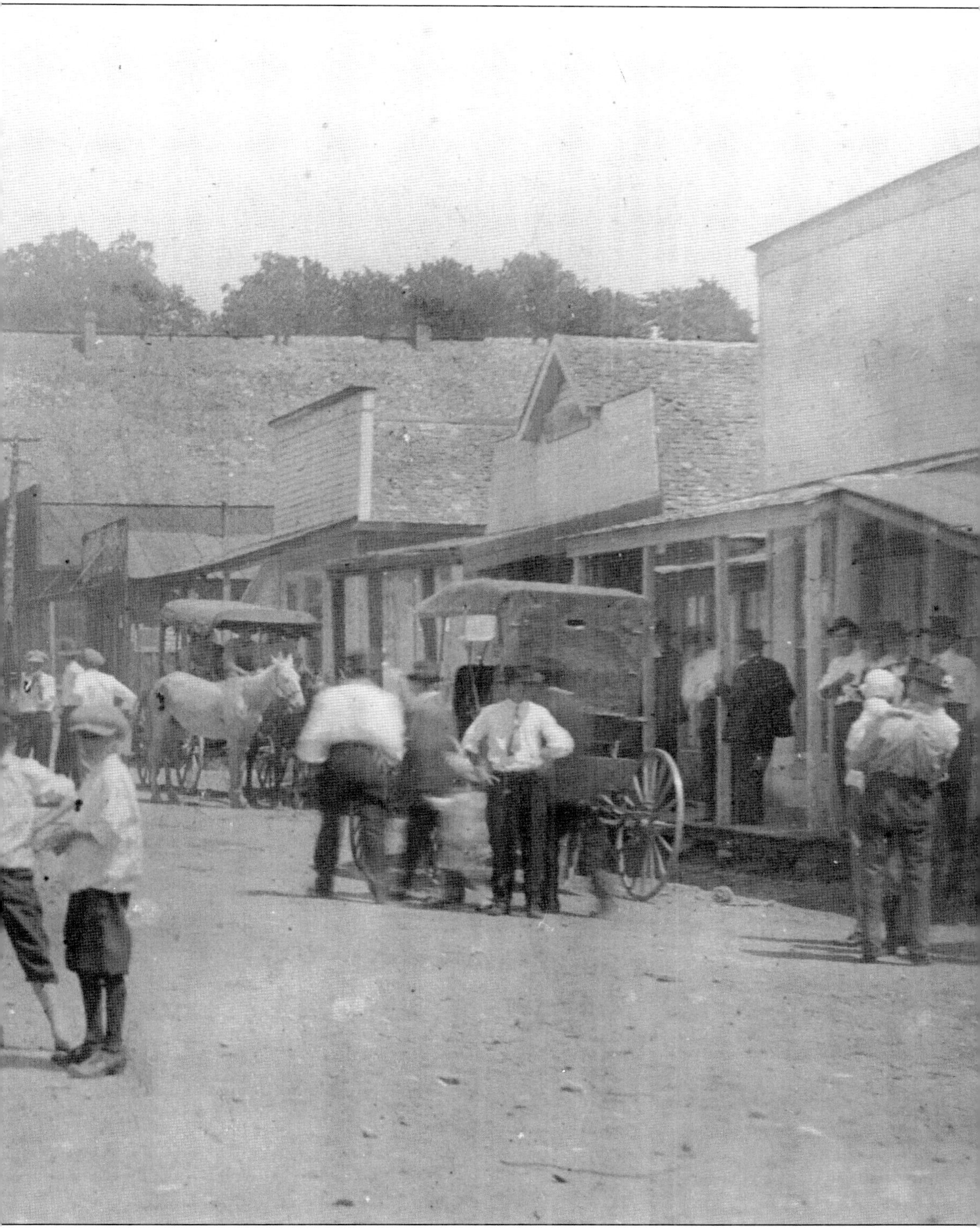

Historical Society)

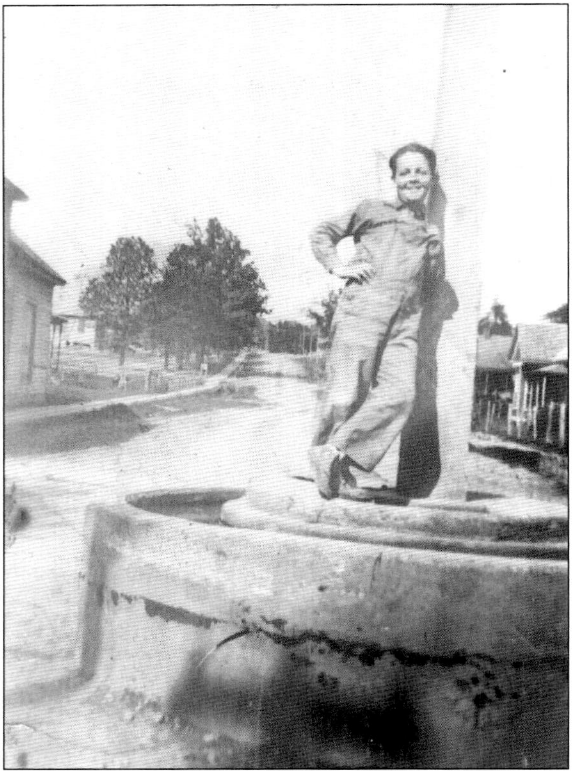

The late C.A. "Dub" Robinson is pictured here standing on the public watering trough at Central Avenue and Pine Street in West Batesville about 1919. This was one of three public wells in town—another was downtown on Main Street, and one was at the intersection of Twelfth and College Streets. (Nancy Britton)

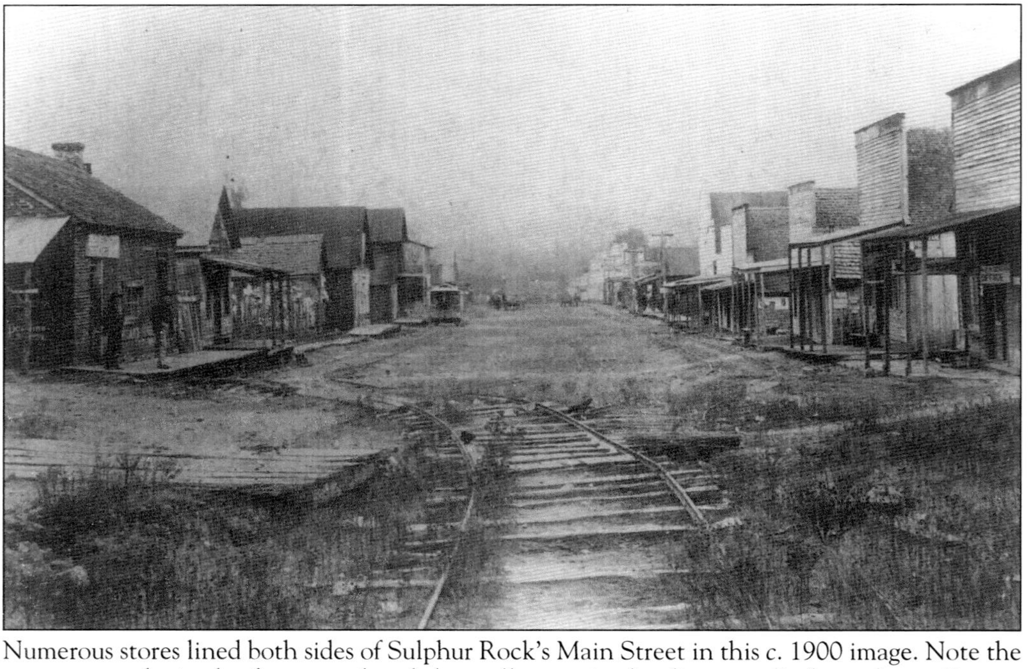

Numerous stores lined both sides of Sulphur Rock's Main Street in this *c.* 1900 image. Note the streetcar tracks in the foreground and the trolley car in the distance. (Independence County Historical Society)

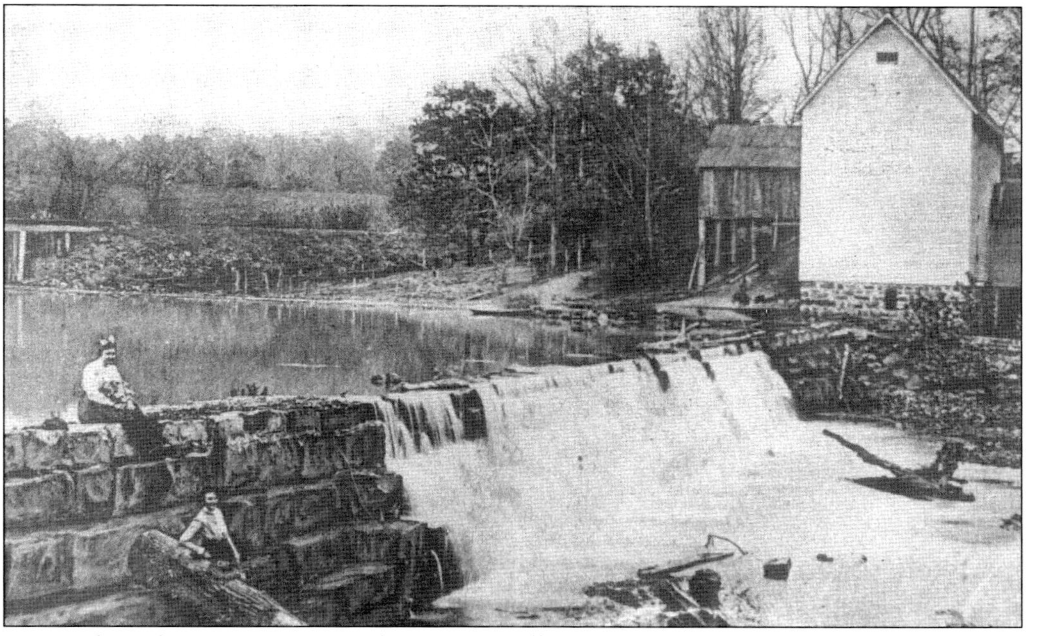

Arising from the Big Spring at Lytle's Spring Mill, Spring Creek flows only a few miles before reaching the river bottom, but on a hillside at this approximate site a water-powered grist mill was constructed, perhaps as early as 1815. John F. Ruddell acquired the property in 1817, and he and his son, William B. Ruddell, operated a mill here until World War I. The mill machinery was dismantled at that time, and a small store opened in the mill house. In 1939, the abandoned building was destroyed by fire. A road runs across the dam now, and only some stone rubble remains of the mill foundation. (Nancy Britton)

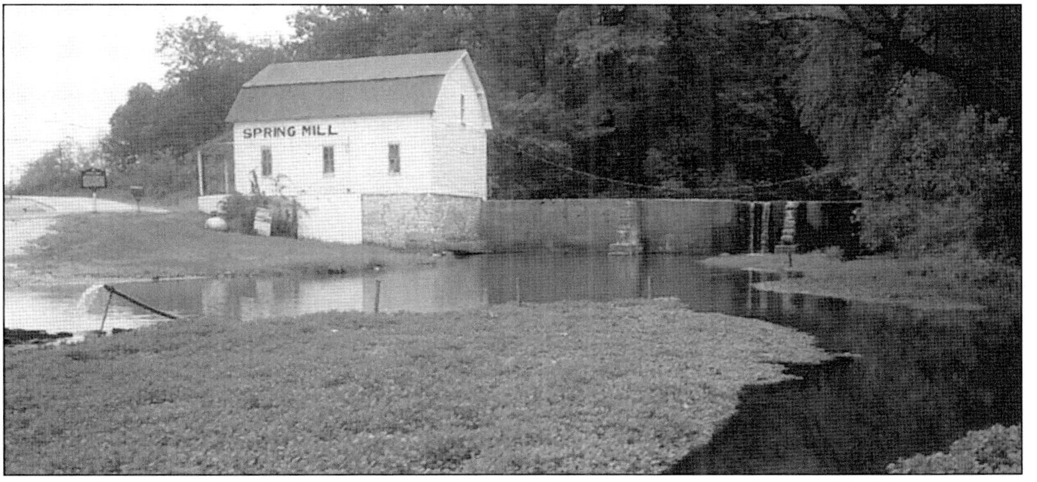

Spring Mill, located on Highway 69 northwest of Batesville, was built in 1867. This date and the name of the builder, Col. J.A. Schnable, were found on a stone tablet built into the rock dam beneath the mill house. After many ownerships, the mill and surrounding property were purchased by J.A. Lytle Sr. in 1917. The family operated the mill and a general store in the mill house for a number of years and the property still belongs to Lytle heirs. It was the last of the 19th century water power mills to operate in the state. (Nancy Britton)

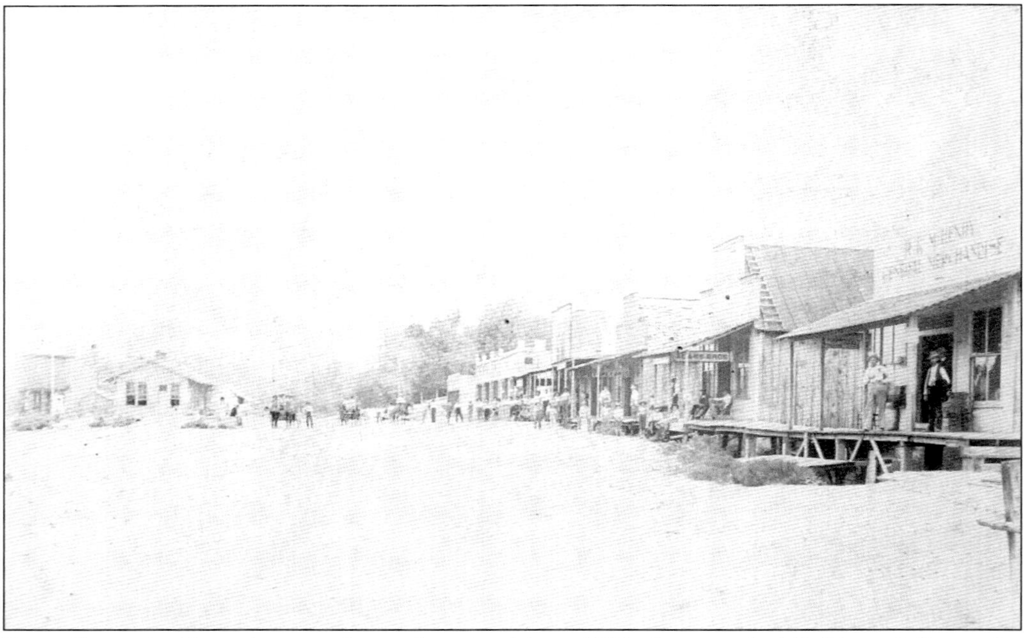

Front Street in Newark was a busy place in this *c.* 1903 photograph. Visible at left are the railroad water tower and the depot. Three of the stores that lined the street were R.K. McHenry, Adams Bros., and Fisher Bros. (Robert D. Craig)

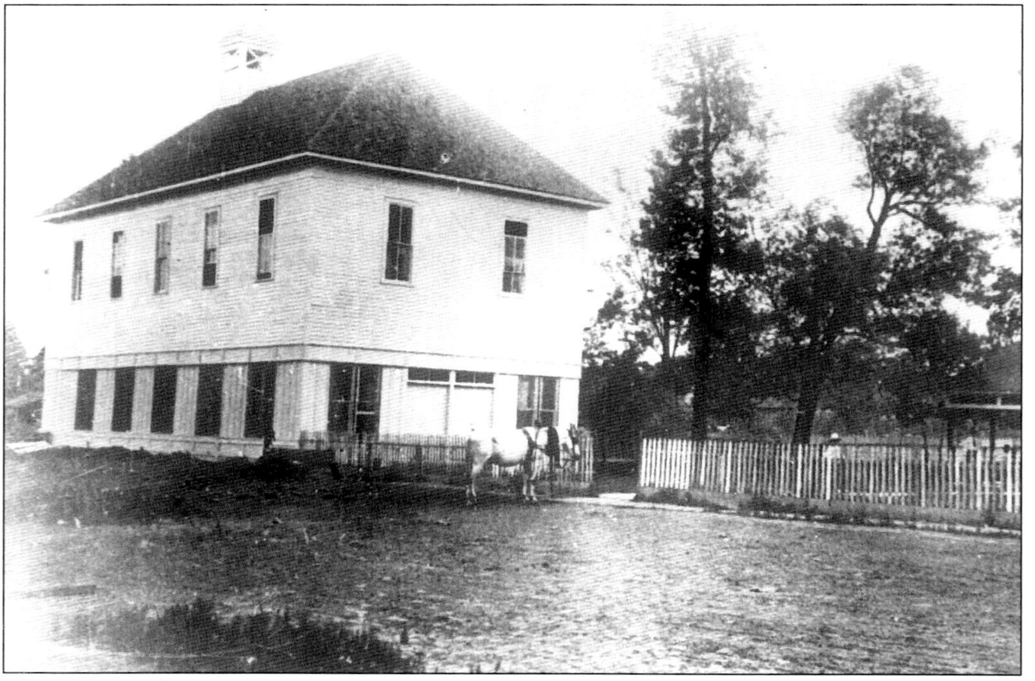

The Town Hall and Lodge Hall at Sulphur Rock was an impressive meeting place for members of the community. This photo dates from 1910. (Butler Center for Arkansas Studies, Central Arkansas Library System)

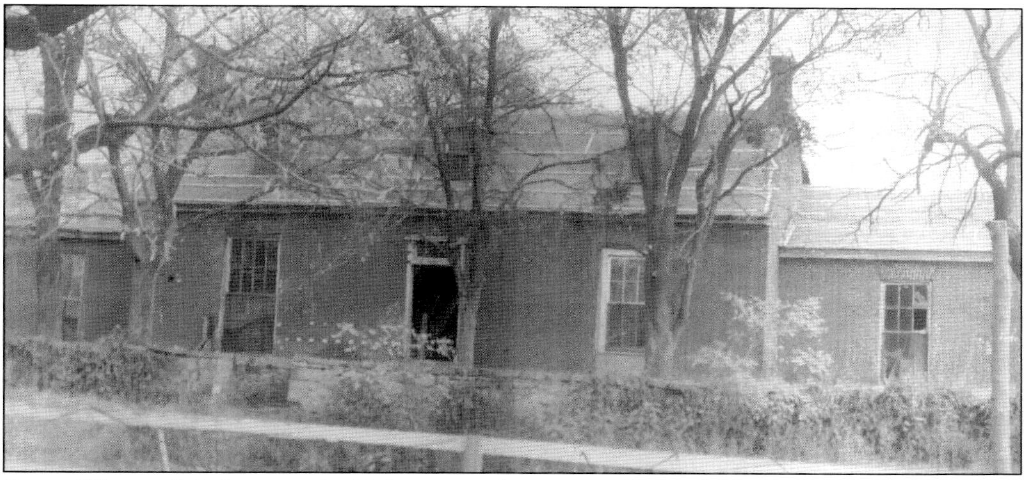

One of Batesville's finest early 19th century homes was built about 1828 by merchant John Ringgold. It was also the residence of his daughter and son-in-law, Lucretia Ringgold and Charles Fenton Mercer Noland, a well-known writer and politician of the time. The house was located on what is now the 300 block of West Main and was constructed of handmade bricks laid in the unusual Flemish bond pattern. It remained the property of Ringgold connections until the 1930s. It was later purchased by the Ringgold-Noland Foundation, a group which tried unsuccessfully to preserve it. After the walls collapsed, bricks from the house were used in the construction of the present Chamber of Commerce Building on Vine Street in 1964. (Regional Studies Center, Lyon College)

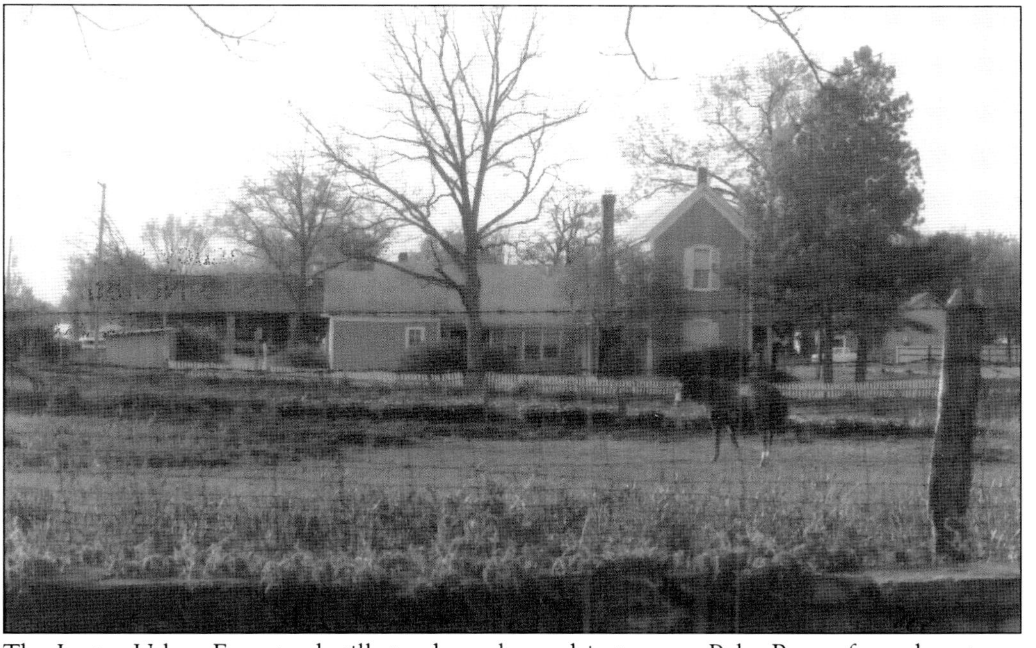

The Luster Urban Farmstead still stands unchanged just across Poke Bayou from downtown Batesville. The 1885 house, complete with outbuildings and pasture lot, was built by James A. Luster and still belongs to his daughter, Mrs. Winnie Luster Atchison. (Independence County Historical Society)

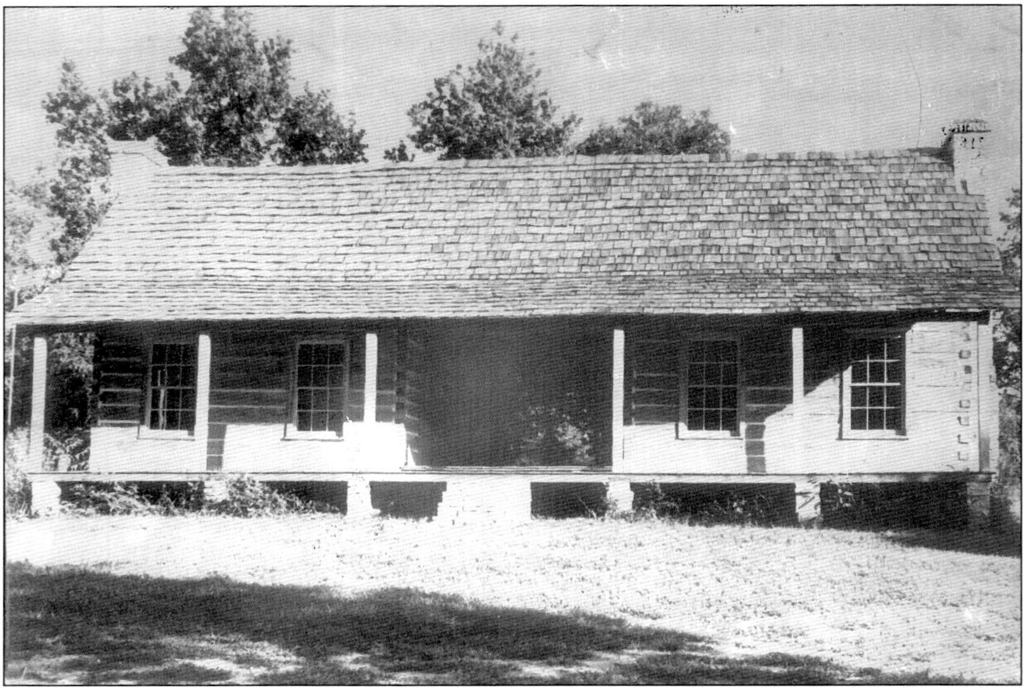

This log dog-trot house was built by the Grigsby family near Bethesda soon after the Civil War. The house was dismantled and moved to the campus of Arkansas (now Lyon) College by Mr. and Mrs. Elmer Kirk. It was rebuilt and dedicated there in 1980. Mrs. Kirk is a descendant of the builder, Charles Grigsby. (Independence County Historical Society)

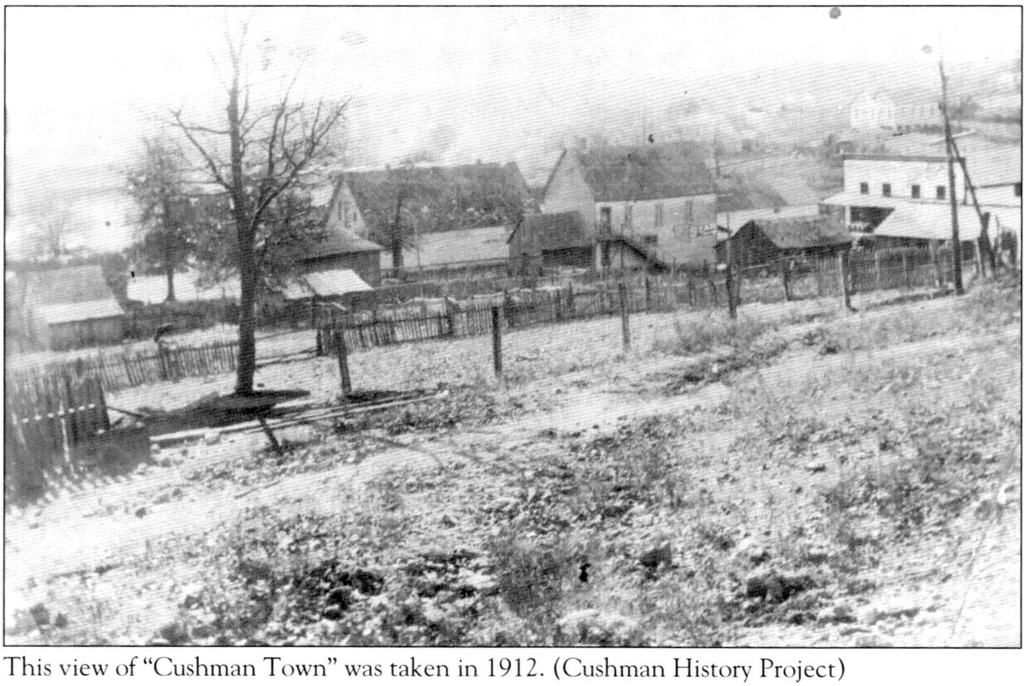

This view of "Cushman Town" was taken in 1912. (Cushman History Project)

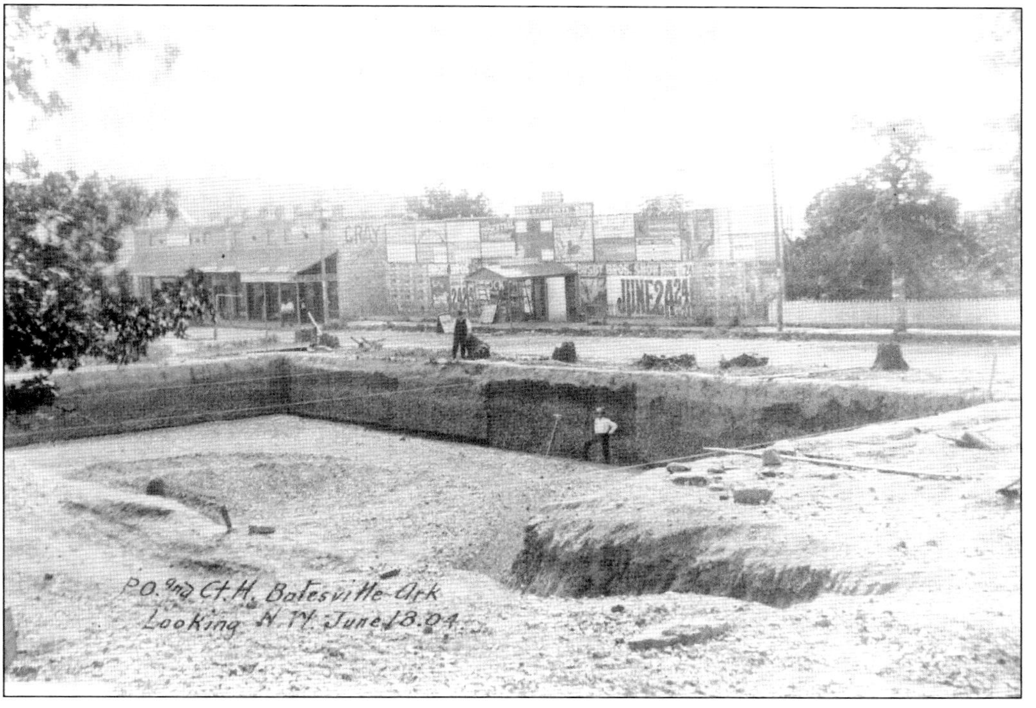

In 1904, construction began on a Batesville landmark. The building served as the post office and housed the federal court for the Eastern District of Arkansas. Today it is the home of the Independence County Regional Library. (Top photo: Wilson Powell, bottom photo: Brian Robertson)

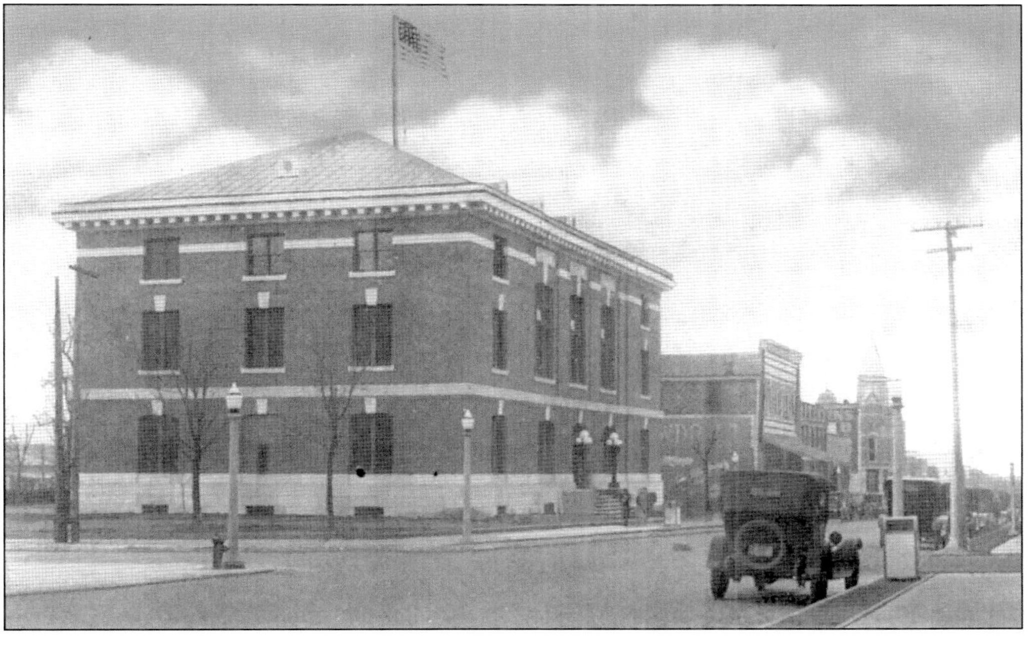

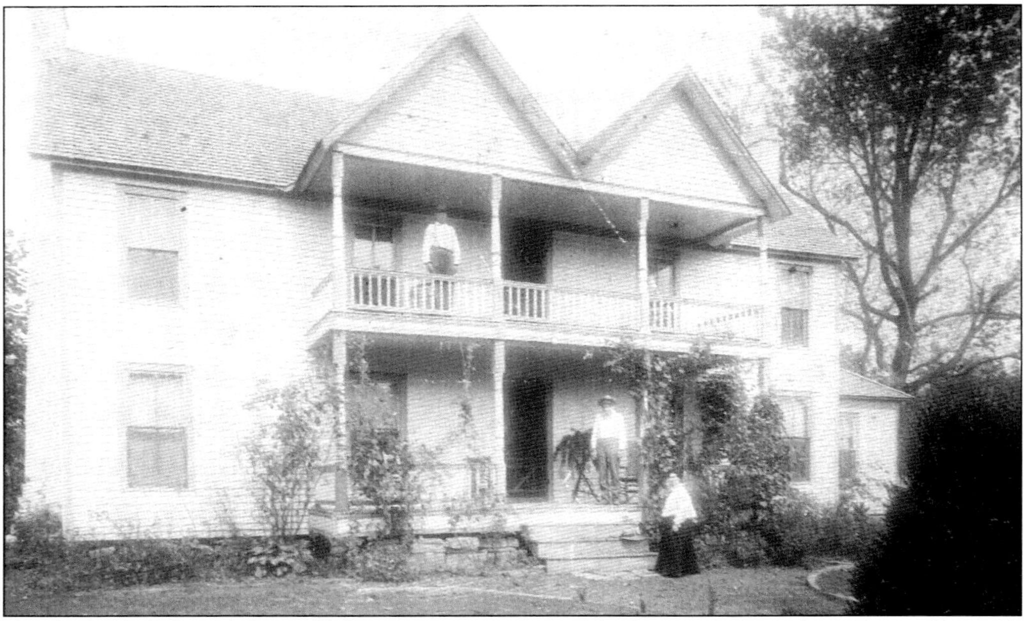

This home at Magness belonged to William D. and Mary Elizabeth Magness. It still stands today. (Mary Crow Shields)

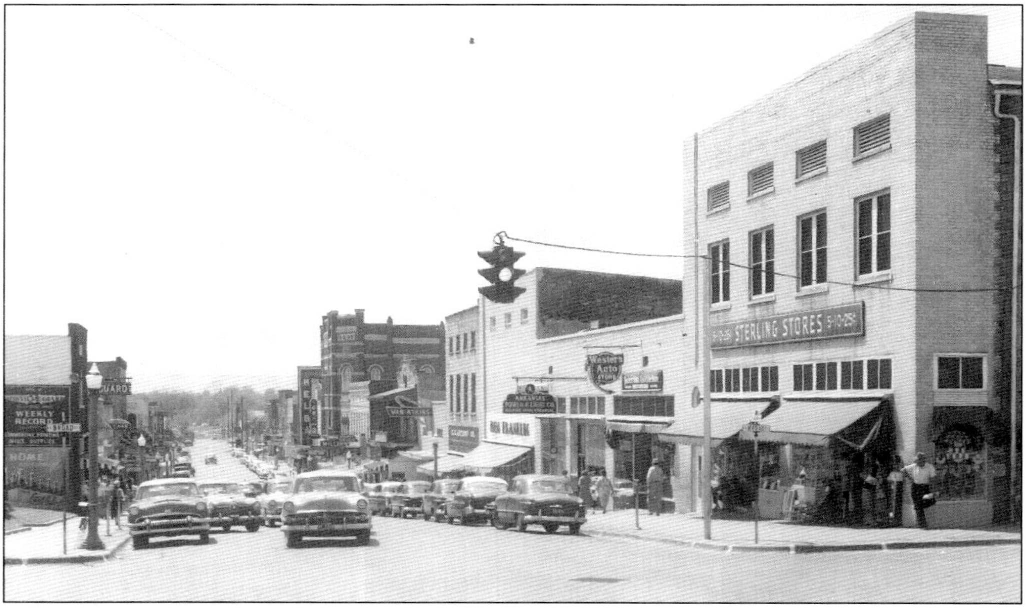

This 1950s view is looking down Main Street in Batesville. (Brian Robertson)

Three

EDUCATION

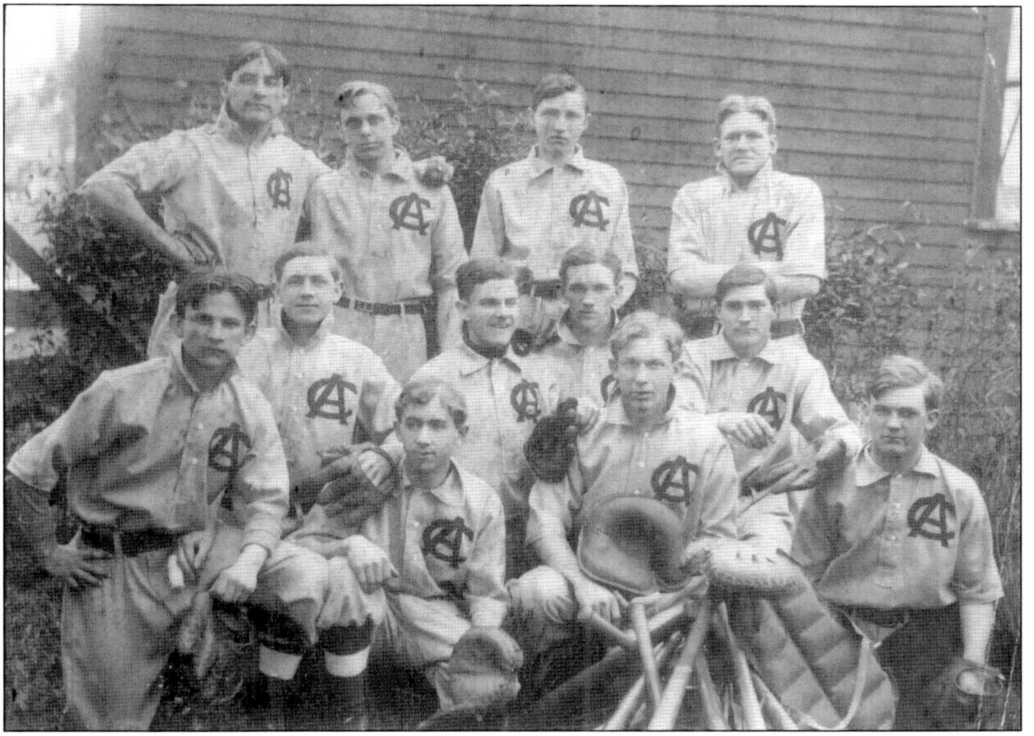

For young men in college, the American pastime of baseball was a very popular pursuit. This was especially true for the fellows that attended Arkansas College around 1906. From left to right are as follows: (standing) Edgar Rogers, Otto McAdams, Duke Ward, and Edward Wilson; (kneeling) "Blackie" Mathis, Stone Schuler, Ludie Winfrey, Stewart Oglesby, Hugh Morrow, Walter Matthews, Russell Raney, and Harold (Jimmie) Ley. (Independence County Historical Society)

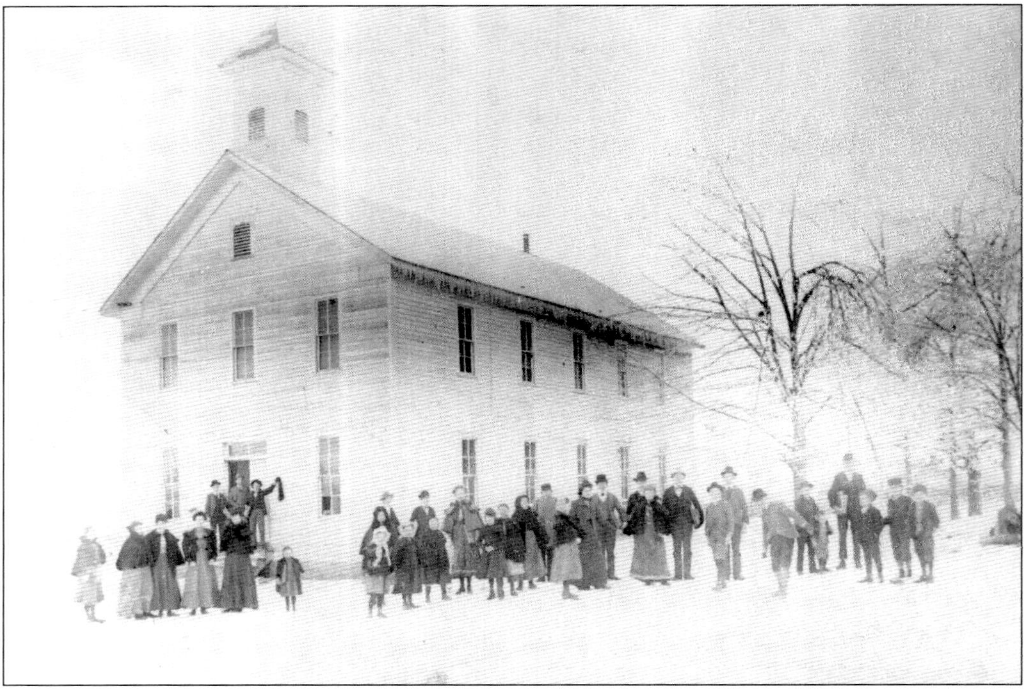

This image of the Pleasant Plains Free School was taken by photographer W.C. Blankenship about 1897. The upstairs rooms were used by the local Masonic lodge. (W.C. Blankenship/ Independence County Historical Society)

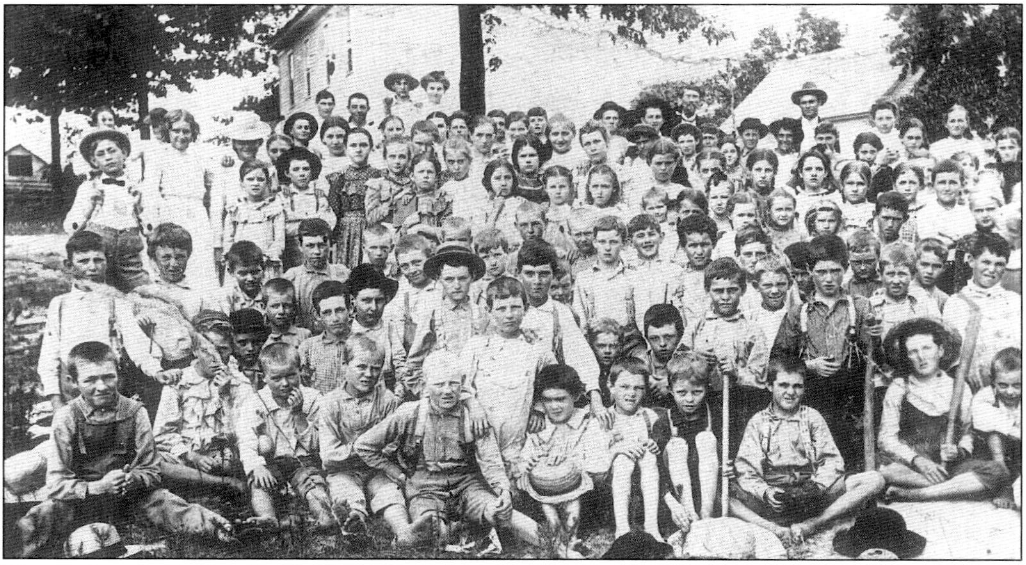

The earliest records of a public school system in Newark date to 1885. In 1903, the state legislature created the Newark Special School District. In 1904, the first school building was replaced when it was bought at auction, cut in half, and turned into two residences. The new building was expanded in 1910. The students in this 1901 view are unidentified, but the teacher was A.A. Henderson. (Mary Crow Shields)

Sidney Pickens has been lauded as an outstanding 20th century Arkansas educator. A graduate of Sulphur Rock Academy and Arkansas College, he served as superintendent of the Batesville schools from 1909 to 1929. During his tenure, Batesville High School became known for its high academic standards and its quality athletic programs. Pickens thoroughly enjoyed competition in both categories. He is credited with giving the name "Pioneers" to the school's athletic teams, and he also created the school motto—"A Pioneer Never Quits!" Pickens was also involved in a number of civic organizations, was a member of the State Board of Education, and taught summer sessions at the University of Arkansas. He served a term as president of the State Teachers' Association and headed the Education Department at Arkansas College for several years. Sadly, Pickens died in 1930 at the age of 49. (Independence County Historical Society)

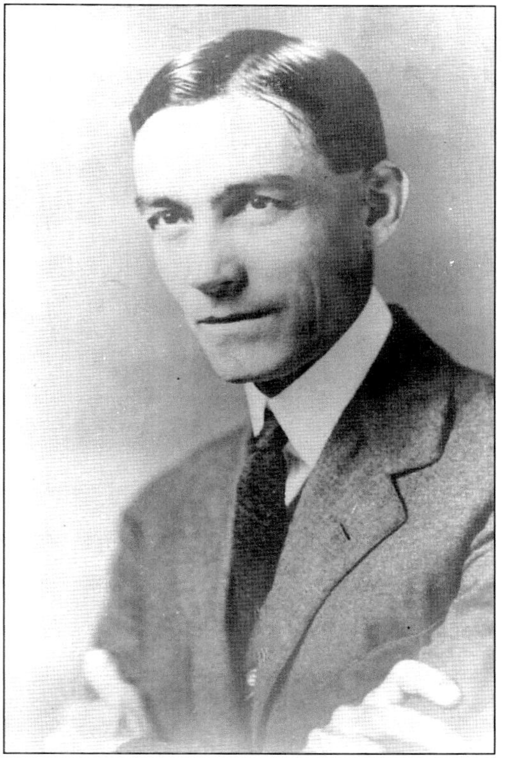

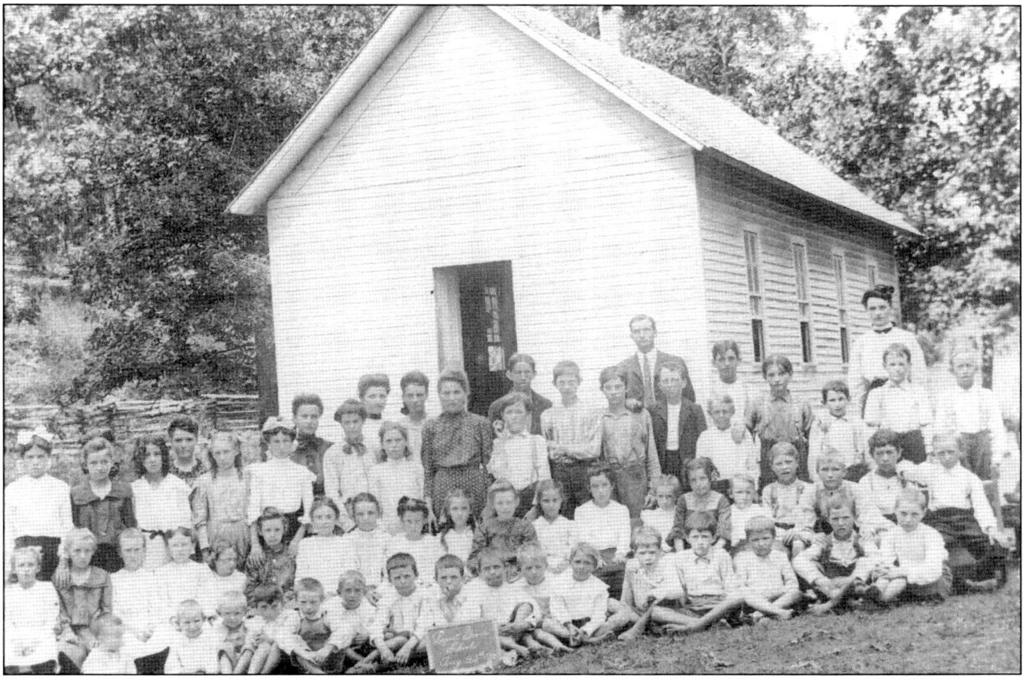

Here is a typical one-room schoolhouse, located at Locust Grove, *c.* 1905. (Kenny Gerhardt)

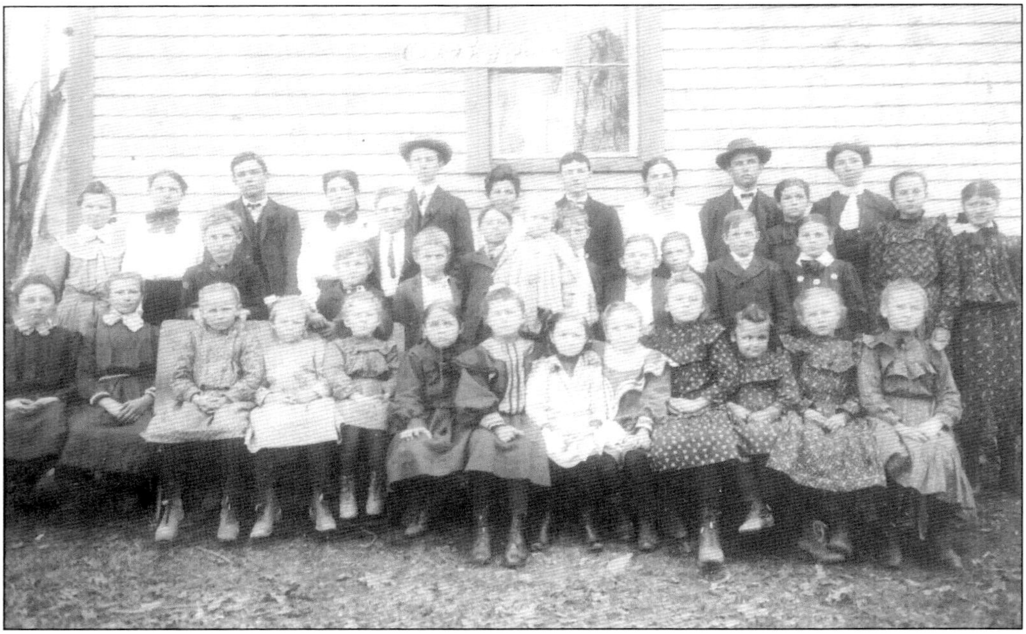

Pictured is the Oak Bluff School near Charlotte about 1905. On the back row, second from the left is the teacher, Lizzie Bevens. (Independence County Historical Society)

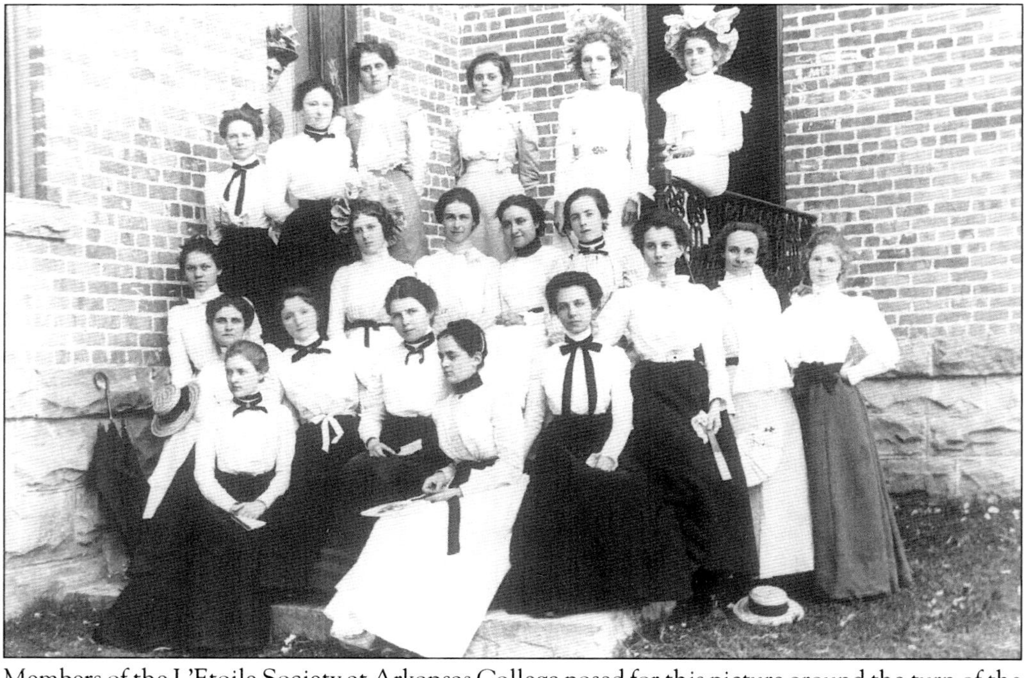

Members of the L'Etoile Society at Arkansas College posed for this picture around the turn of the century. Notice the young man in a girl's hat peeping out the door on left. (Old Independence Regional Museum)

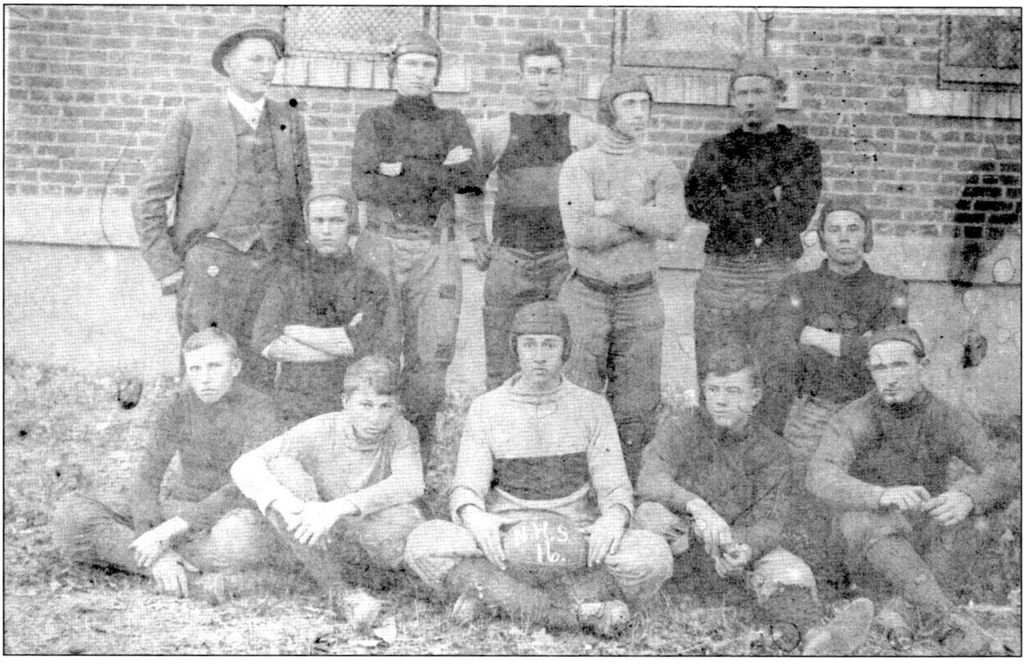

In 1916, Newark fielded a championship football team. The Newark boys defeated Little Rock to claim the state championship. From left to right are as follows: (standing) Coach Walter Isgrig, Herman Williamson, Ernest Henderson, Lynn Galloway, and Dick Holderby; (kneeling) Cecil Norris and French Roe; (sitting) M.L. Arnold, Horace Hoyt, Frank Martin Jr., John Pascoe, and Douglas Hall. (Billy Joe Freeze)

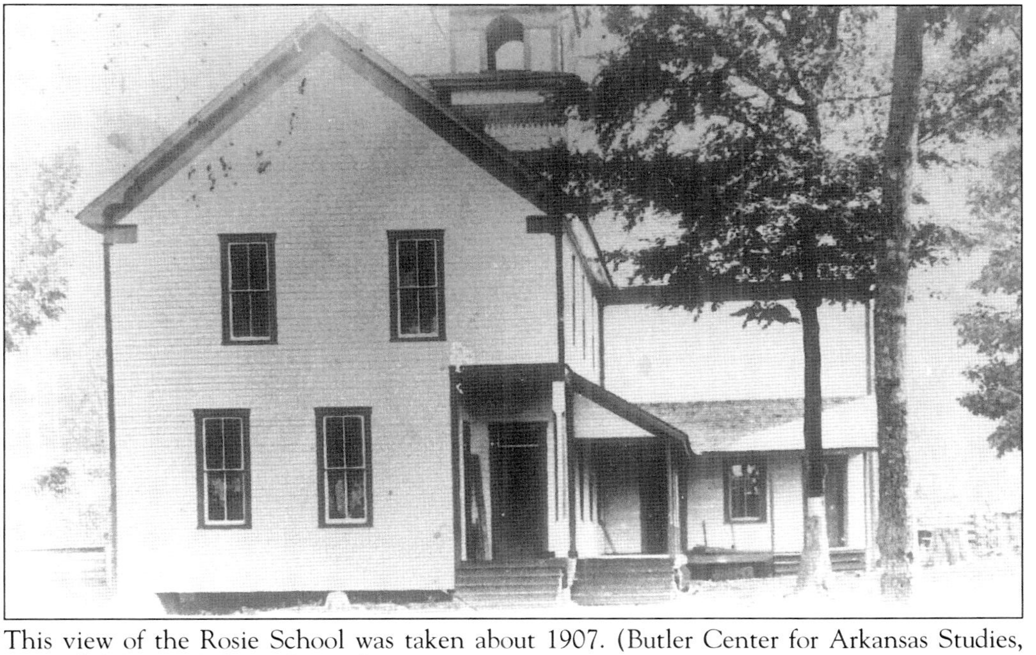

This view of the Rosie School was taken about 1907. (Butler Center for Arkansas Studies, Central Arkansas Library System)

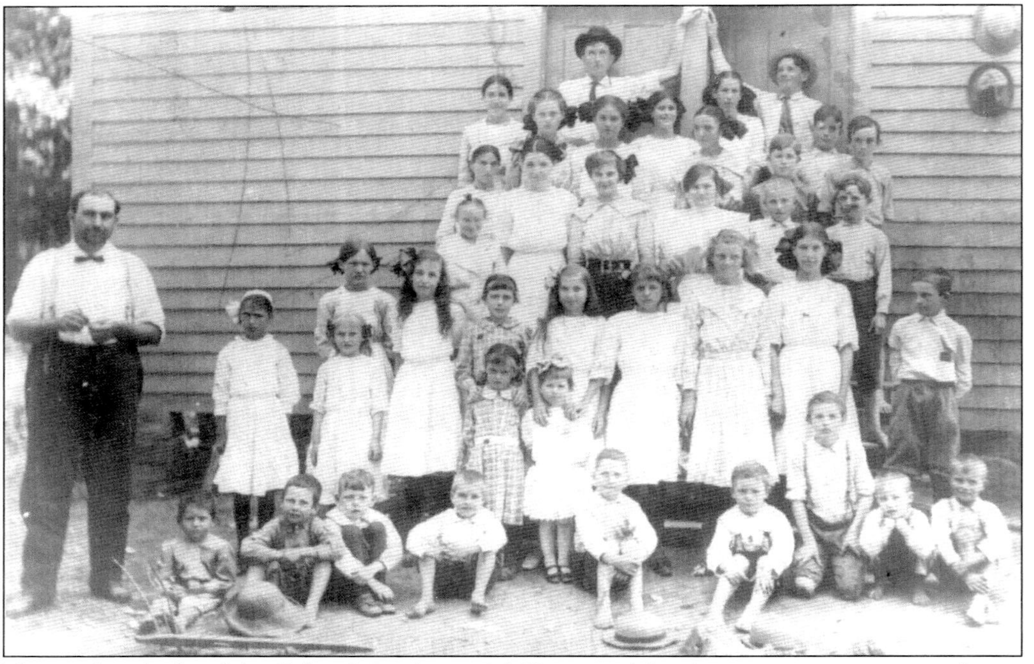

The student body of the Baker School near McHue posed for this picture one summer day in 1910. Teacher Claud McClendon is standing at left. (Wilson Powell)

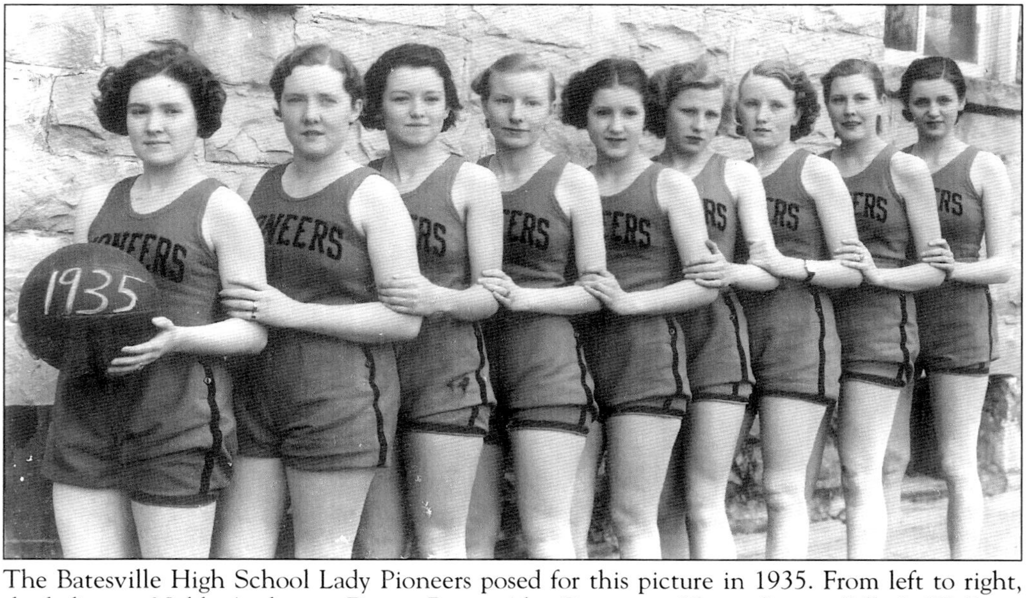

The Batesville High School Lady Pioneers posed for this picture in 1935. From left to right, the ladies are Noble Anderson, Donna Bracy, Alta Carpenter, Elnora Staggs, Billy Jo Wallace, Marie Blue, Trudy Brown, Geraldine Sims, and (?) Ferguson. (Wilson Powell)

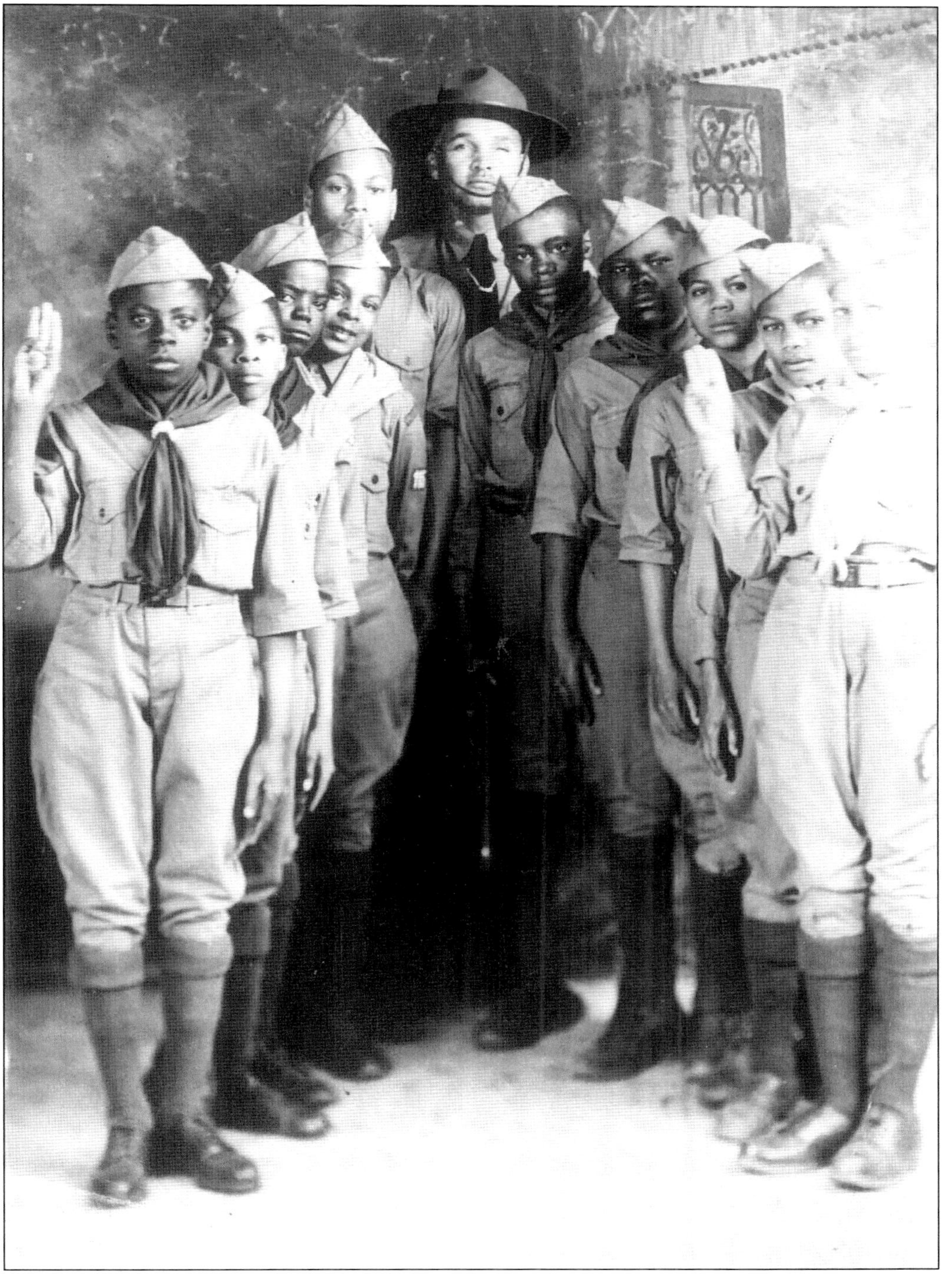

These eager young men are members of the Miller School Boy Scout Troop. The scouts are, from left to right, E.L. Finley, Goldman McCurn, Richard Sims, Richard Sales, Norman Smith, Johnnie Brown (Leader), Herbert Abner, Charlie Harper, (?) Bell, Eugene Lexion, and Hinston Rucker. (Regional Studies Center, Lyon College)

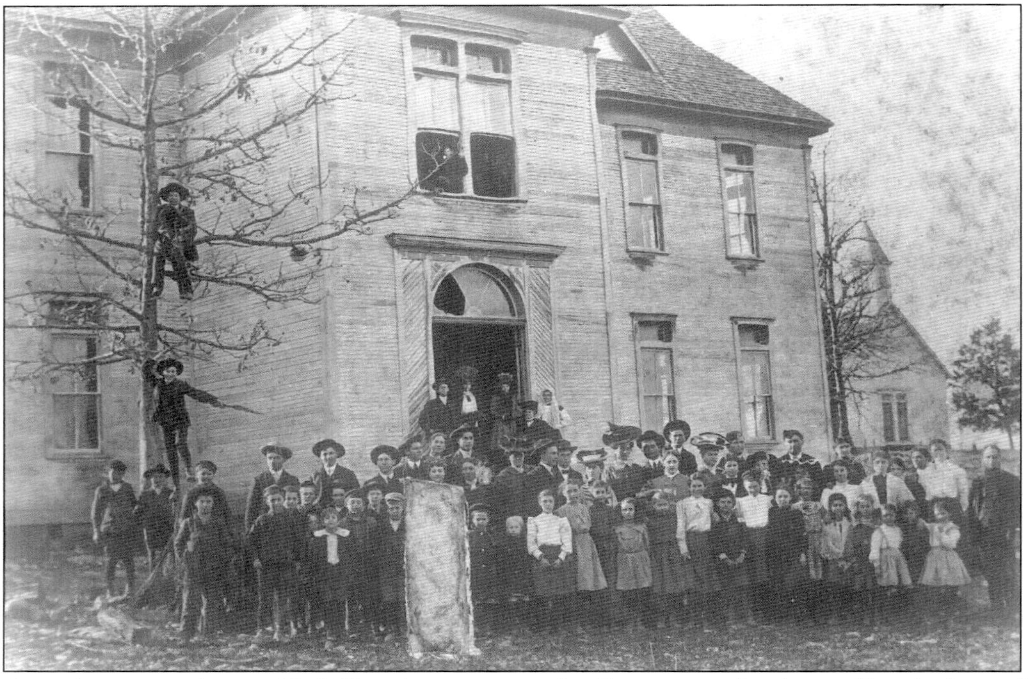

According to an August 21, 1890, advertisement, the "Jamestown Academy offers the best of inducements to youth of both sexes. Healthy locality, churches, preaching, and Sunday School each Sunday. Tuition $1.50, $2.25, $3.00, according to grade. Book Keeping $2.00 per mo. extra. Music terms reasonable." (Independence County Historical Society)

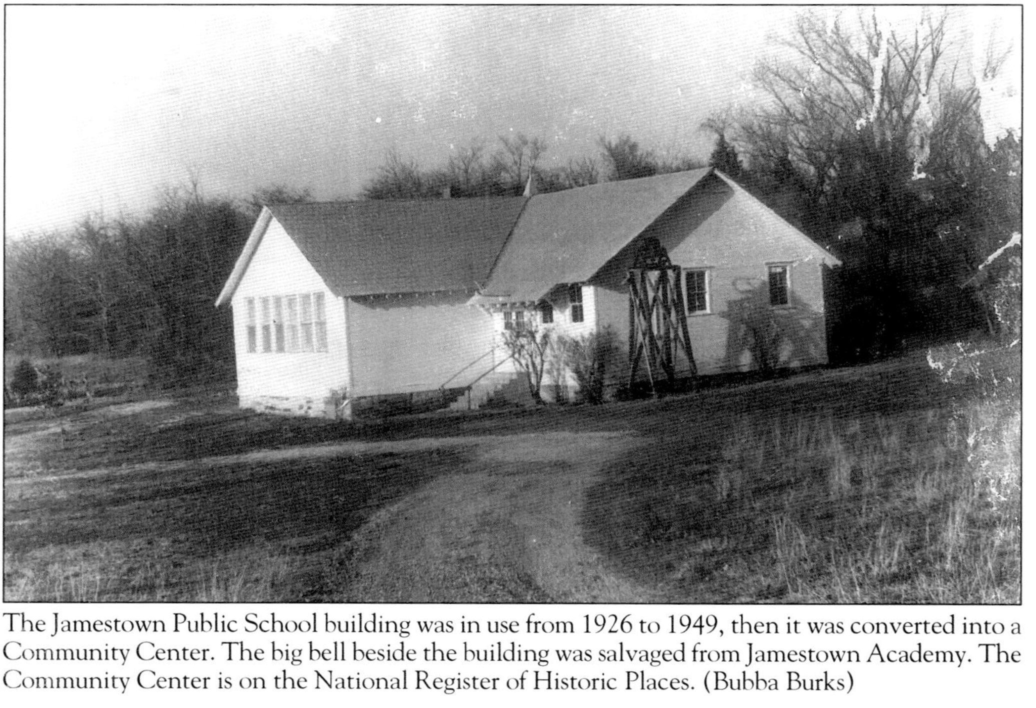

The Jamestown Public School building was in use from 1926 to 1949, then it was converted into a Community Center. The big bell beside the building was salvaged from Jamestown Academy. The Community Center is on the National Register of Historic Places. (Bubba Burks)

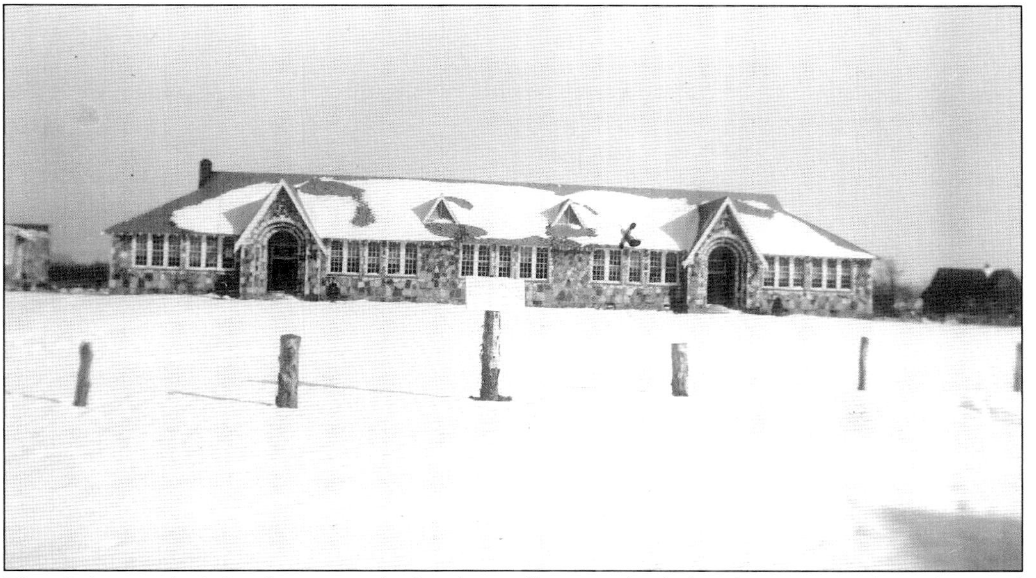

The Oil Trough School, a typical "Ozark giraffe," was built by the WPA. The colors and placement of sandstone rocks led to the appellation. (Sandra Cox)

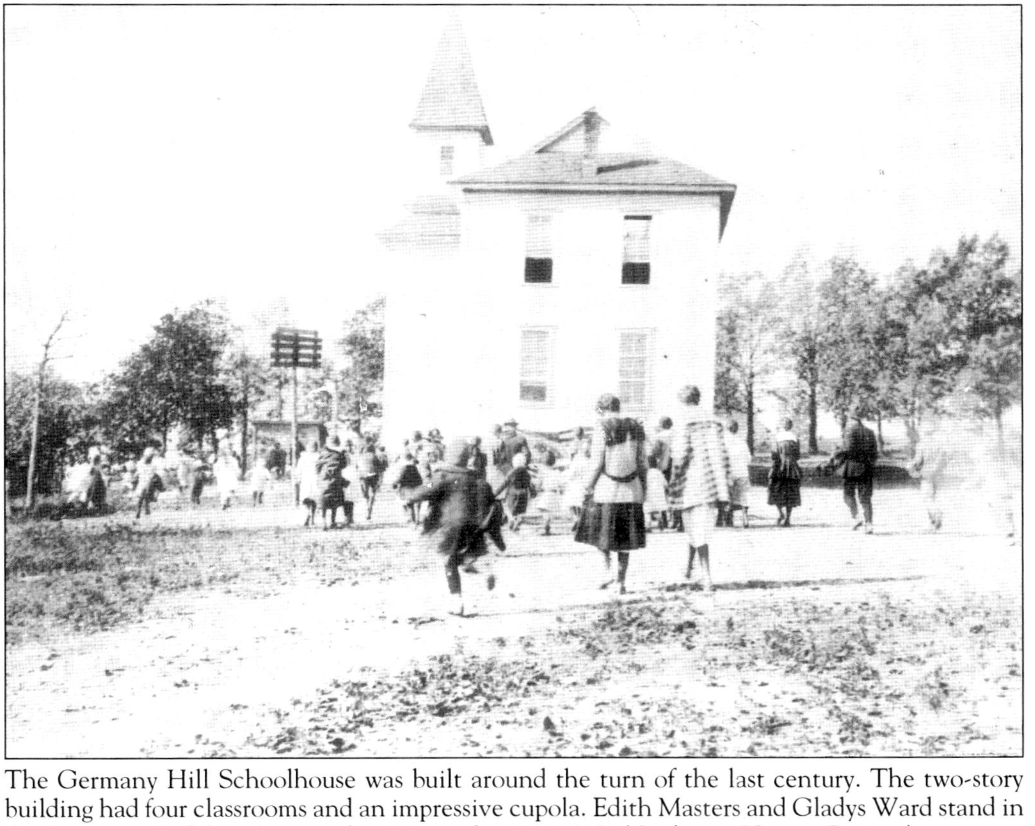

The Germany Hill Schoolhouse was built around the turn of the last century. The two-story building had four classrooms and an impressive cupola. Edith Masters and Gladys Ward stand in the foreground of this picture taken November 11, 1918. (Cushman History Project)

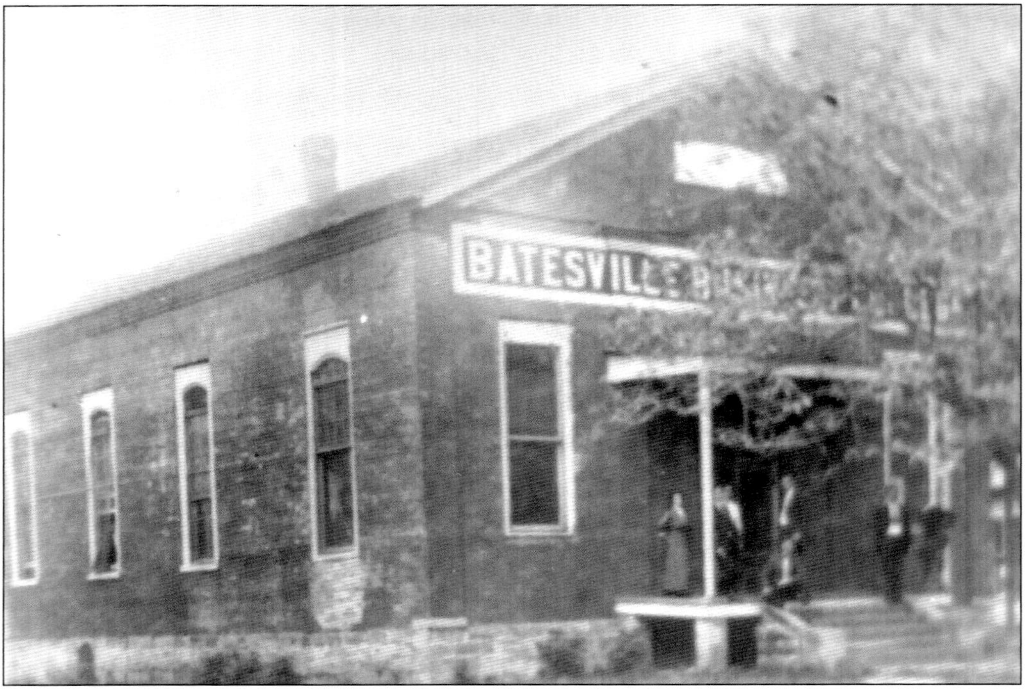

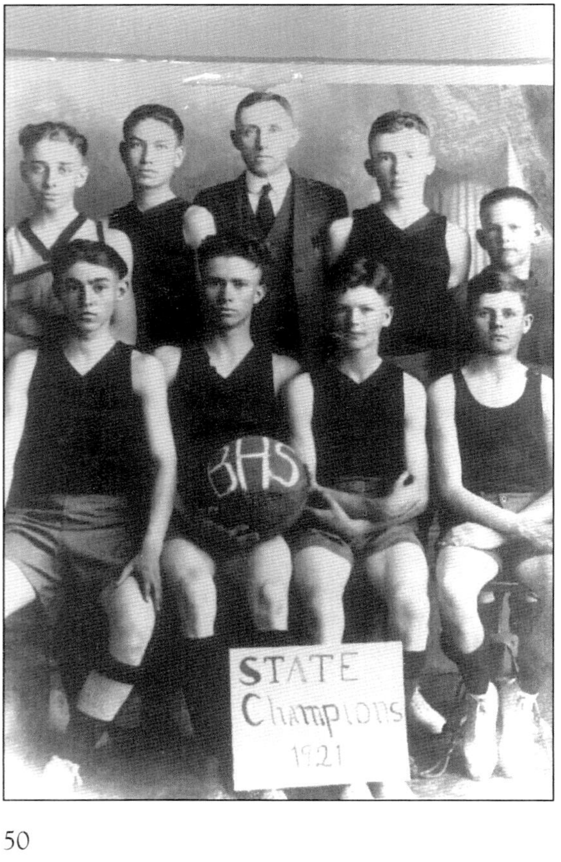

The Batesville Business College reported an enrollment of 60 students from February to October 1914, and was actively recruiting more. The board of directors of the local institution included D.D. Adams, F.B. Adams, A.L. Crouch, Dr. F.A. Gray, J.A. Hinkle, Samuel A. Moore, and T.J. Walbert. The Business College was housed in the original 1849 sanctuary of the Presbyterian Church. (Nancy Britton)

The Batesville Pioneers were the state basketball champions in 1921. (Regional Studies Center, Lyon College)

The Isaac J. Long Memorial Building, constructed in 1892, was the crowning edifice of the original Arkansas College campus. The first floor contained classrooms, the library, and an office for the curator. The second floor housed more classrooms, the museum, and the Erosophic Society. When the college moved to its present location, this building was razed. It was replaced by the current sanctuary of First Presbyterian Church in 1968. (Brian Robertson)

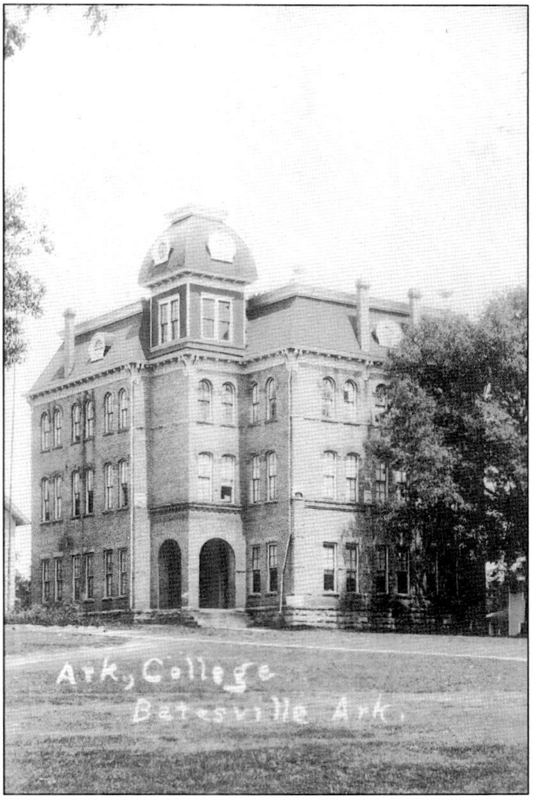

The Cushman School got its first school bus in 1930–31 when Tom Shell converted a truck into a bus. Doubtless the young students eagerly awaited the arrival of their new mode of transportation to and from school. (Cushman History Project)

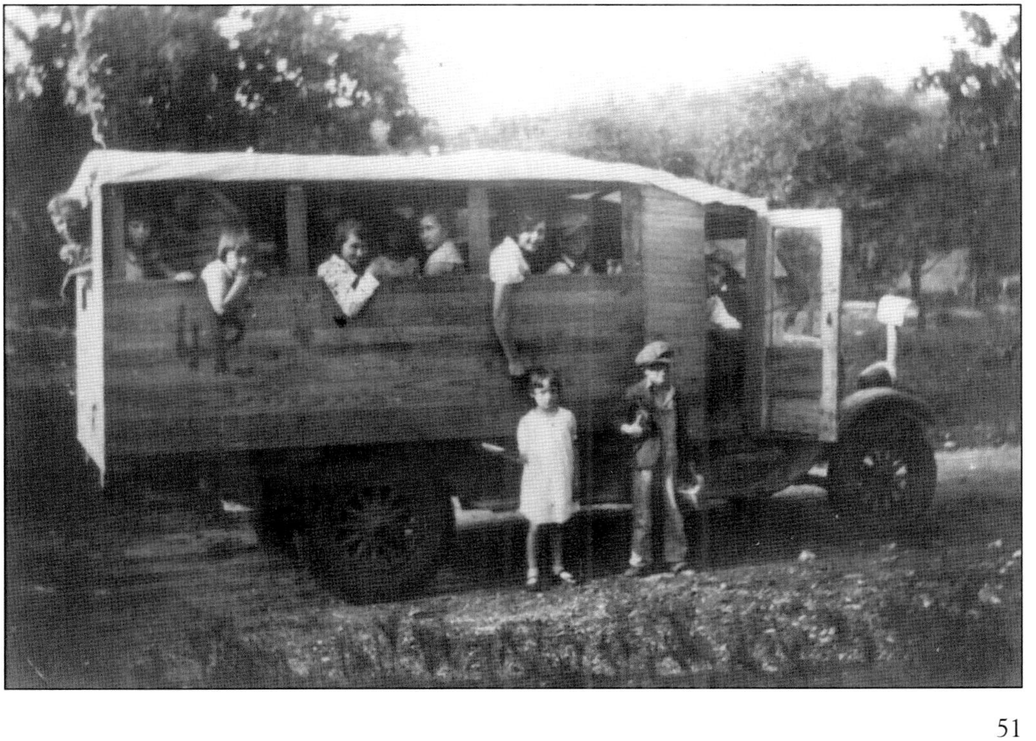

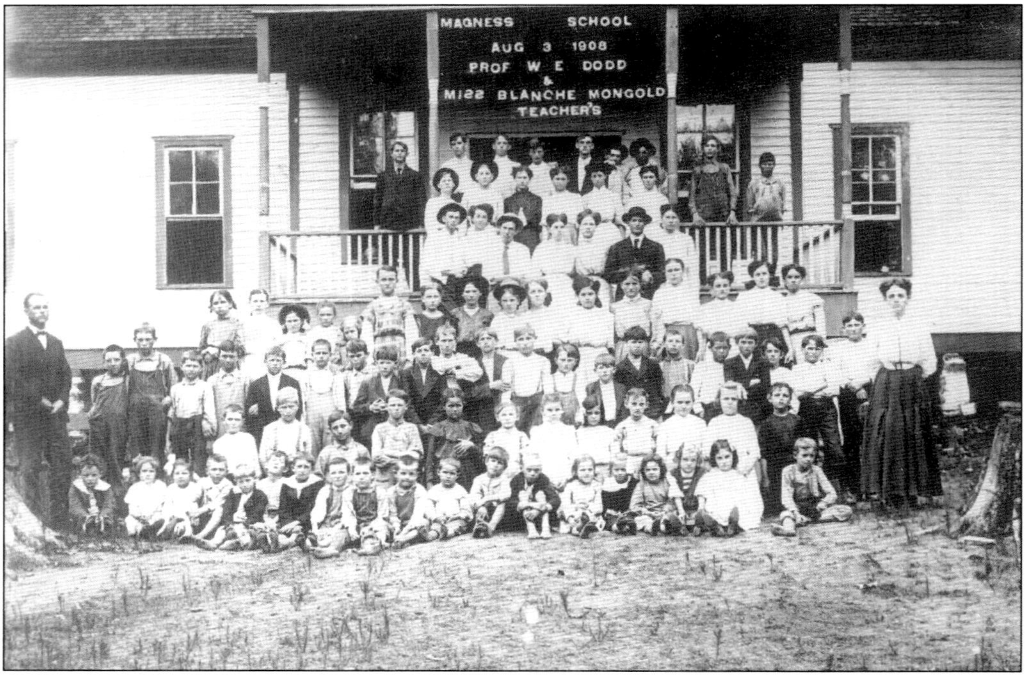

The Magness School District was created by order of the county court about 1875. The school was expanded in 1905, but soon after a new building was created to accommodate the large number of students. This view of the school was taken August 3, 1908. The teachers were W.E. Dodd (left) and Blanche Mongold (right). (William Perry Magness)

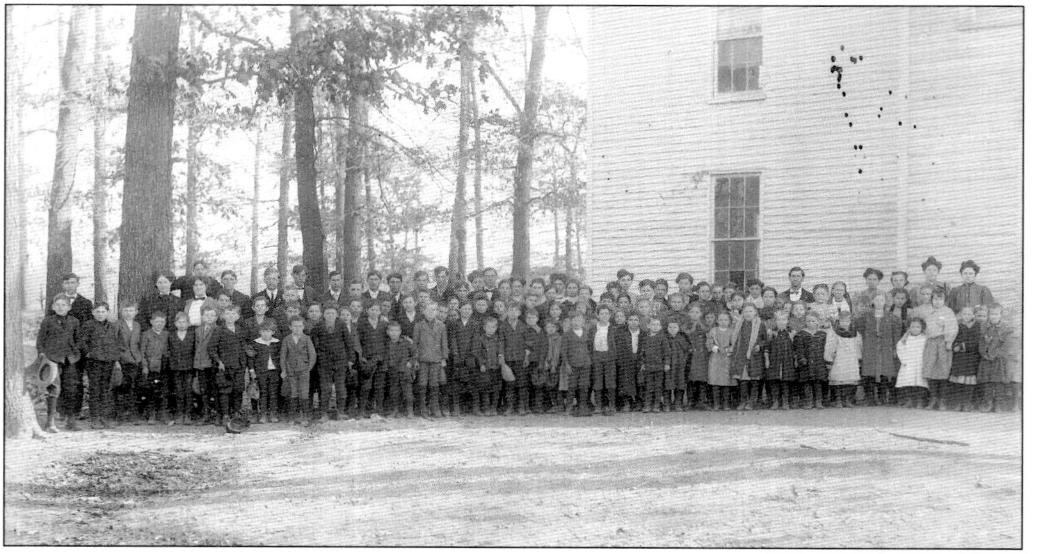

In 1872, a group of leading citizens in Sulphur Rock decided to get together and start an academy to educate the children in the local area. The Sulphur Rock Male and Female Academy operated for a number of years before being turned over to the public school system in 1906. In this March 15, 1908, photo, the building was the Sulphur Rock High School. It was in use until 1935, when it was destroyed by fire. (Wilson Powell)

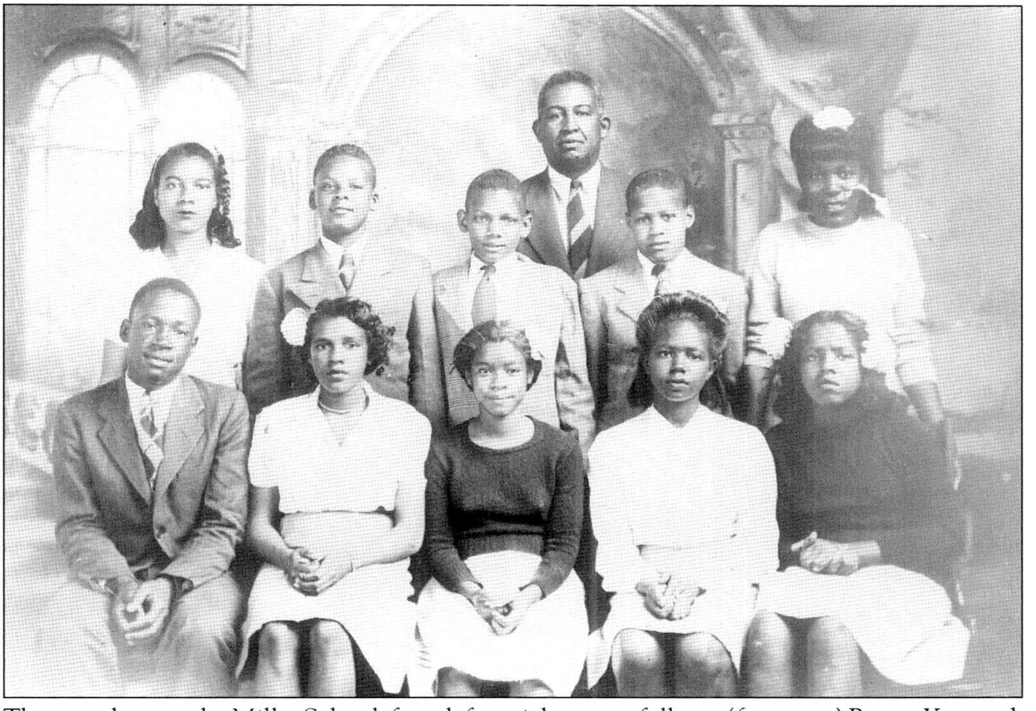

These students at the Miller School, from left to right, are as follows: (front row) Rayon Kennard, George Edna White, Anita Brown, Hannah Mae Kitchens, and Coquette Crawford; (back row) Ida McCurn, Richard Sales, Eugene Lexion, Mr. Miller, Hinston Rucker, and Mildred Barris. (Regional Studies Center, Lyon College)

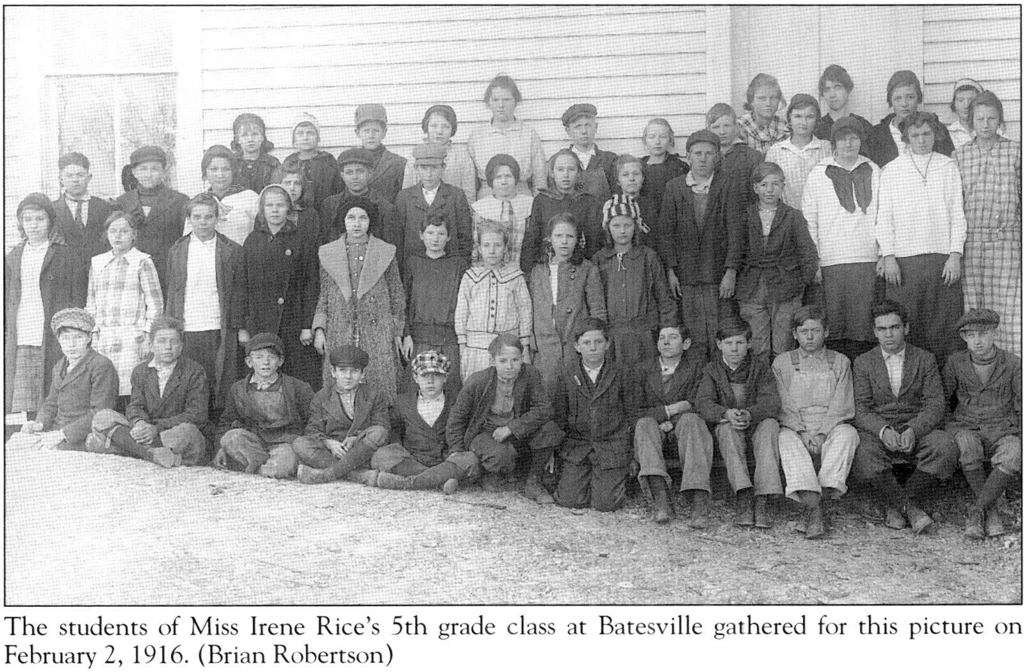

The students of Miss Irene Rice's 5th grade class at Batesville gathered for this picture on February 2, 1916. (Brian Robertson)

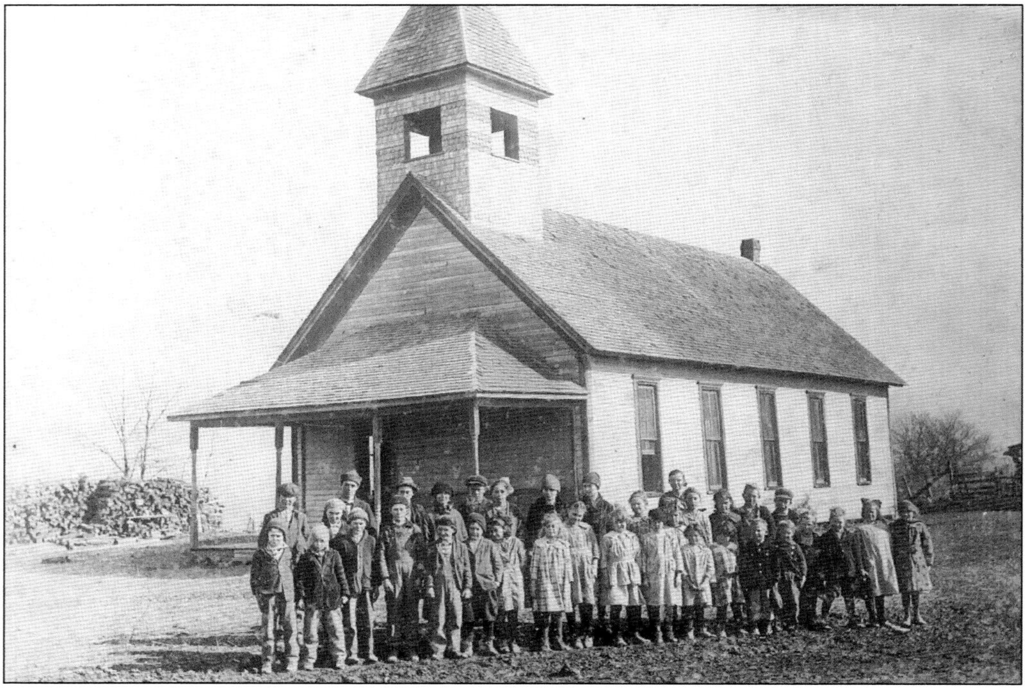

The White School was located in the bottoms, south of Newark. It was believed to have been started in 1889, when Theodore Maxfield deeded two acres of land for a school building. The building burned down in 1914. It was rebuilt, but was burned down by arsonists in 1918. A new building was built and served the community for a number of years as a school and church building. (Sandra Cox)

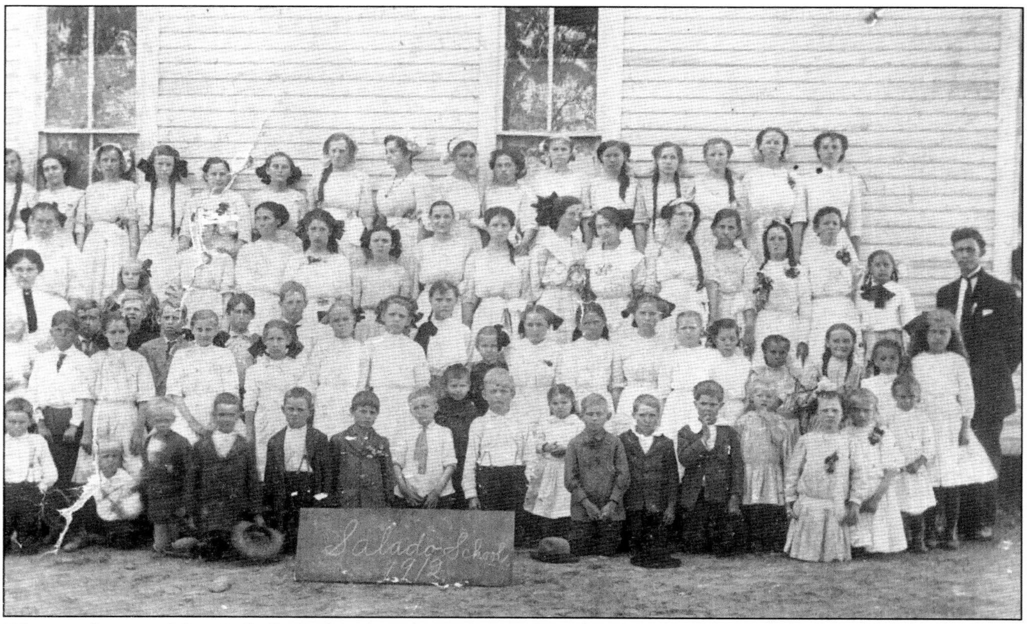

The students of the Salado School gathered together for this 1912 photo. (Wilson Powell)

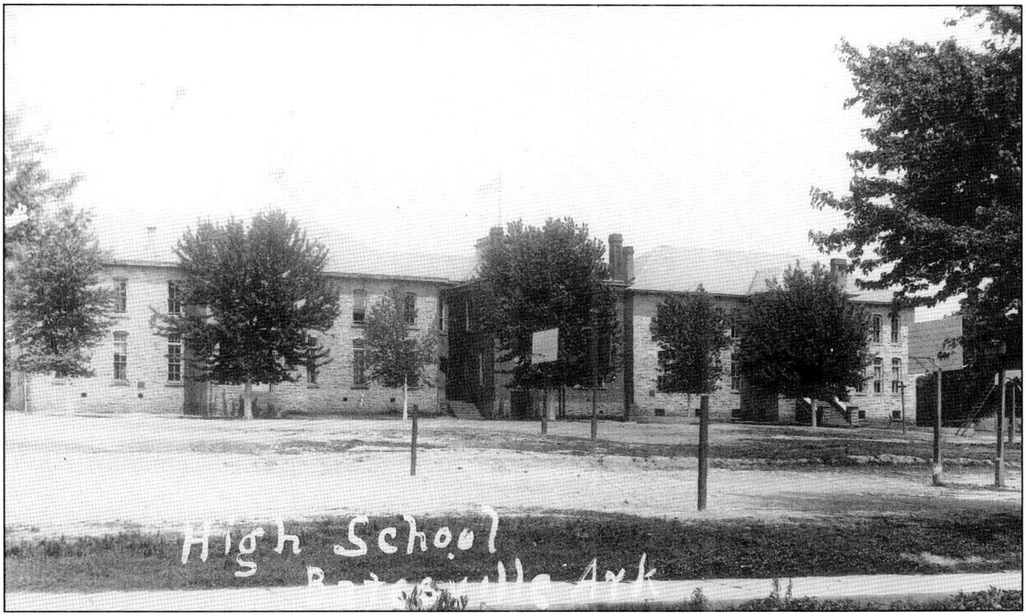

The old Batesville High School, located on Seventh Street between Vine and Oak Streets, served the school district for a number of years. Built in 1892, it was razed in 1961. (Brian Robertson)

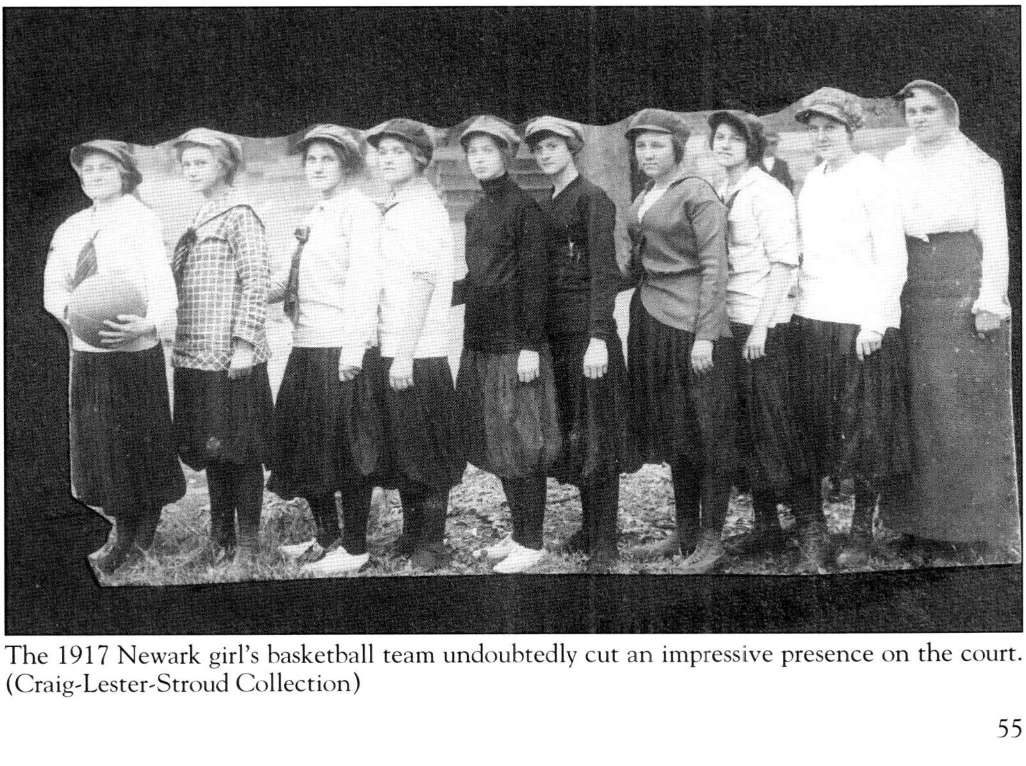

The 1917 Newark girl's basketball team undoubtedly cut an impressive presence on the court. (Craig-Lester-Stroud Collection)

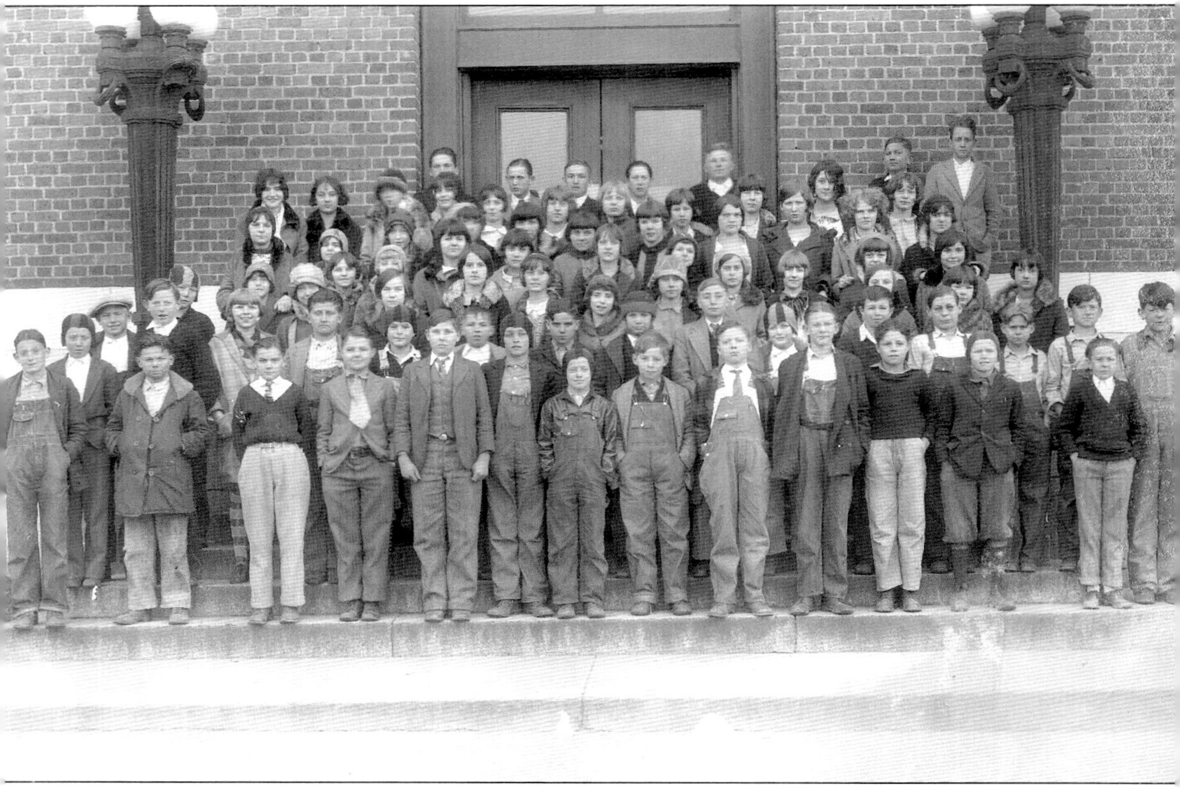

This unidentified group of Batesville students is gathered on the post office steps in downtown Batesville. (Wilson Powell)

Four

Religion

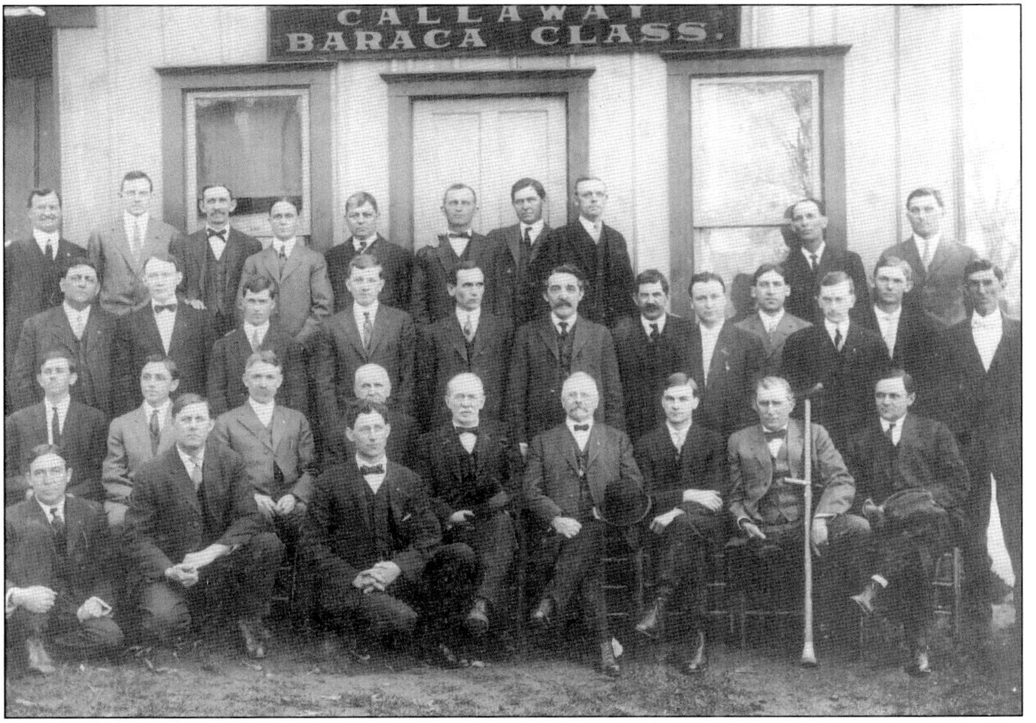

Lined up here is the Callaway-Baraca Sunday School Class of First Baptist Church in Batesville. The Baraca movement was an interdenominational Sunday School organization for young men. (Wilson Powell)

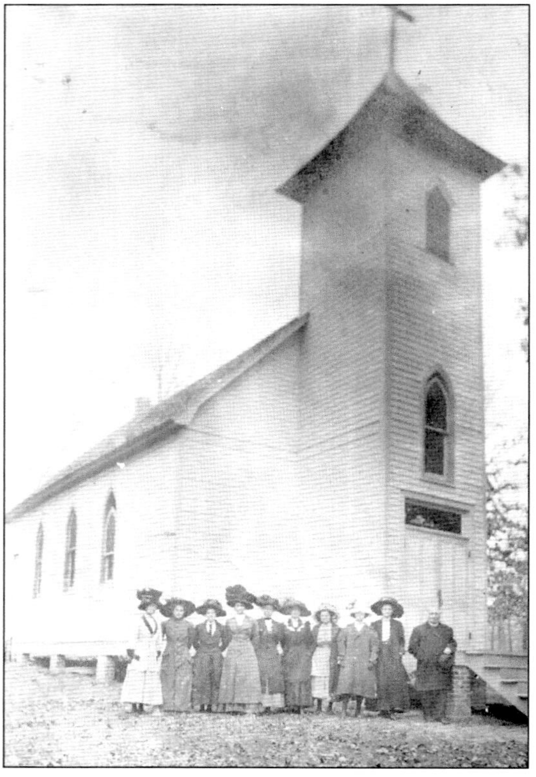

St. Fidelis Roman Catholic Church was built in 1909 in the woods east of Batesville. Today it would have been located on the slight rise of ground between the present Maple and College Streets, facing what is now Eighteenth Street. A priest came from Newport to conduct services. The church was vandalized in 1921, some say by the Ku Klux Klan. Considered desecrated, it was vacated and razed. Members of the congregation stored the windows, altar, and other furnishings in their homes until another sanctuary would be erected some 15 years later. (Independence County Historical Society)

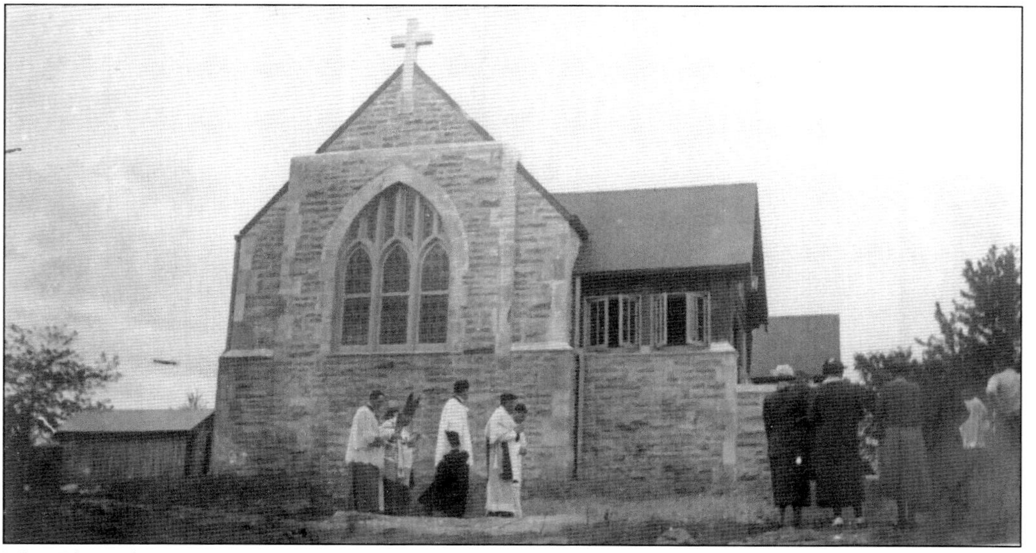

The Blessed Sacrament Roman Catholic Church was dedicated in Batesville in 1936. This lovely building was a Charles Thompson design. It stood on a lot facing College Street, just east of St. Louis Street. It was used until the congregation outgrew it and bought a larger building downtown at Fifth and Boswell in 1965. Blessed Sacrament then became the Parish Hall and was used for meetings. It was eventually razed to make room for a supermarket. (Independence County Historical Society)

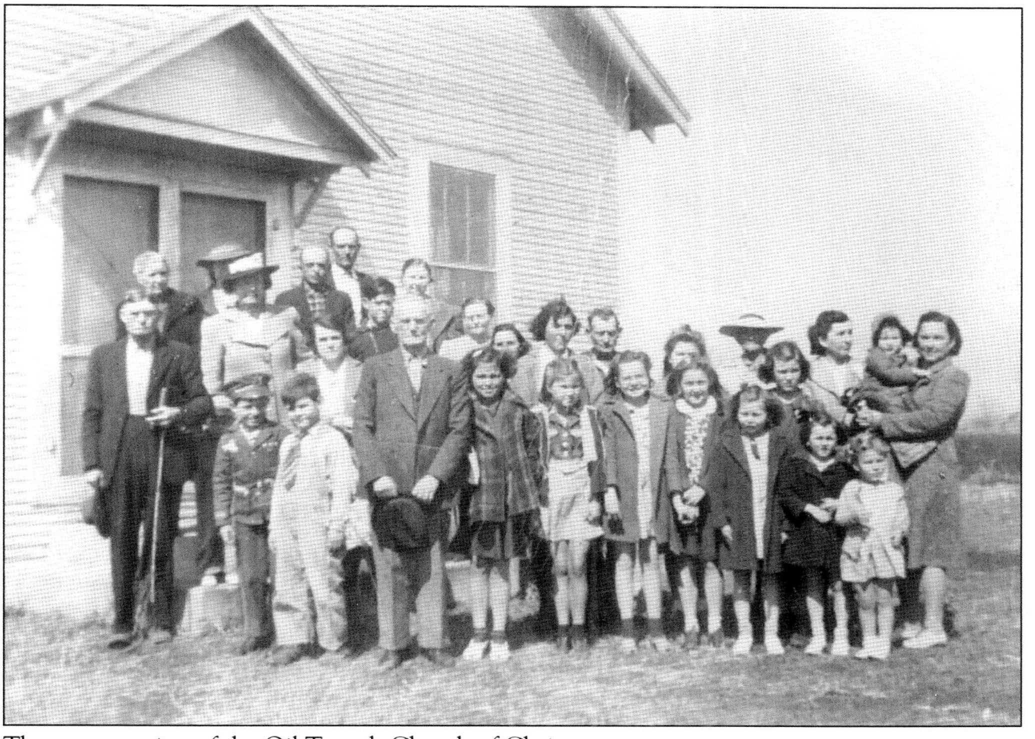

The congregation of the Oil Trough Church of Christ stands in front of their frame church that was destroyed by a tornado in 1944. The members built a new rock church, which was also destroyed by a tornado in 1968. (Sandra Cox)

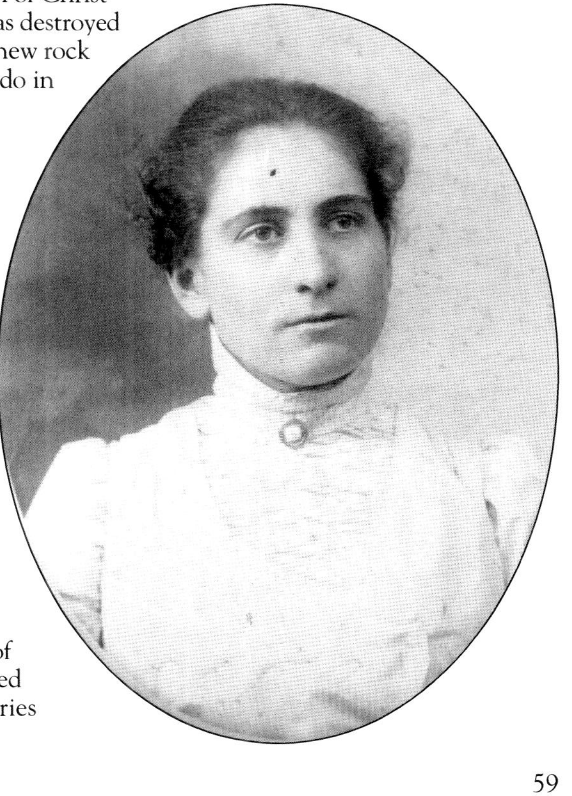

Following the death of her fiance, Miss Esther Case dedicated herself to religious work. In 1894, she became the first woman from Arkansas to go into foreign missionary work for the Methodist Episcopal Church, South. She taught in mission schools in Mexico for many years, then worked for the General Board of Missions until her death in 1932. She visited every continent where Methodist missionaries were working. (Nancy Britton)

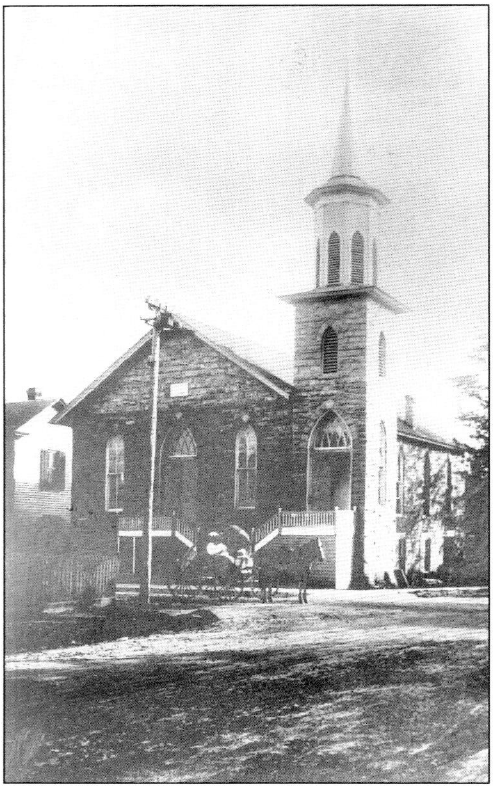

The second sanctuary of the Methodist Episcopal Church, South, in Batesville was completed in 1883 and used until 1913. It stood at the southwest corner of Third and College Streets, facing Third. The gable end of the parsonage can be seen next door. (Nancy Britton)

The groundbreaking for the new First Methodist Church, South, in Batesville was held in 1913. The man designated #5 in front is V.Y. Cook, who donated the land for the church; #13 is the pastor, Reverend T.Y. Ramsey. In the background is the magnificent home of the M.A. Wycough family. It is still standing in 2001, reduced to two stories because of a fire. (First United Methodist Church)

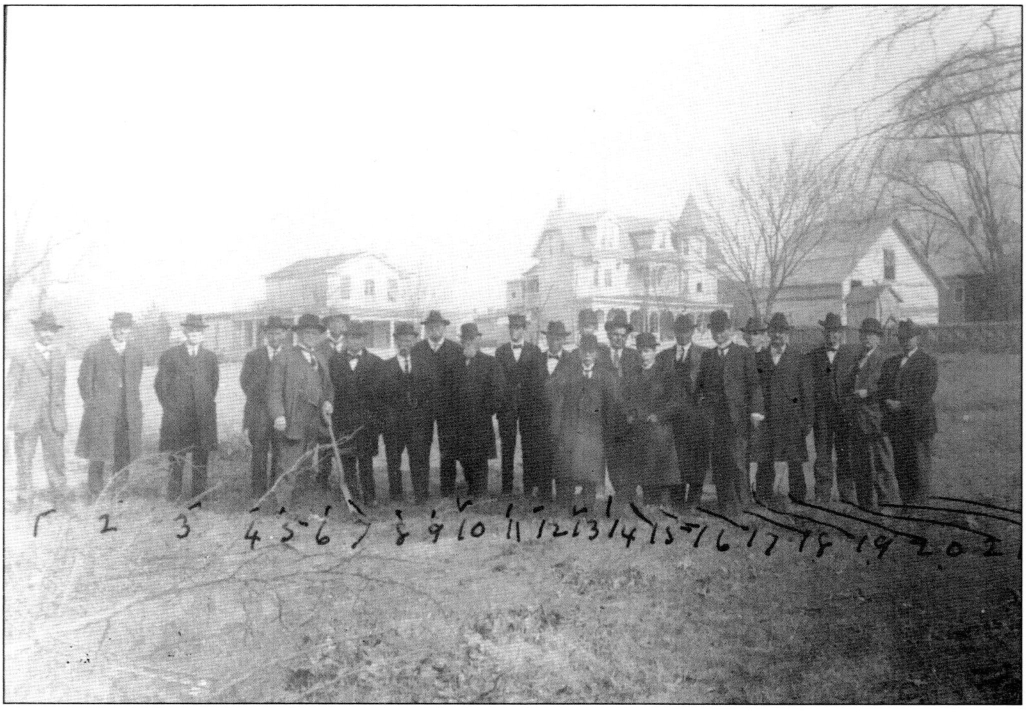

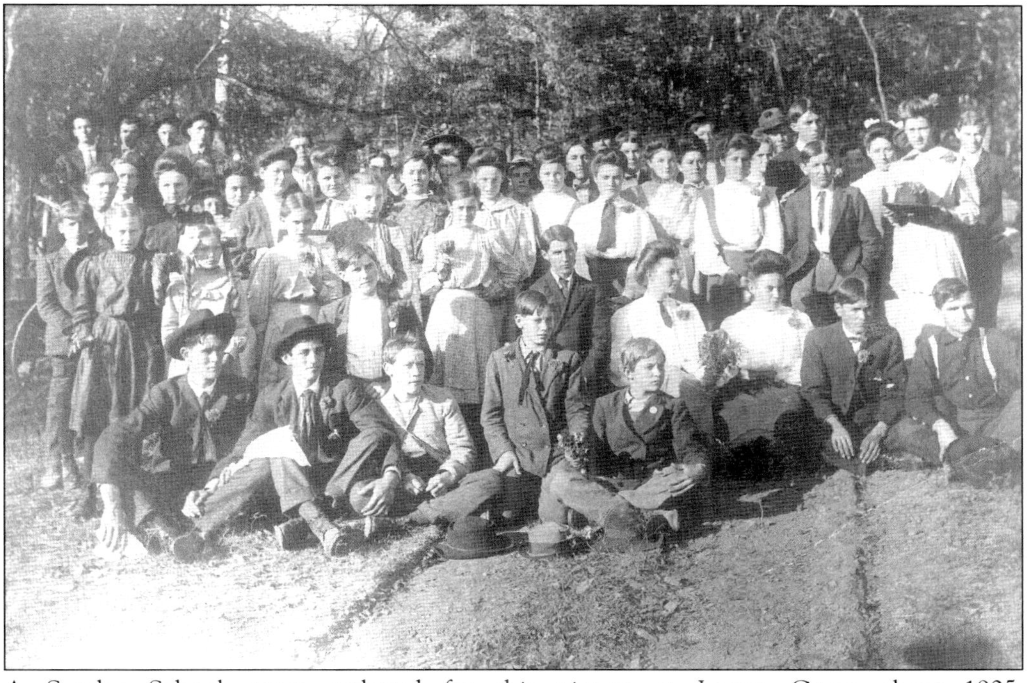

A Sunday School group gathered for this picture at Locust Grove about 1905. (Kenny Gerhardt)

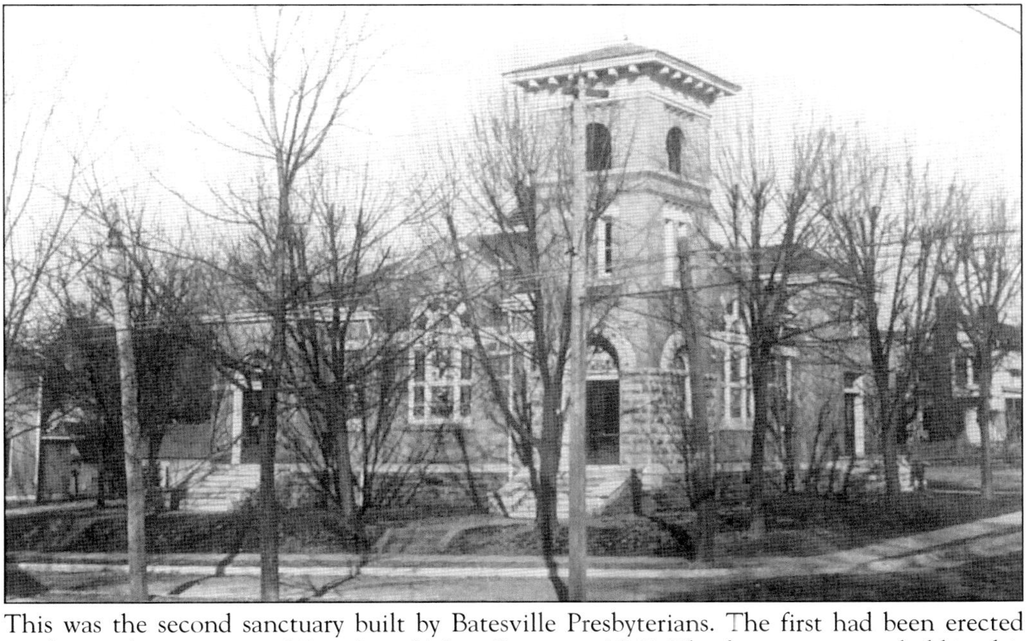

This was the second sanctuary built by Batesville Presbyterians. The first had been erected on the northeast corner of Fourth and Main Streets in 1849. The first service was held in this church, located on the northwest corner of Seventh and College Streets in January 1911, and the last service in June 1968. After the congregation had moved into the present sanctuary, this building was torn down. The site remains a vacant lot today. (Brian Robertson)

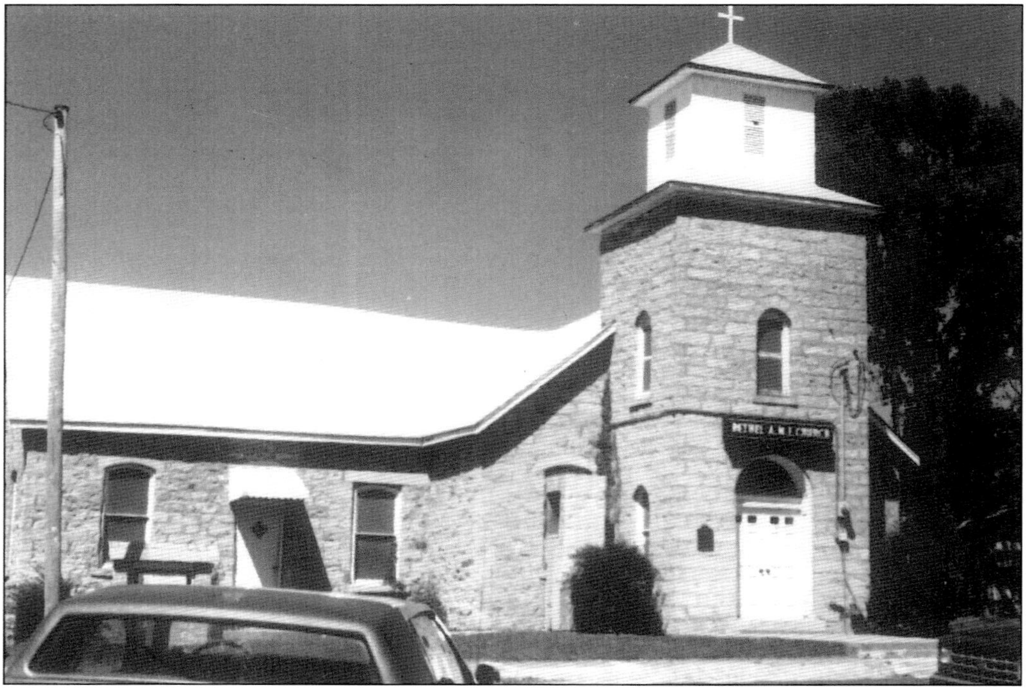

The first mention of the AME Church in Batesville is a deed for this lot at Ninth and Oak Streets to the "trustees of the AME Church: Charles Findley, Samuel Greer, and Sandy Willis" by William Byers in 1871. A small frame building was erected, but it burned in 1881. The lot was then mortgaged to Simon Adler for $235 and the money used to construct the present building. The note was marked "paid in full" on April 22, 1886. Much of the work on the building was done by members who were stone masons and carpenters. One of the early preachers was M.F.A. Easton, who was also a teacher at the Freedmen's School in the 1870s. Bethel AME Church is the oldest church building in Batesville. (Independence County Historical Society)

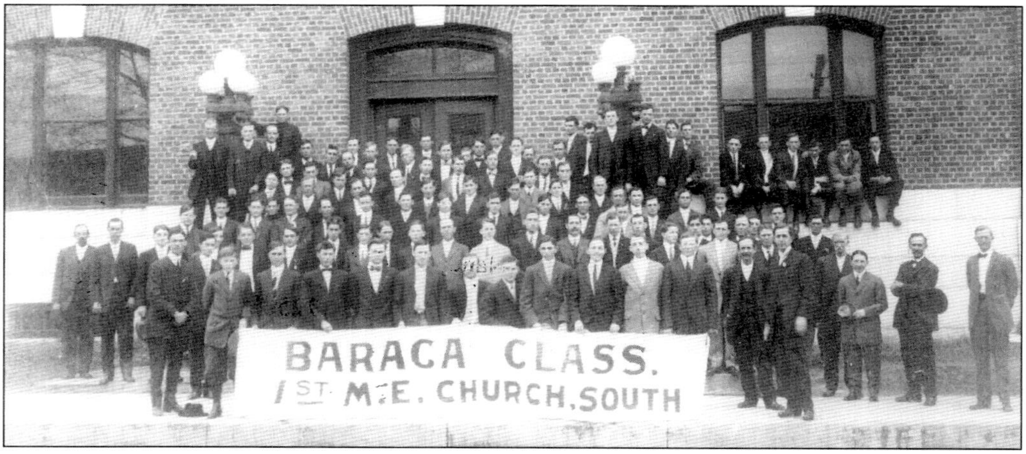

This photo of the Baraca Sunday School Class of First Methodist Church was made about 1915. The class was meeting in the Federal Building (now the public library) on Main Street at the time because it had grown so large. They also met for a time in the Melba Theater downtown. The teacher, Sidney Pickens, stands at left on the front row. (First United Methodist Church)

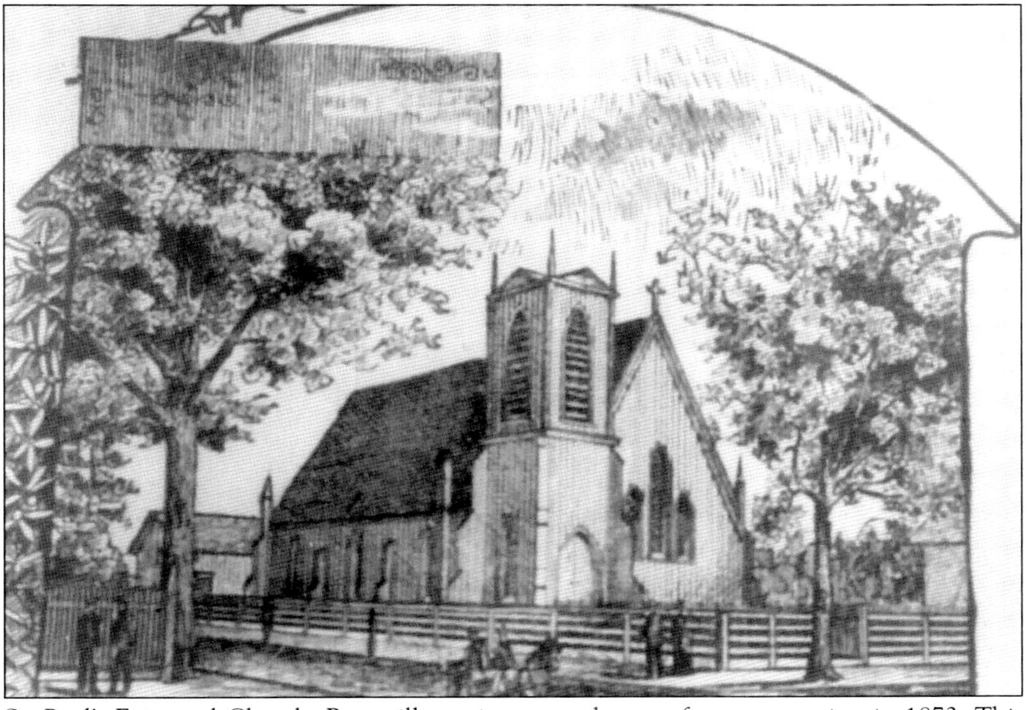

St. Paul's Episcopal Church, Batesville, as it appeared soon after construction in 1873. This engraving is from Hempstead's *Pictorial History of Arkansas*.

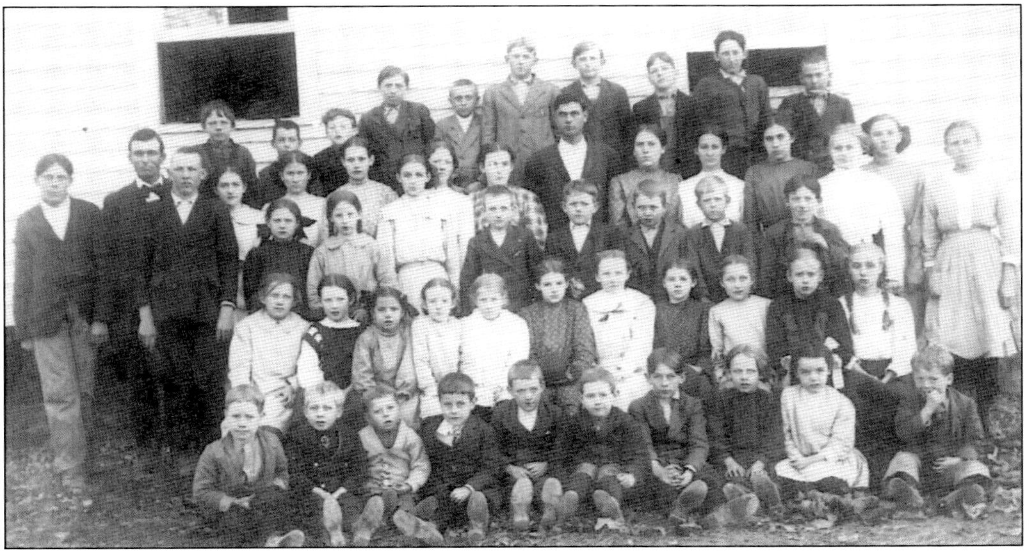

Campground United Methodist Church at Bethesda can trace its history back to 1841, when 10 acres of land were deeded to the church by Rev. Juba Estabrook to be used for camp meetings. The original church building stood by an old spring and people came from miles away to worship there. The meetings sometimes lasted for weeks and two small log cabins were built near the church for worshippers to camp in. The children of the congregation posed for this picture about 1905. (Doyle McSpadden)

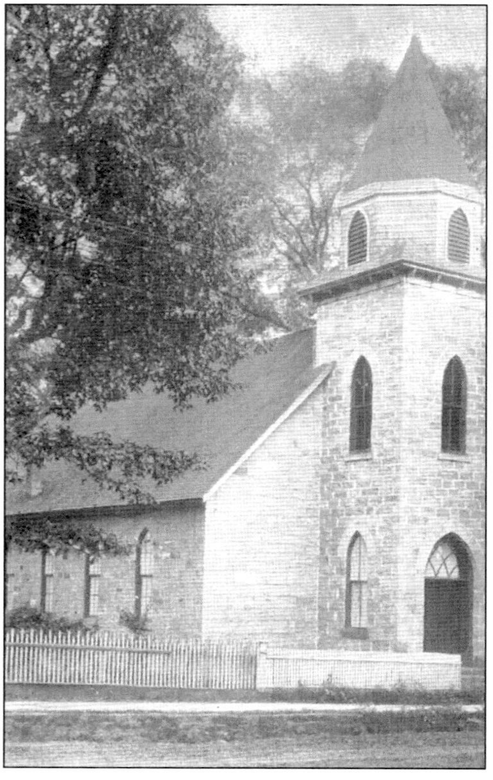

"Batesville Baptist Church Number One" was organized in 1847. Early services were held in homes and schools, until a small frame structure was built at Ninth and Oak Streets in 1851. This building proved to be too small and it was sold in 1861. The congregation met variously in the courthouse, Soulesbury Institute, and other churches on Sunday afternoons until this sanctuary was built of stone in 1881. It was used until 1925, when it was torn down and replaced by the present church. Many of the materials from the 1881 church were reused in building the new one. (Brian Robertson)

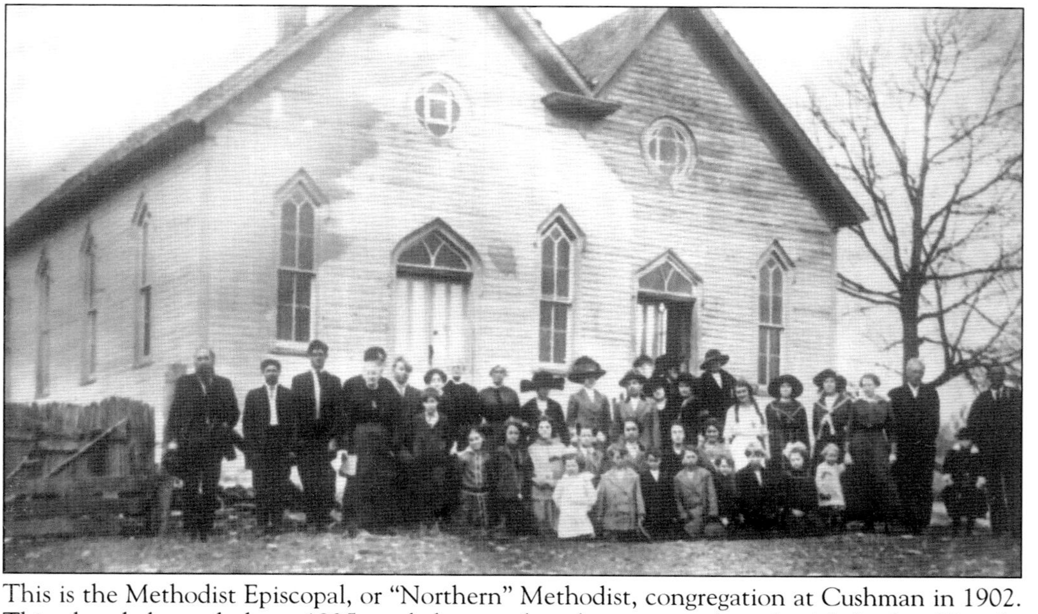

This is the Methodist Episcopal, or "Northern" Methodist, congregation at Cushman in 1902. This church burned about 1925, and the members began attending the Methodist Church, South. These two branches of Methodism in America were reunited officially in 1939. (Cushman History Project)

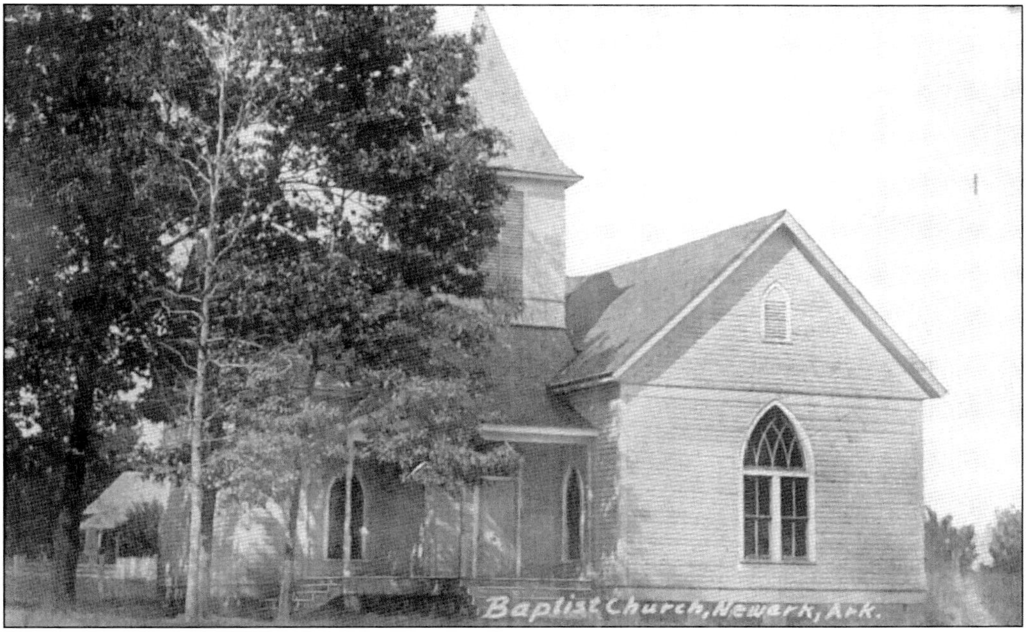

The Newark Baptist Church was organized as the Missionary Baptist Church of Jesus Christ on April 22, 1901. Plans were made for a new church building in 1903. The church held ice cream socials and box suppers as fundraisers for the new construction. The new building was completed in 1905 with the addition of a 500 pound bell. This image dates from c. 1909. (James Logan Morgan)

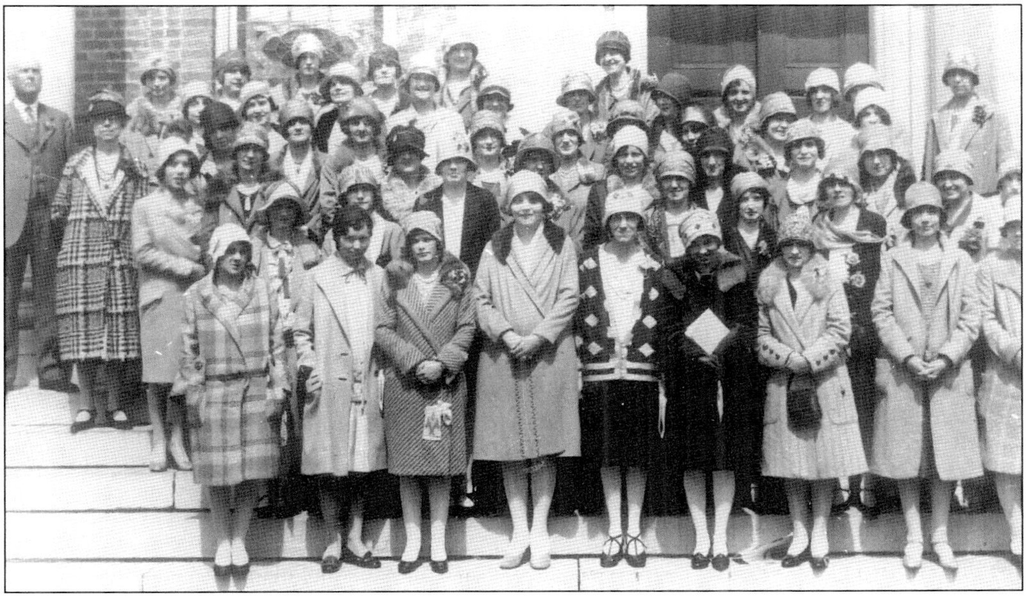

The Jones Bible Class of First Methodist Church, Batesville, was a Sunday School class for young women. They are posed here on the steps in front of the church with their longtime teachers, Mr. and Mrs. W.P. Jones. Judging by the popular cloche hat style, the photo was probably made in the early 1930s. (First United Methodist Church)

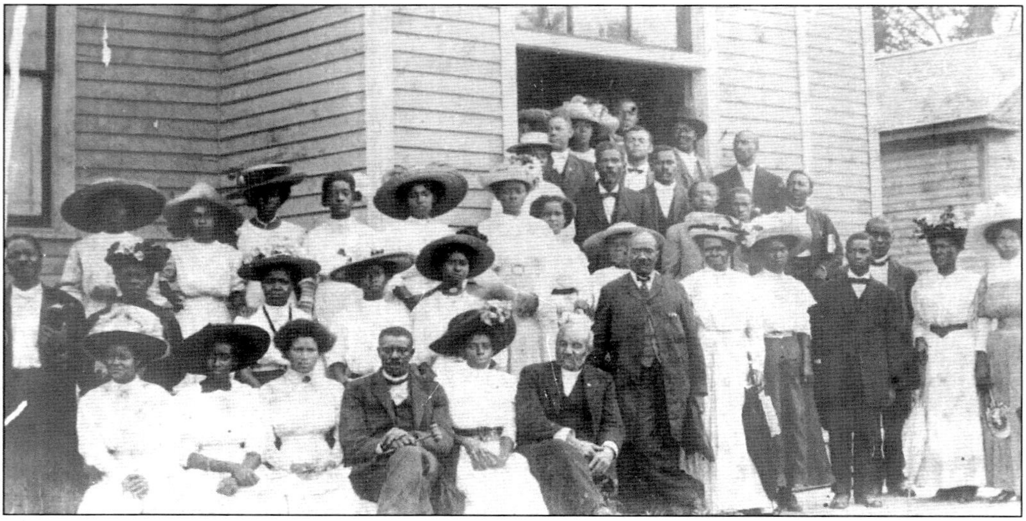

The congregation of Batesville's Lafferty Methodist Episcopal Church gathered in front of their church c. 1905. The building was constructed in 1864 by white members of the ME or Northern branch of the Methodist Church. In 1883, the white ME members walked across the street and joined the ME Church, South. At that time they turned this building over to the black ME congregation, which had been meeting elsewhere. Lafferty built a new sanctuary about 1917, and this building was torn down. When Lafferty was closed in 1968, its two remaining elderly members transferred to First United Methodist Church on Main Street. The pulpit and Bible from Lafferty were also moved there and placed in a small chapel. (Arkansas History Commission)

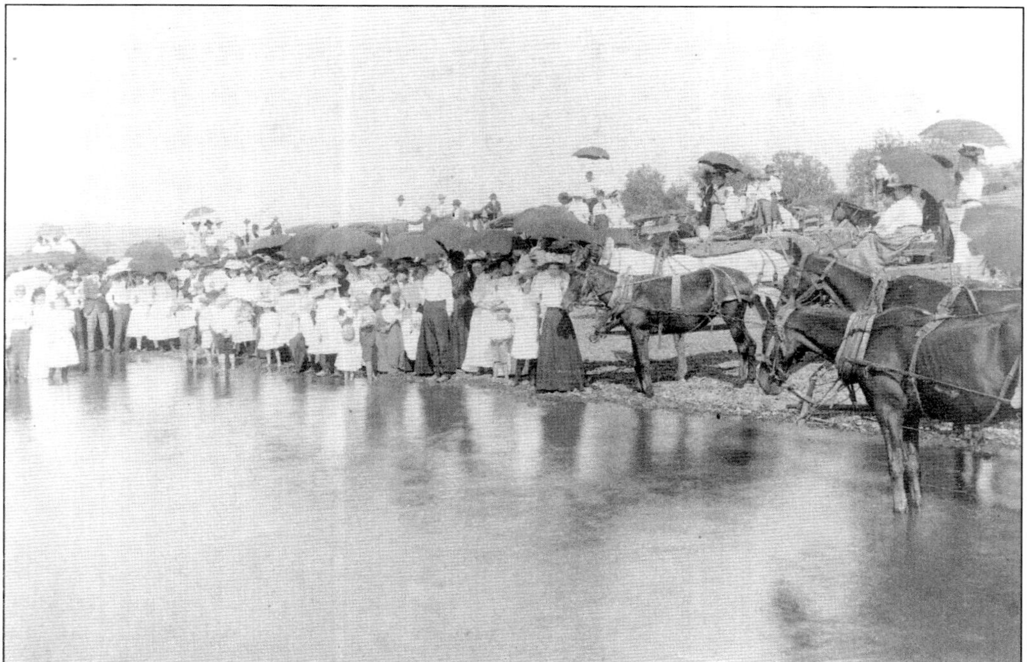

A baptizing in the White River about 1905. The site was near Locust Grove at the approximate site of the Gainor Ferry. (Independence County Historical Society)

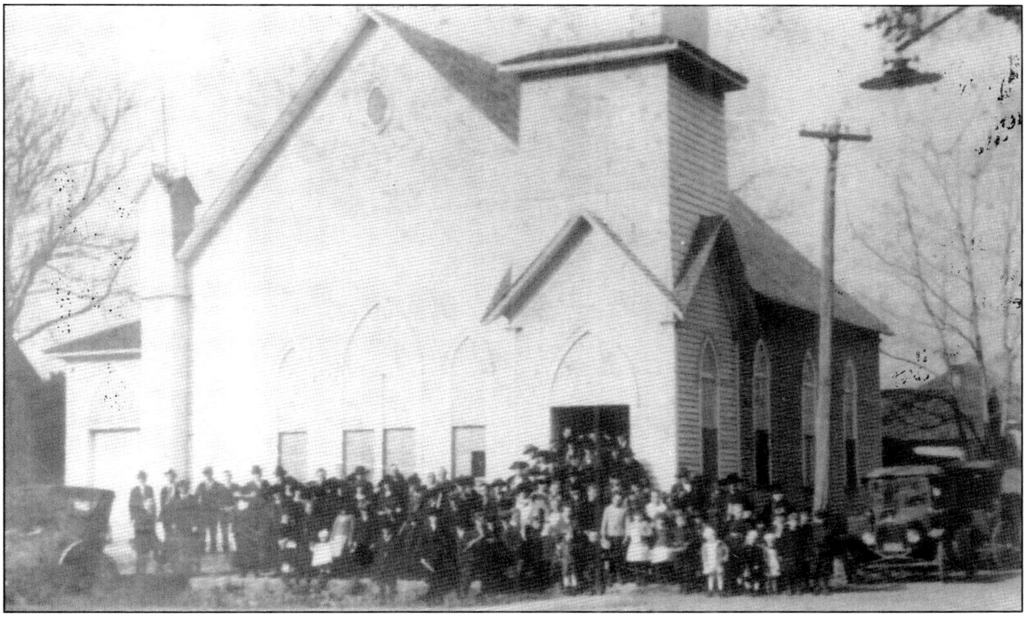

This church building was erected on the northwest corner of Fifth and Boswell Streets in Batesville in 1893 by Cumberland Presbyterians. From 1910 to 1953, it was used by the Christian Church. It then became the property of a Church of Christ congregation and was rocked with limestone slabs. In 1965 the building was purchased by the Roman Catholic Church and dedicated as St. Mary's. The Catholics used the building until their present sanctuary was completed in 1979. This building was torn down at that time to create parking for the post office. (Independence County Historical Society)

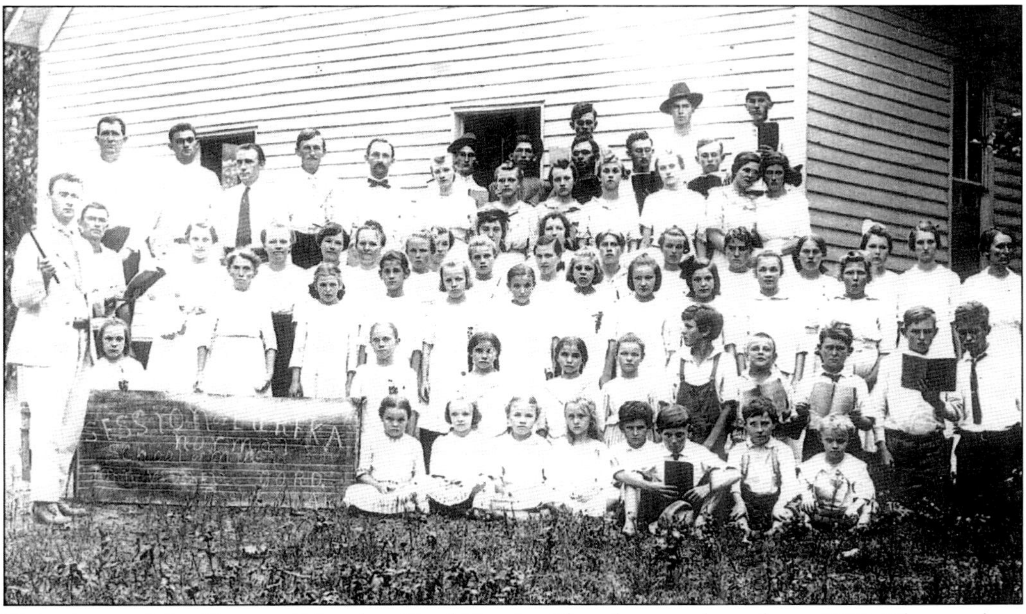

This photo of the Singing School at Cord Baptist Church was taken about 1910. The teacher, standing at the left, was John Mitchell. (Independence County Historical Society)

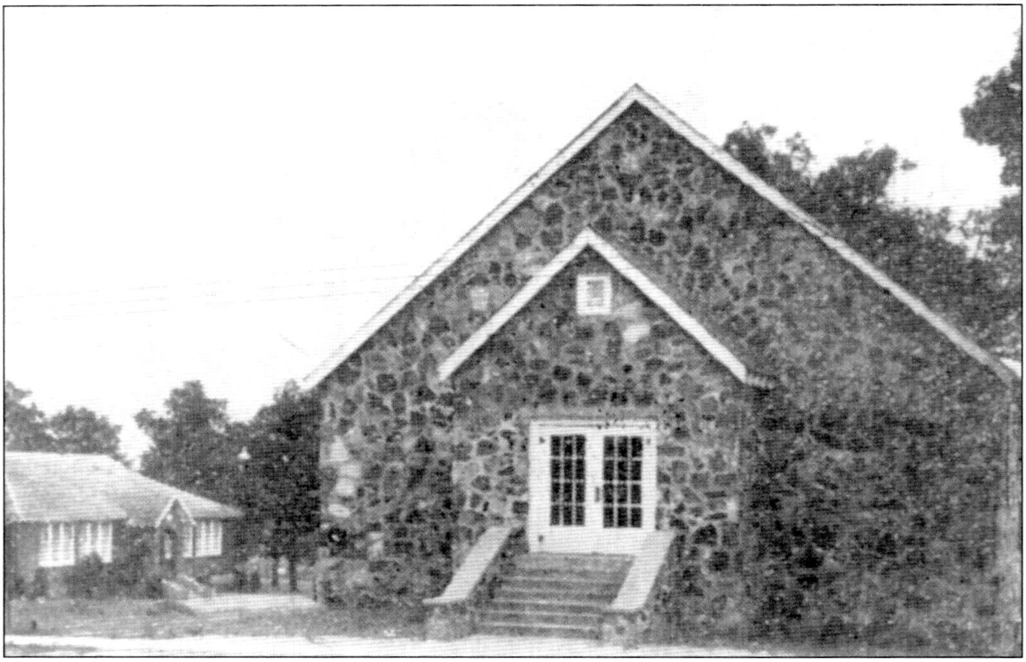

The congregation of Calvary Baptist Church, Batesville, began building this rock sanctuary in 1940, and held the first service in it in September 1943. It faced the present sanctuary, completed in 1954, across Lyon Street. It was razed in 1979. (Independence County Historical Society)

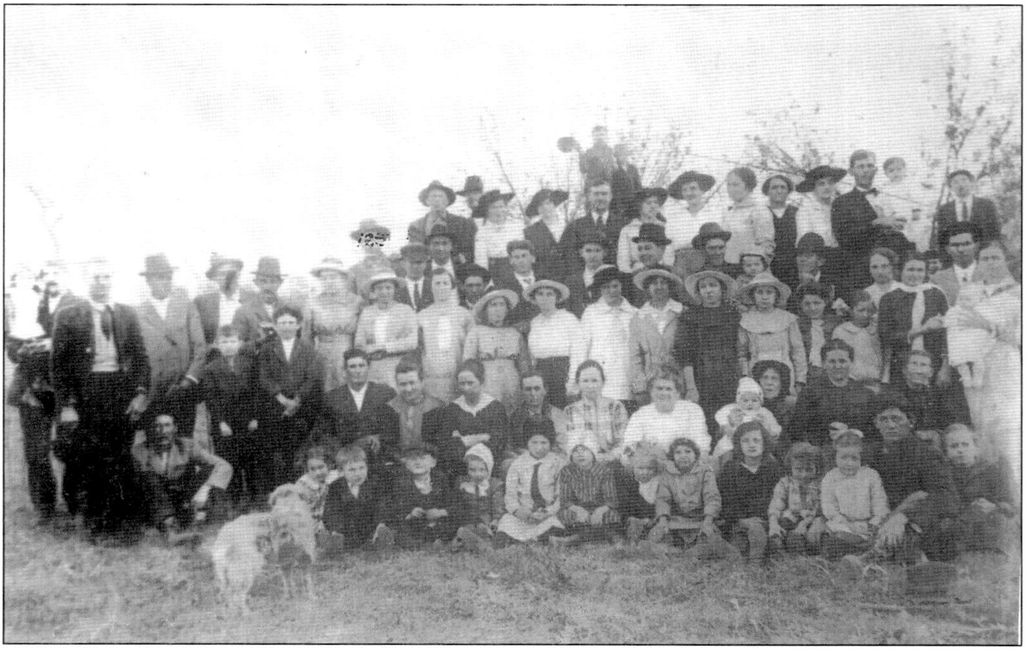

The congregation of Floral Baptist Church in a photograph taken about 1917. Standing, second from left, is Reverend John C. James. (Independence County Historical Society)j

Five

AGRICULTURE

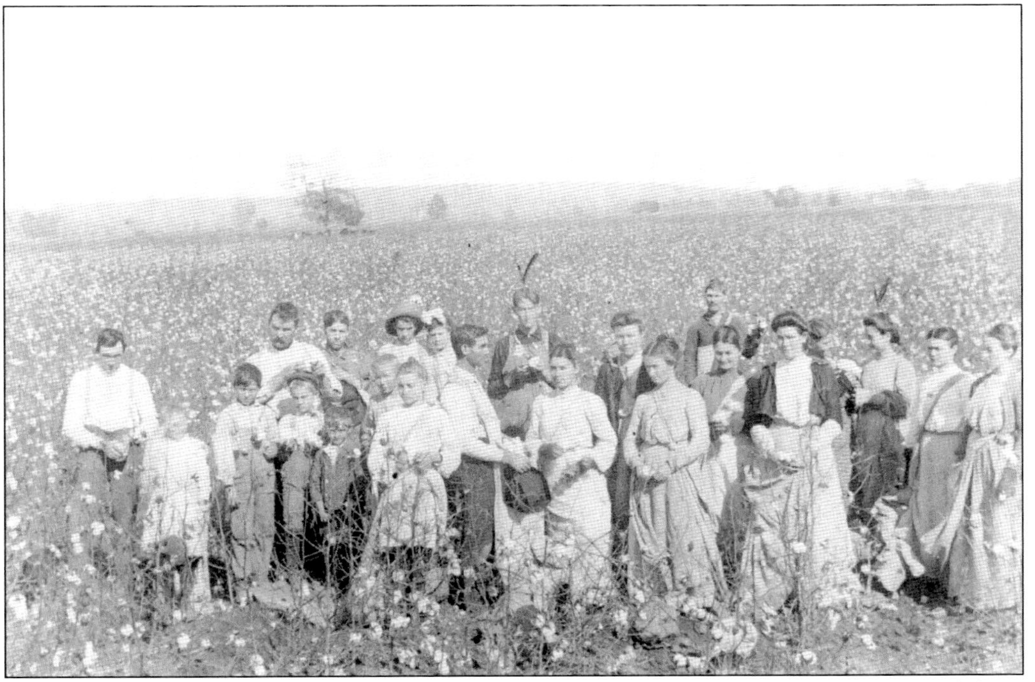

These cotton pickers in the Greenbrier Bottoms stopped from their back-breaking work long enough to have this picture made about 1905. (Kenny Gerhardt)

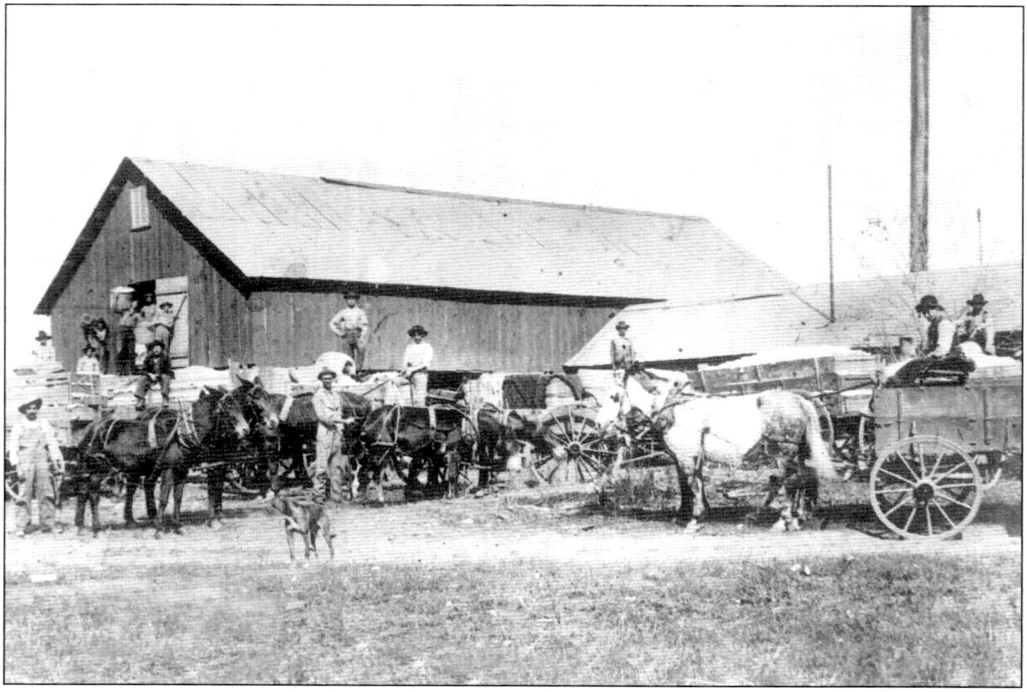

J.U. Martin operated this cotton gin at Sulphur Rock. He also ran a gin at Magness and was very successful in the ginning business for a number of years. Martin retired from the business in the early 1920s. Walter Reaves, another noted ginner, stands in the center of the picture, and his brother, Claud, is driving the waterwagon. (Wilson Powell)

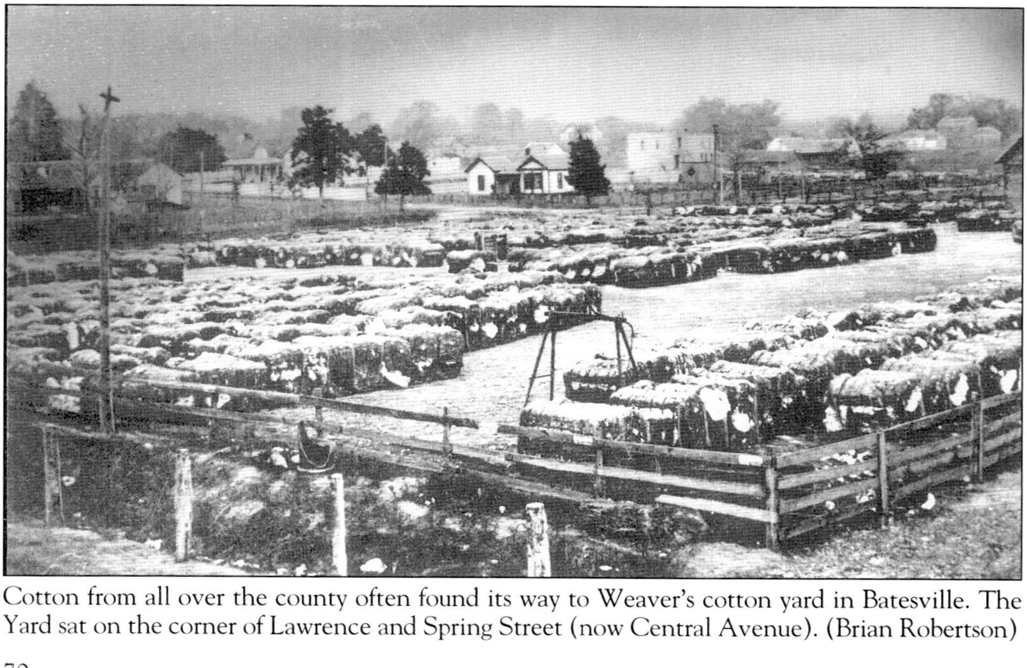

Cotton from all over the county often found its way to Weaver's cotton yard in Batesville. The Yard sat on the corner of Lawrence and Spring Street (now Central Avenue). (Brian Robertson)

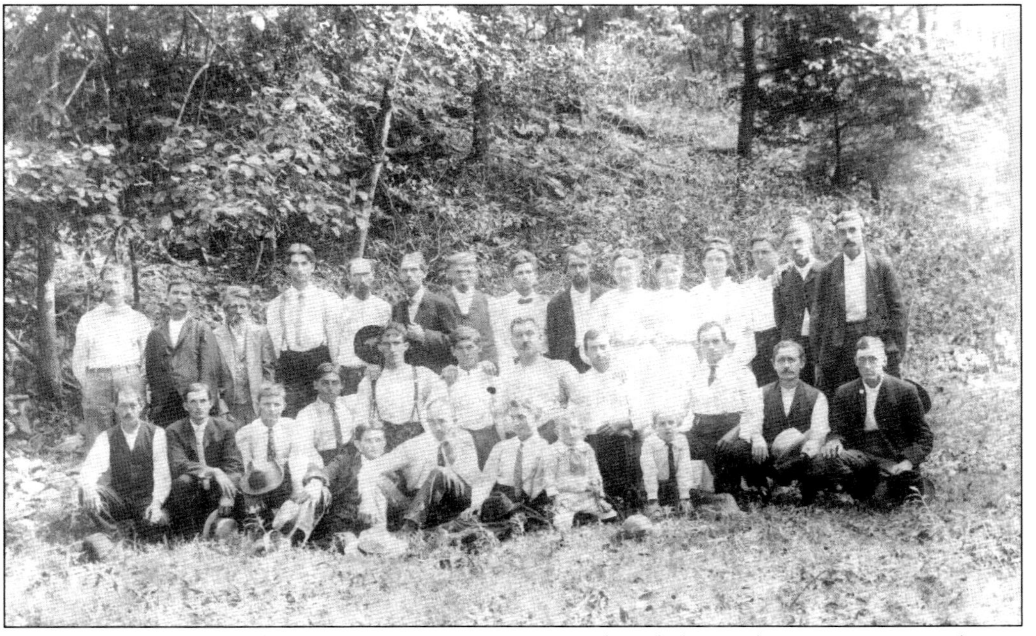

The Agricultural Wheel Cooperative Association was founded in Arkansas in 1882 and soon gained wide appeal among discontented farmers. There was an association in Independence County by 1887; two years later there were 38 known community groups in the county. Wheelers operated a cooperative store on Broad Street in Batesville from 1887–1894, and participated in the Union Labor Party campaigns of 1890. This group may be the Locust Grove Wheel or a similar organization of a later date. (Independence County Historical Society)

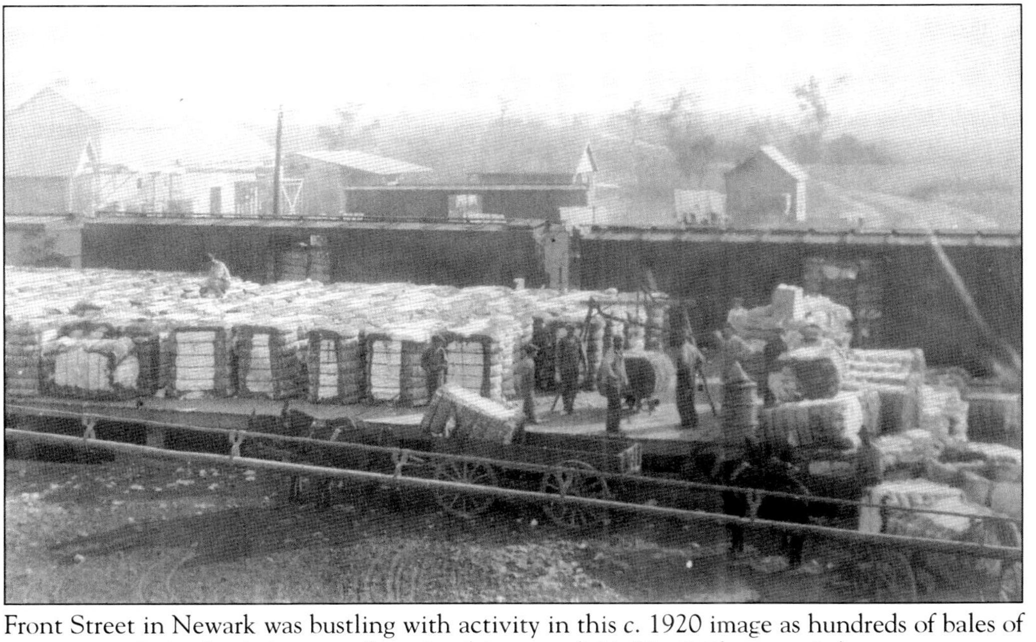

Front Street in Newark was bustling with activity in this c. 1920 image as hundreds of bales of cotton were being loaded onto railcars for shipment. (J.V. "Bug" Chapman Jr.)

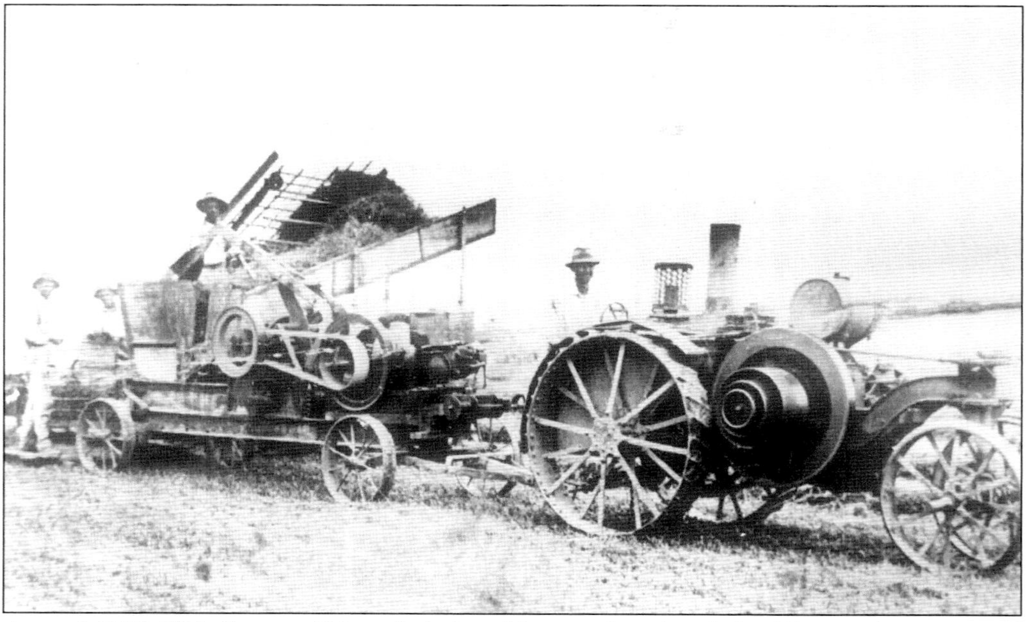

Around 1915, W.J. Freeze of Newark designed his windrow hay baler. The machine received a great deal of interest from many farm implement companies around the country, but Freeze eventually gave up his idea of manufacturing them after spending several years dealing with government bureaucracy in an effort to secure a patent. A patent was finally issued in 1922, but by that time Freeze had gone onto other ventures. When his patent expired in 1937 several companies came out with designs similar to his. (Billy Joe Freeze)

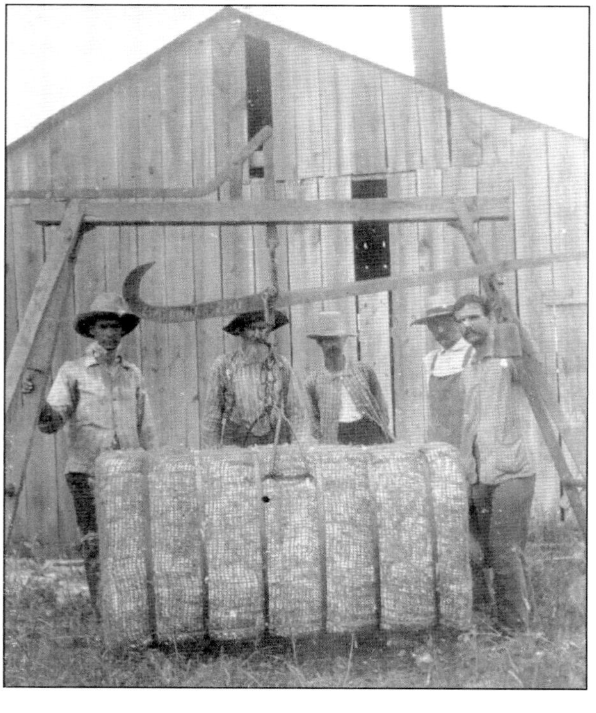

This is the first bale of cotton processed at the Wyatt Gin near Gainor's Ferry. The photo was made in the fall of 1902. (Regional Studies Center, Lyon College)

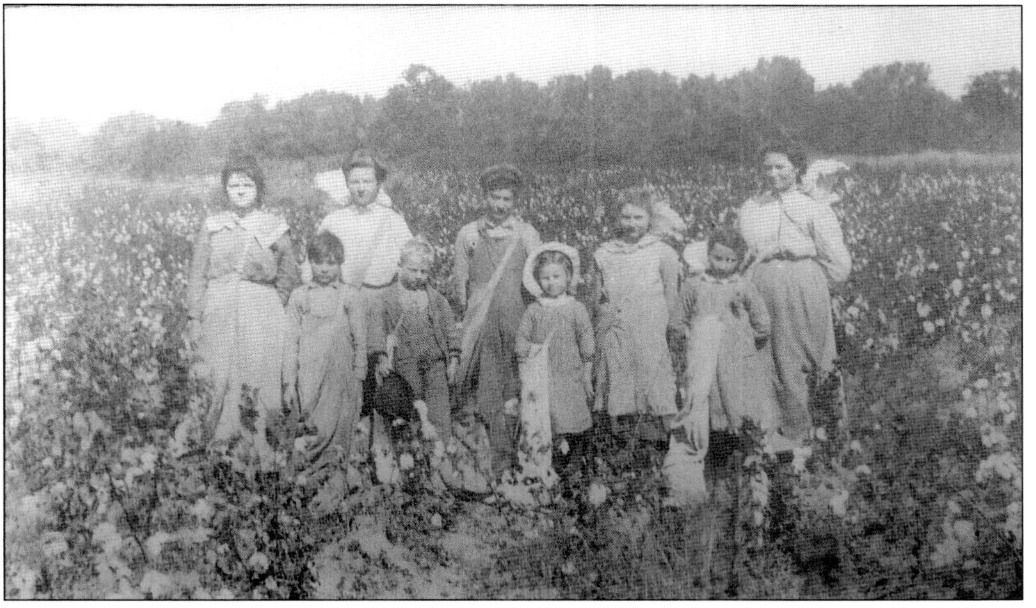

This photo of cotton pickers was made in the Oil Trough Bottoms about 1910. Pictured, left to right, are: (back row) Mary Cook, Almer Bell, Ira Bell, Clara Bell, and Ida Bell (Strother); (front row) Albert Bell, Oscar Strother, Sarah Strother, and Leona Strother Hembrey. The Strother family lived on Hutchinson Mountain and traveled back and forth to Oil Trough in a farm wagon. The Bell family lived in another part of the county and commuted the same way. (Wilson Powell)

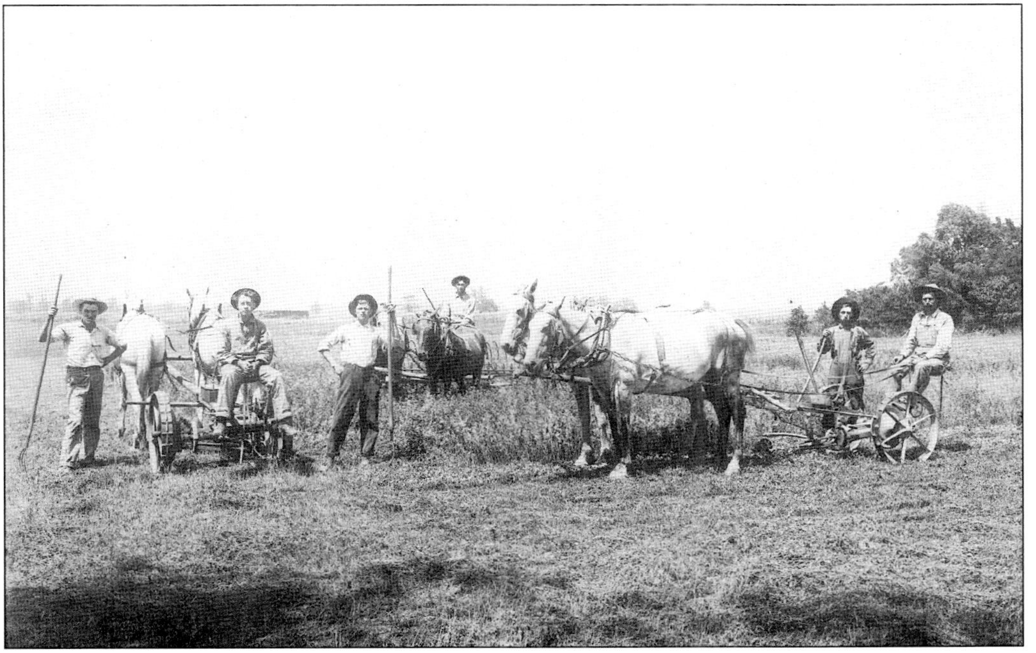

These men are working in Dr. Alfred Williamson's alfalfa field at Akron in 1909. (Wilson Powell)

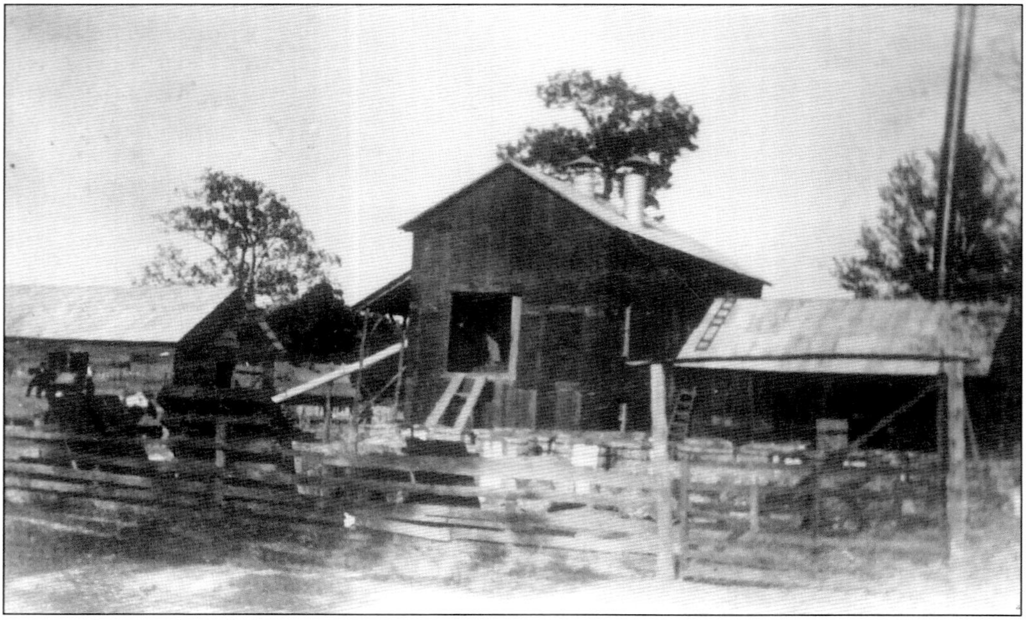

Ben Desha purchased this steam gin in the Desha community from the Searcy family in 1919. It eventually came under the management of Desha Lester who later moved and modernized it. The Desha Gin Company was the last ginning company to operate in the county. (Regional Studies Center, Lyon College)

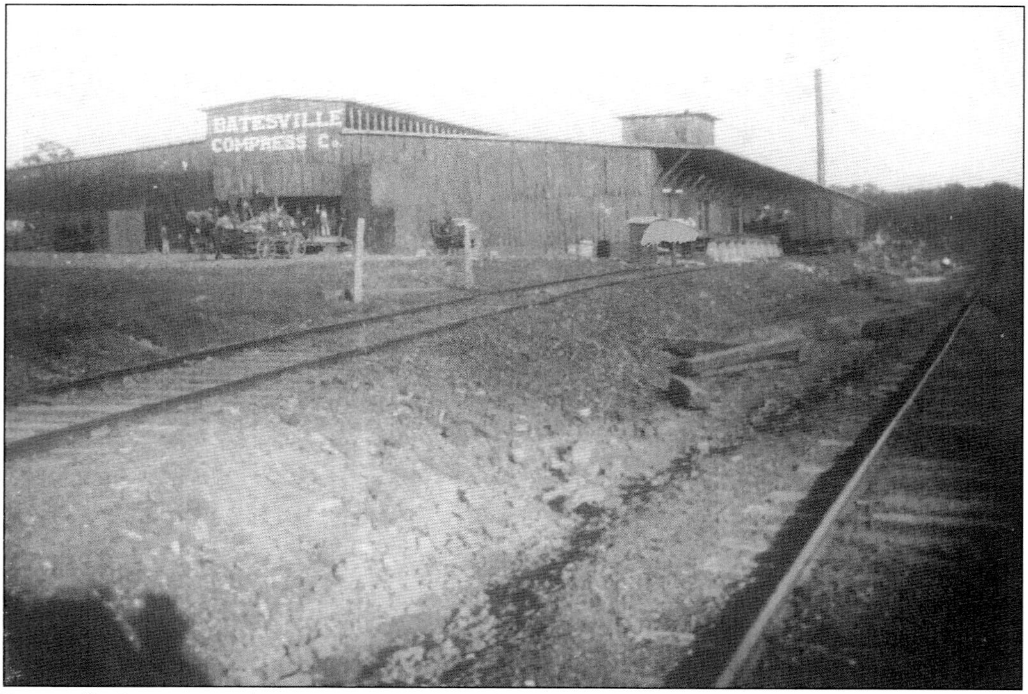

Batesville Compress, where cotton was pressed into bales for shipping, was located on Lawrence Street in Batesville. (Old Independence Regional Museum)

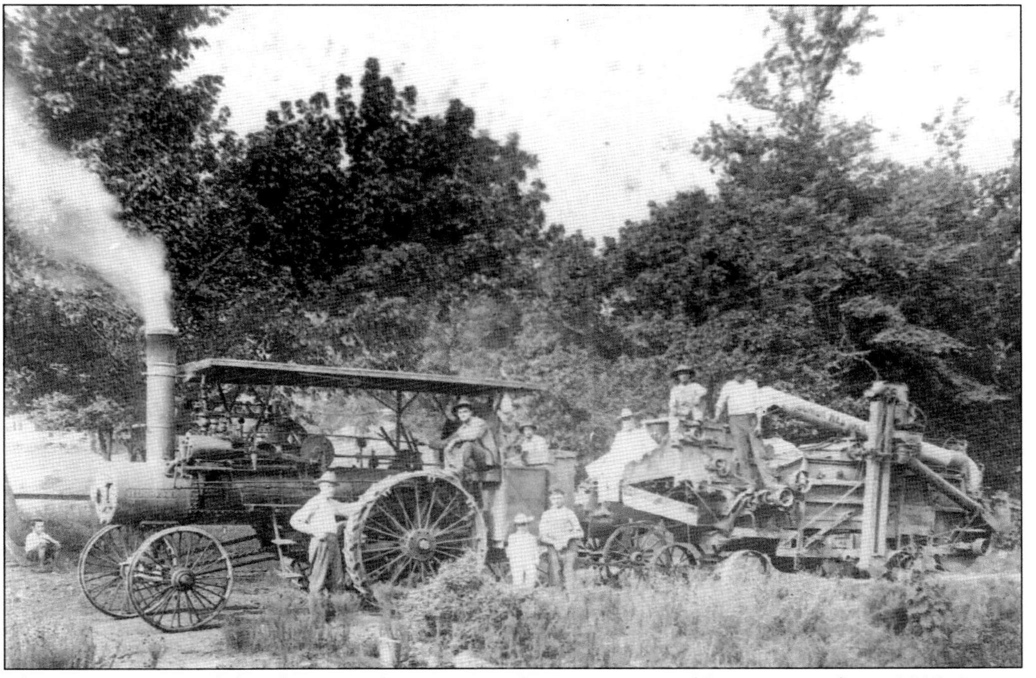

This steam-powered threshing machine was working just west of Jamestown about 1918. It was probably one of the last of its kind to thresh wheat in Independence County. Clint Barnes is seated with one foot on the rear wheel. His father, J.M. Barnes, is standing with his hand on the wheel, and the co-owner of the machine, Billy Pate, is seated in the center on the separator. (Wilson Powell)

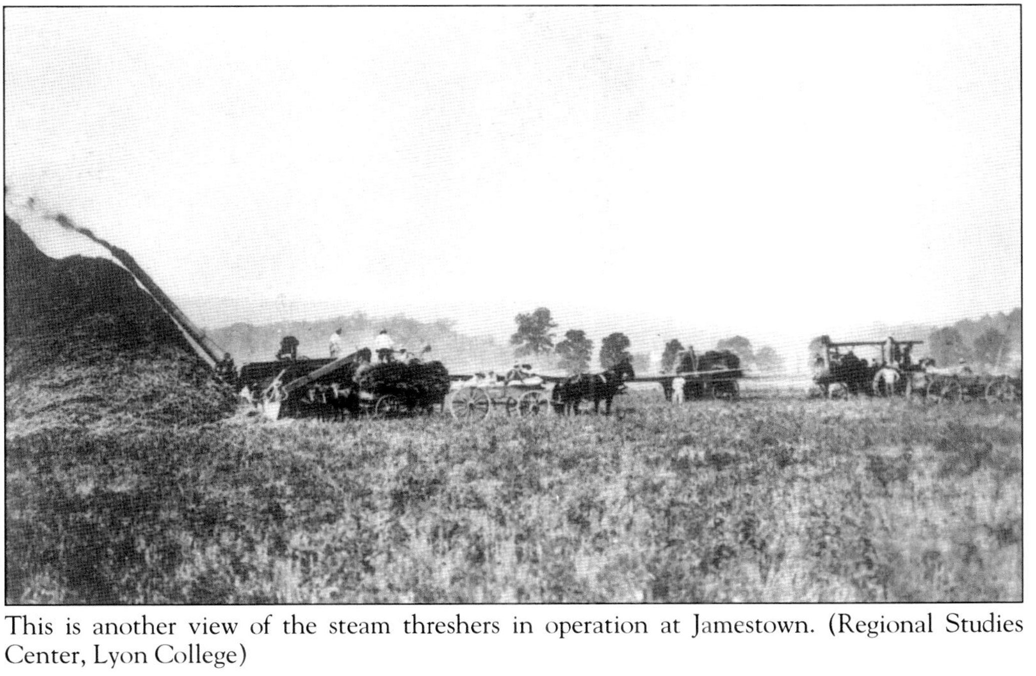

This is another view of the steam threshers in operation at Jamestown. (Regional Studies Center, Lyon College)

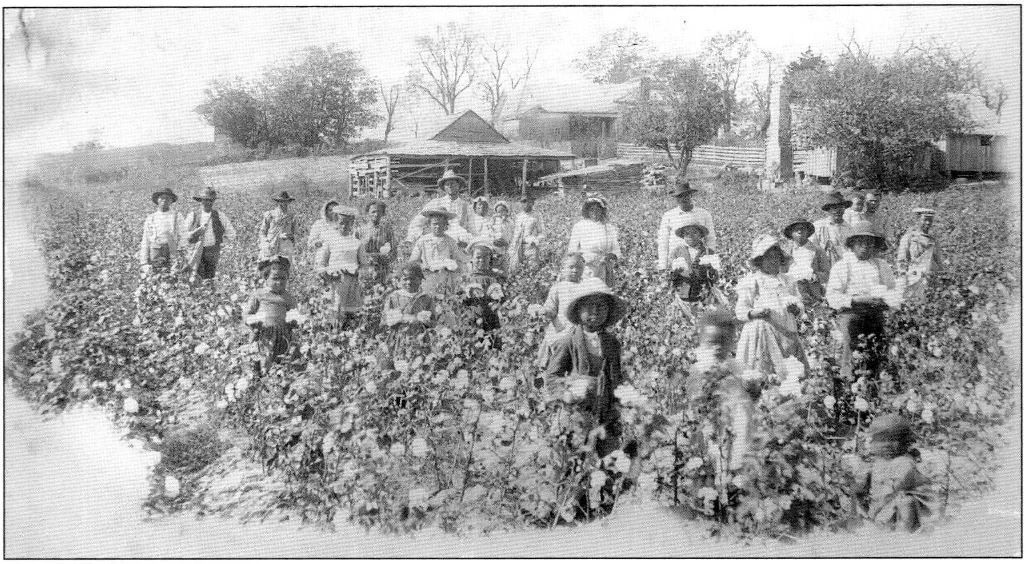

These families were picking cotton on Harry Case's farm near Moorefield. (Wilson Powell)

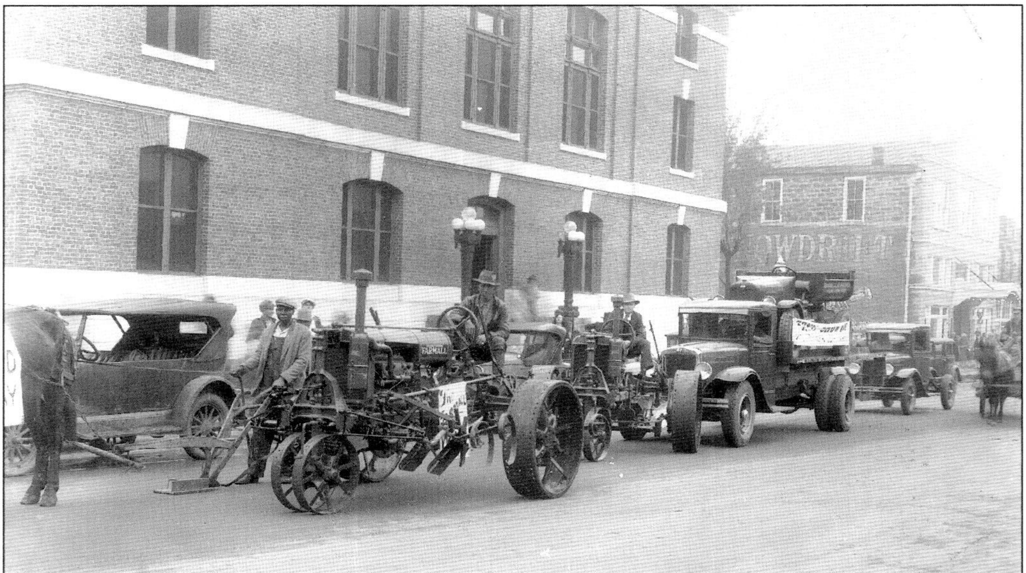

This 1930 parade up Main Street in Batesville was in honor of the opening of an International Dealership in the city by Will Duvall. Undoubtedly farmers in the area were eager to see the exhibition of implements. Driving the first tractor is Steve Davis of Sulphur Rock. Louis Grider, International salesman from Jonesboro, is driving the second tractor. Driving the truck behind him is Leslie Kent. (Wilson Powell)

Six

Business and Industry

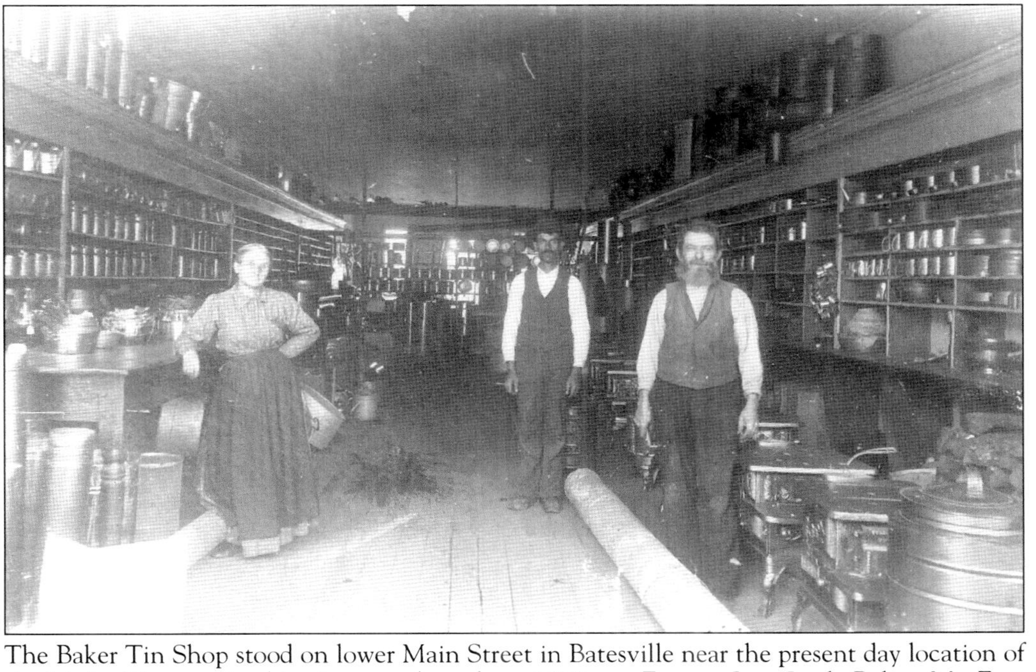

The Baker Tin Shop stood on lower Main Street in Batesville near the present day location of the Melba Theater. In this picture, taken about 1900, are Frances Jane Leale Baker, Mr. Fox, and the proprietor, G.A. Baker. (Dora Le Ferguson)

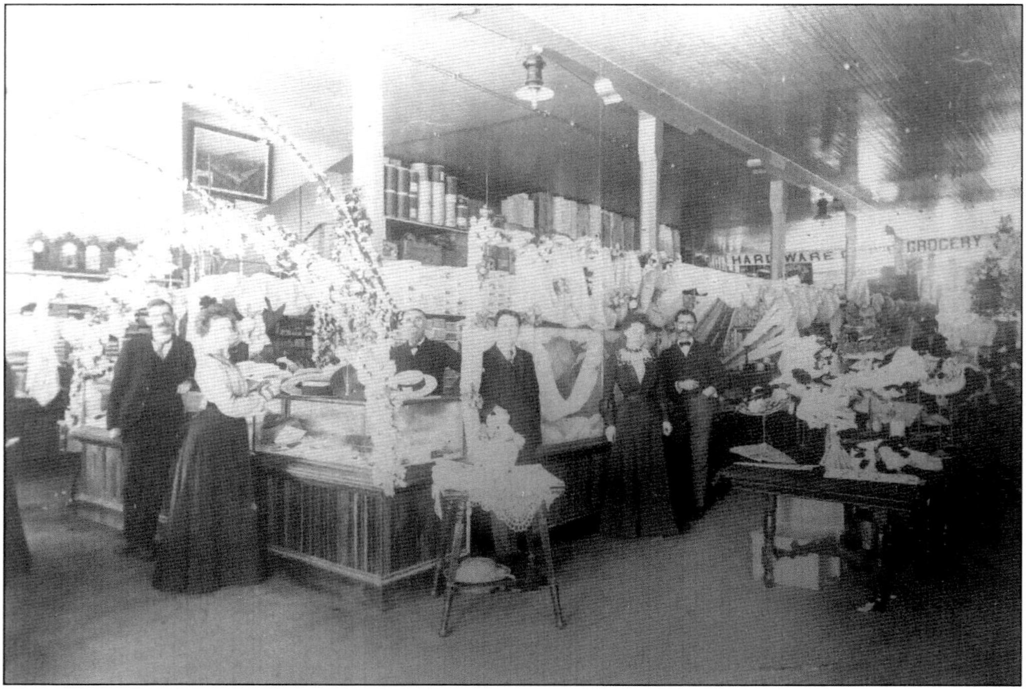

When the Maxfield Store opened in Batesville during the spring of 1899 it was a festive occasion. In this photo the proprietors are proudly displaying the variety of wares available to potential buyers. (Independence County Historical Society)

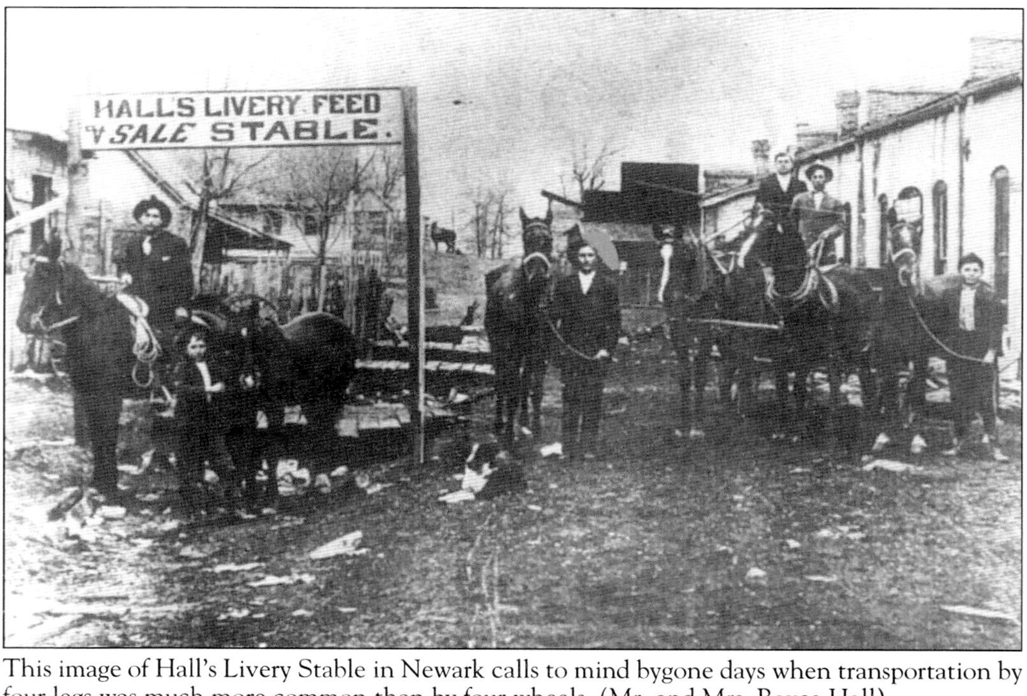

This image of Hall's Livery Stable in Newark calls to mind bygone days when transportation by four legs was much more common than by four wheels. (Mr. and Mrs. Boyce Hall)

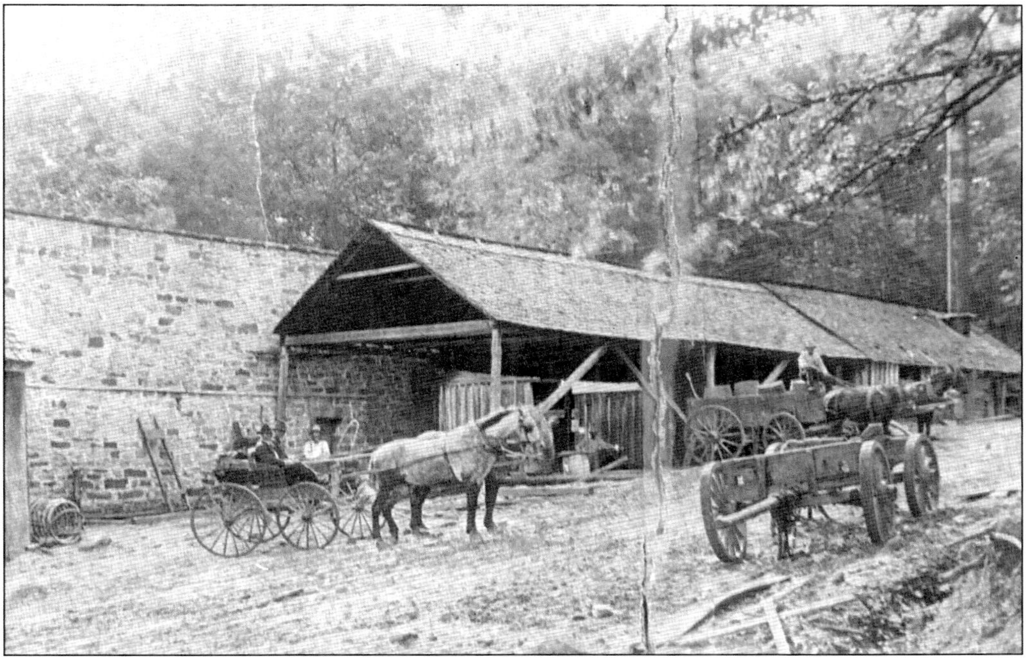

This is a photo of R.W. Earnheart's Distillery near Bethesda about 1905. Already a successful farmer in Washington Township, Earnheart established his distillery in 1887 and operated it until 1914. At least two brands of whiskey were sold under the Earnheart label—"Earnheart's Old Standard Whiskey" and "Arkansaw Straight Corn Whiskey." Earnheart and his sons also had a saloon and hotel on Main Street in Batesville. (Wilson Powell)

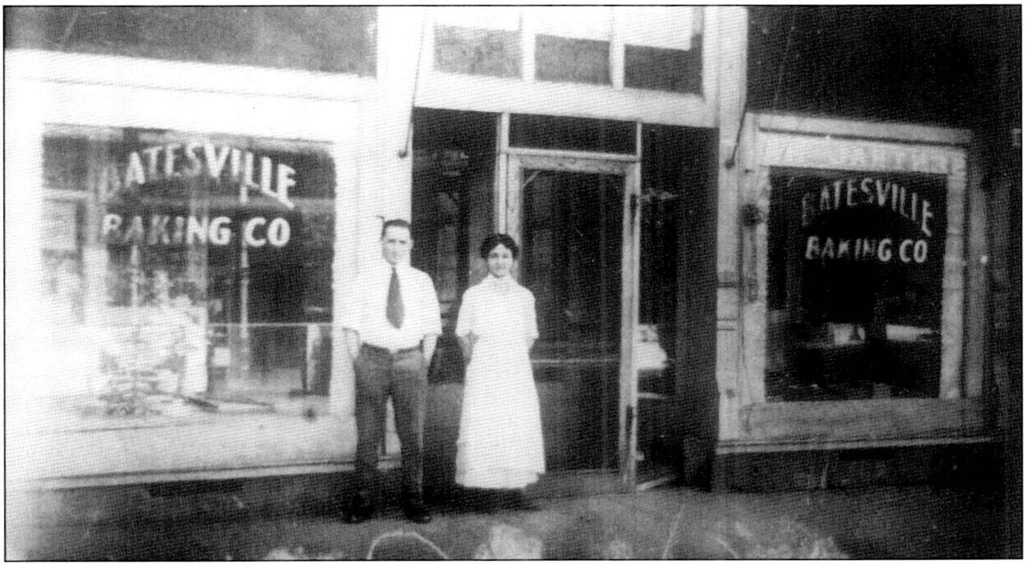

The Batesville Baking Company was located at 312 East Main Street below the Landers Theater. The company delivered bread on in-town and out-of-town routes with the aid of two delivery trucks. The owner, Mr. Mac Albright, is standing in front of the store with his sister. (Old Independence Regional Museum)

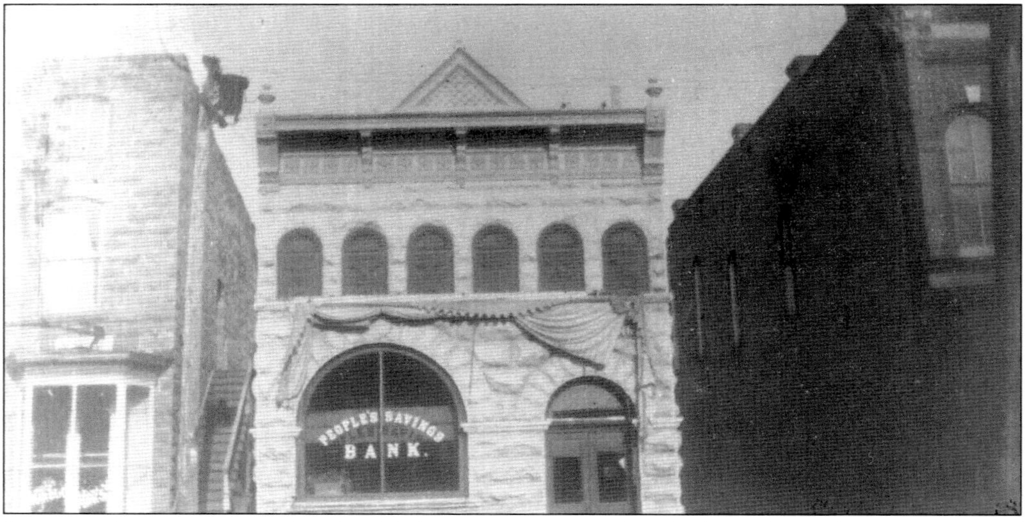

Simon Adler, one of the earliest Jewish businessmen to settle in Independence County, organized the People's Savings Bank in 1891. It was the second banking house in Batesville and stood on lower Main Street. (Independence County Historical Society)

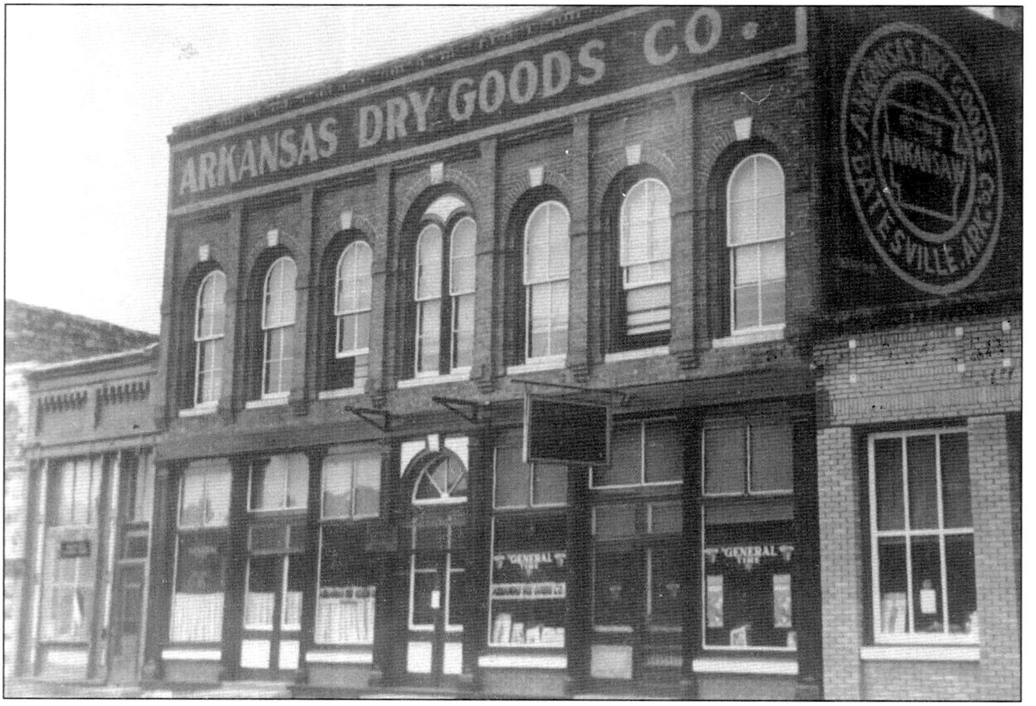

Adler Hall was constructed by Simon Adler on the site of the Batesville Institute after that impressive building burned in 1880. Adler operated a general merchandise store on the ground floor; the second floor housed his offices and a large open auditorium known as an opera hall. Theatrical performances, banquets, and dances were held here up until the 1940s. The keystone above the center second-story window is engraved with the letter "A." (Independence County Historical Society)

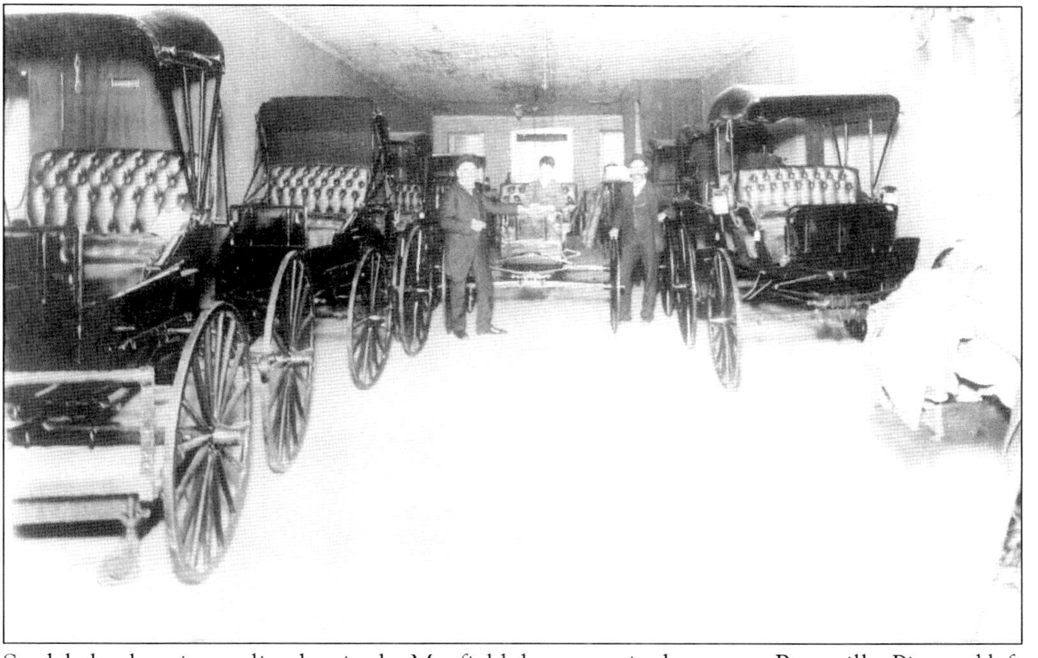

Studebaker buggies are lined up in the Maxfield showroom in downtown Batesville. Pictured left to right are Theodore, Fred, and C.W. Maxfield. (Independence County Historical Society)

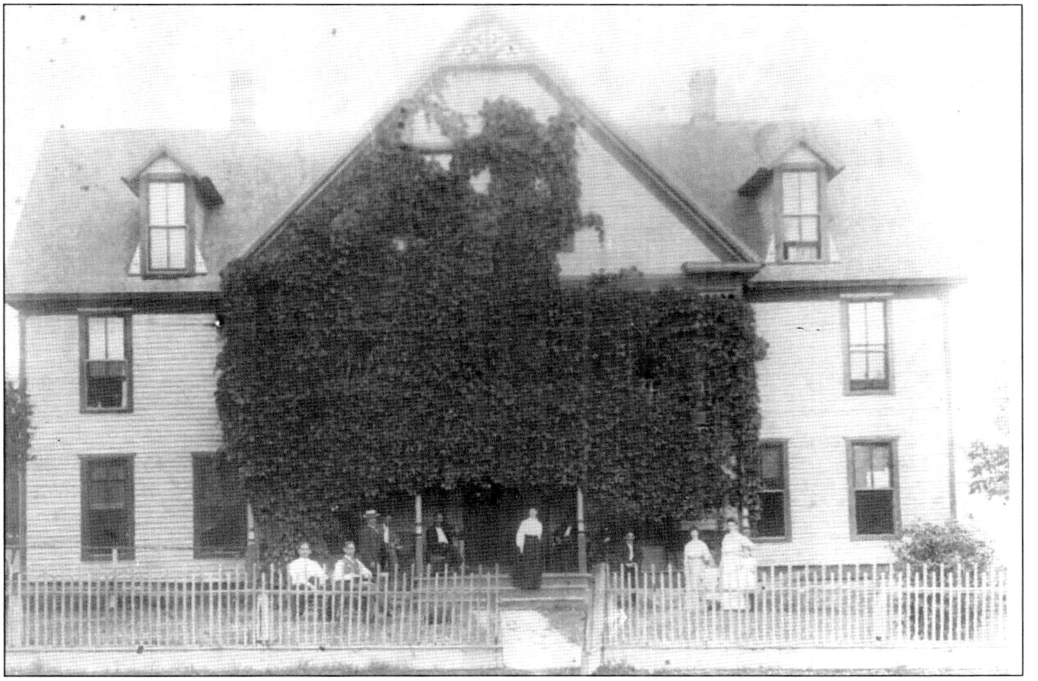

The Baker Hotel, built in 1900, catered to a number of visitors to the local area. It stood on the present site of the empty Coca-Cola Bottling Company plant on the corner of Central and College in Batesville. (Regional Studies Center, Lyon College)

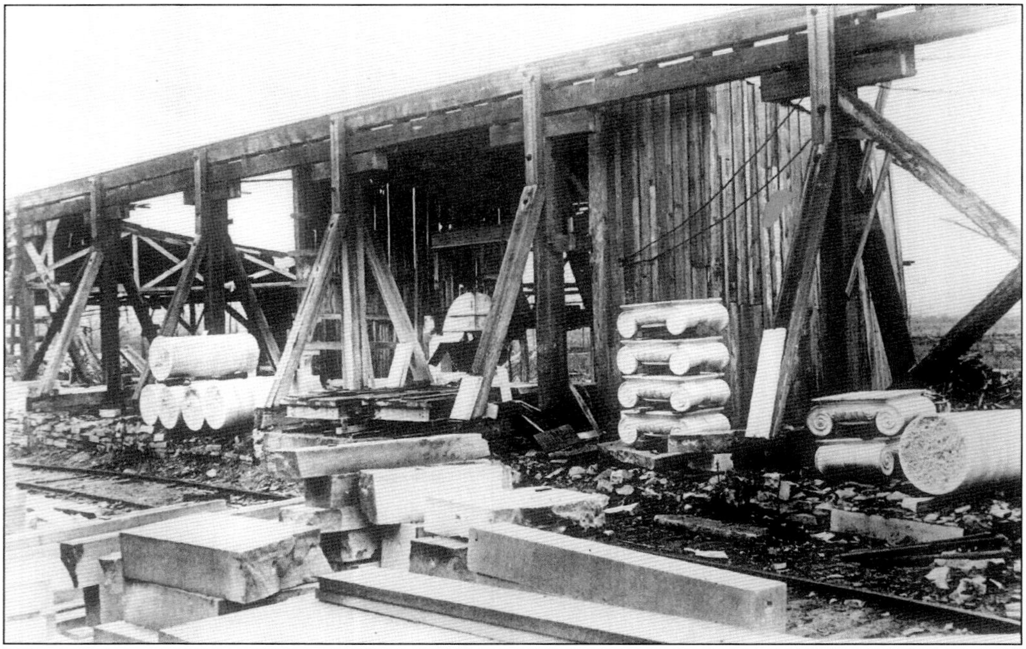

The Pfeiffer Stone Company had been incorporated in 1881, but the event that really put it on the map was the planned construction of "a million dollar state capitol" in Little Rock in 1899. The decision to use Batesville marble was a boon for the company. During peak times work was done day and night. A common laborer could expect to make $1.50 for a 10 hour day while more skilled men earned 25¢ to 30¢ per hour. (Top photo: Butler Center for Arkansas Studies, Central Arkansas Library System, bottom photo: Wilson Powell)

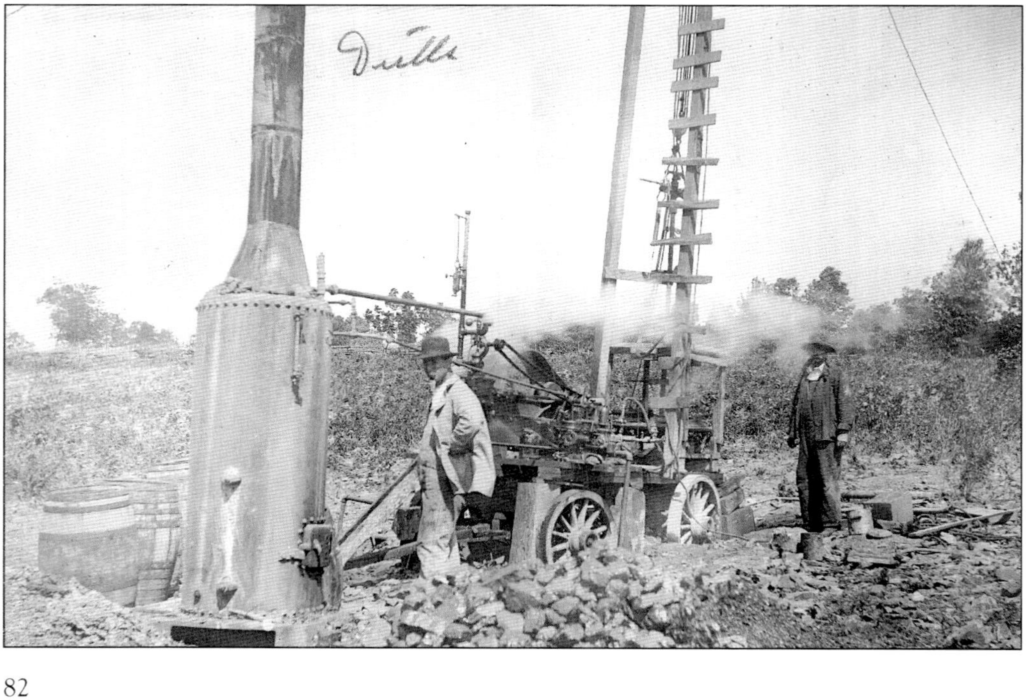

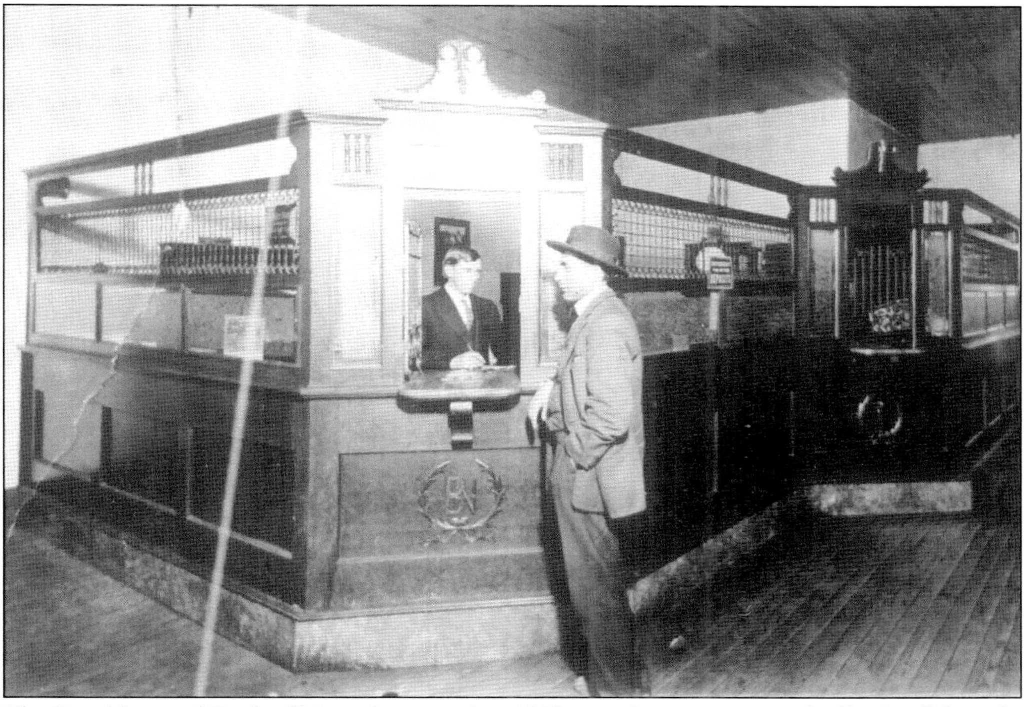

The First National Bank of Newark, created in 1908, was the successor to the Bank of Newark. Edgar Chesser waits on a lone customer in this *c.* 1915 photo. (Ellis B. Chesser)

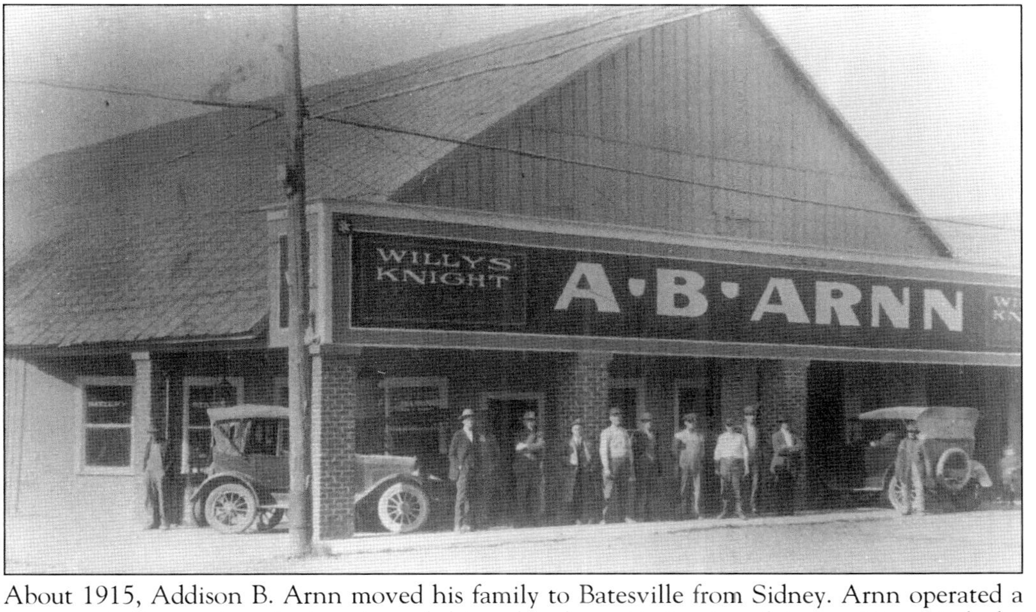

About 1915, Addison B. Arnn moved his family to Batesville from Sidney. Arnn operated a livestock business where he bought and shipped mules to St. Louis and Kansas City. With the changing of the times he switched from mules to automobiles. This store was located on the northeast corner of Central and College in Batesville. (George A. Toney Collection, Butler Center for Arkansas Studies, Central Arkansas Library System)

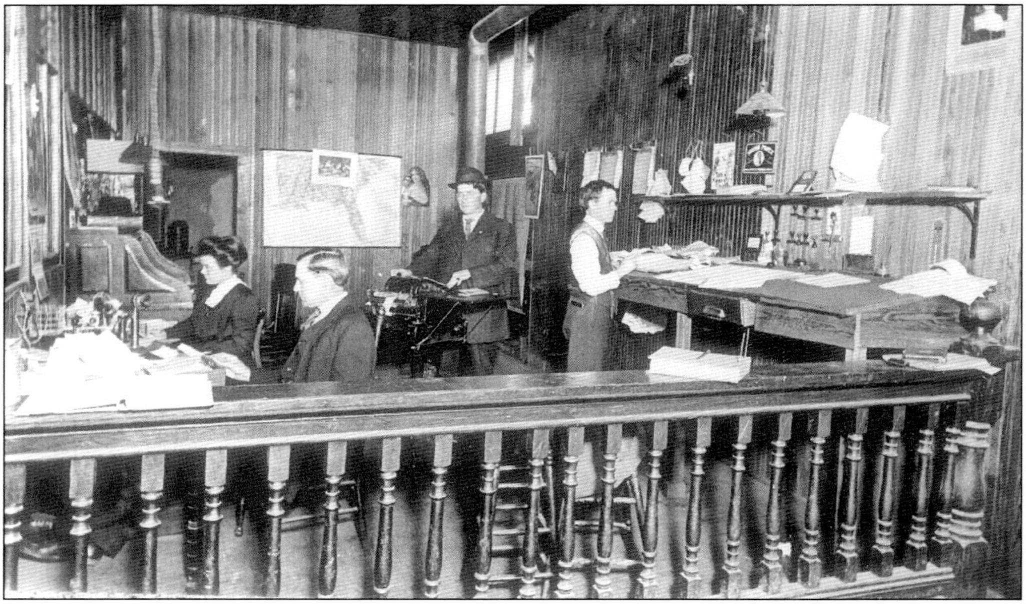

The office of Yeatman-Gray Grocery Company was located in Adler Hall in Batesville. Pictured left to right are Ouida Thomas Dorr, unknown, Claude Dorr, and unknown. (Independence County Historical Society)

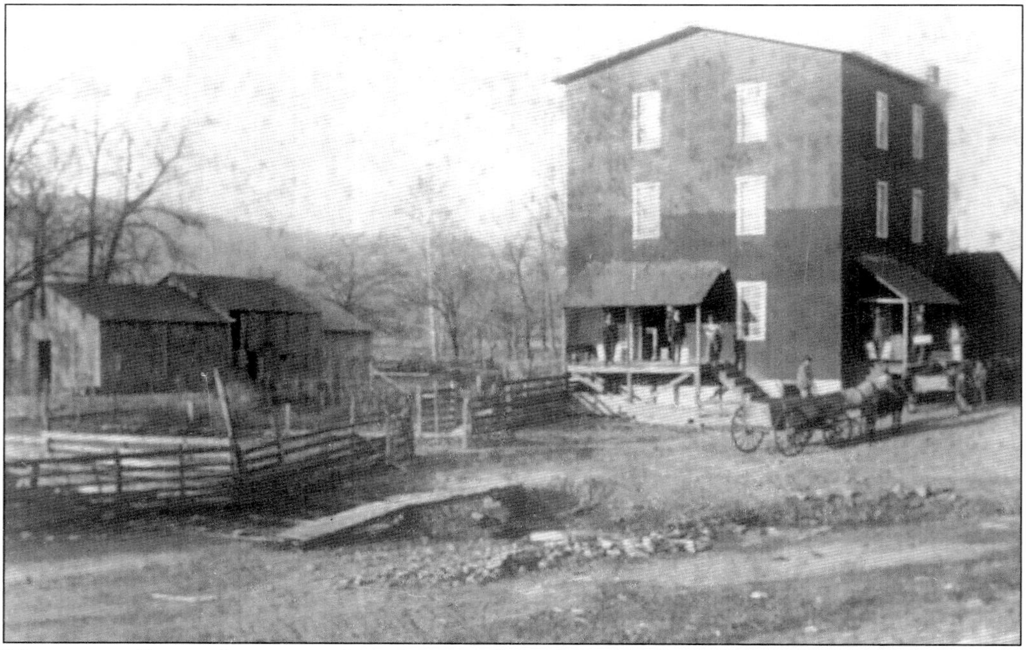

The grist mill, seen here in a 1910 photograph, was operated in Jamestown for many years by W.B. Pate. Pate and an early partner named Young installed new equipment which enabled them to separate bran and shorts and to manufacture three grades of flour—Magnolia, Pearl, and Harvest Bell brands. These were sold to wholesale grocery dealers in the area. In later years, Pate's partner was Herbert Snapp. (Bubba Burks)

The *Newark Journal* began publication in 1901 under the direction of Oscar Franklin Craig. In March 1915, the newspaper purchased a Linotype machine to improve its plant. The machine was operated by O.F. Craig's thirteen-year-old son, Roy M. Craig. The younger Craig was sent to the Mergenthaler Linotype School in New Orleans. He was recognized as the youngest person in the country to complete the training. (Robert D. Craig)

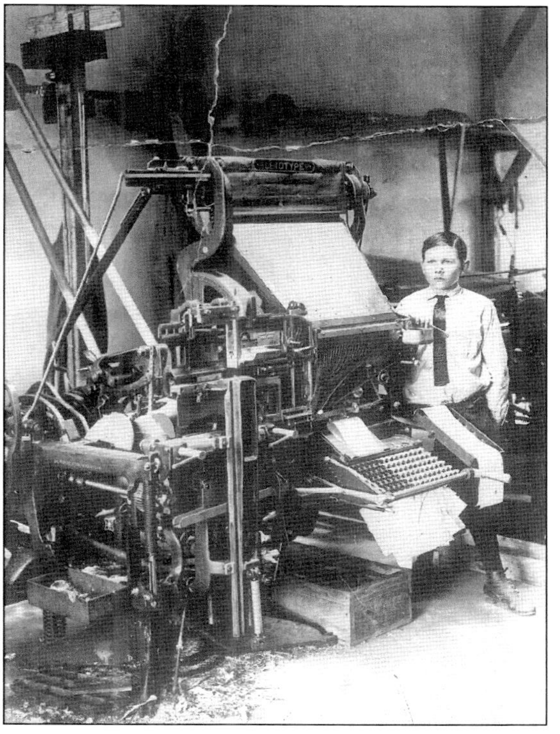

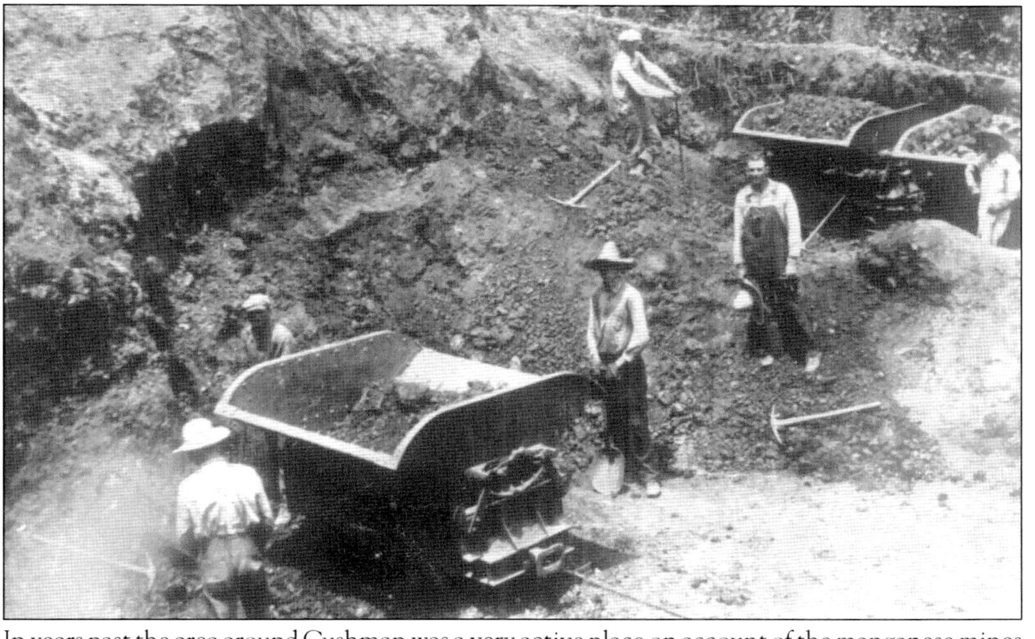

In years past the area around Cushman was a very active place on account of the manganese mines that dotted the countryside. By working in the mines, locals found a way to supplement their farming income in lean years. In 1886 the railroad was extended from Batesville to Cushman in order to cash in on the booming manganese economy. Two of the people identified in this open pit mine are Gilbert McDoniel and Wesley Smith. (Cushman History Project)

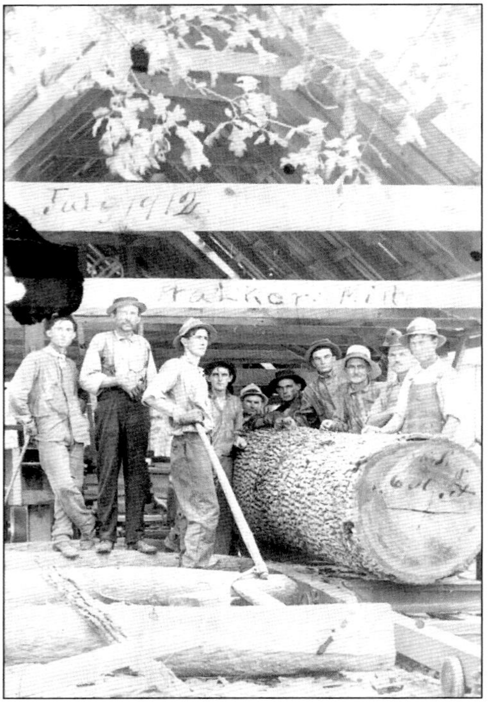

The timber industry was big business in many parts of Independence County. This image taken in July 1912, shows some of the workers at Walker's Sawmill in the eastern part of the county. (Ann Benson Nicholas)

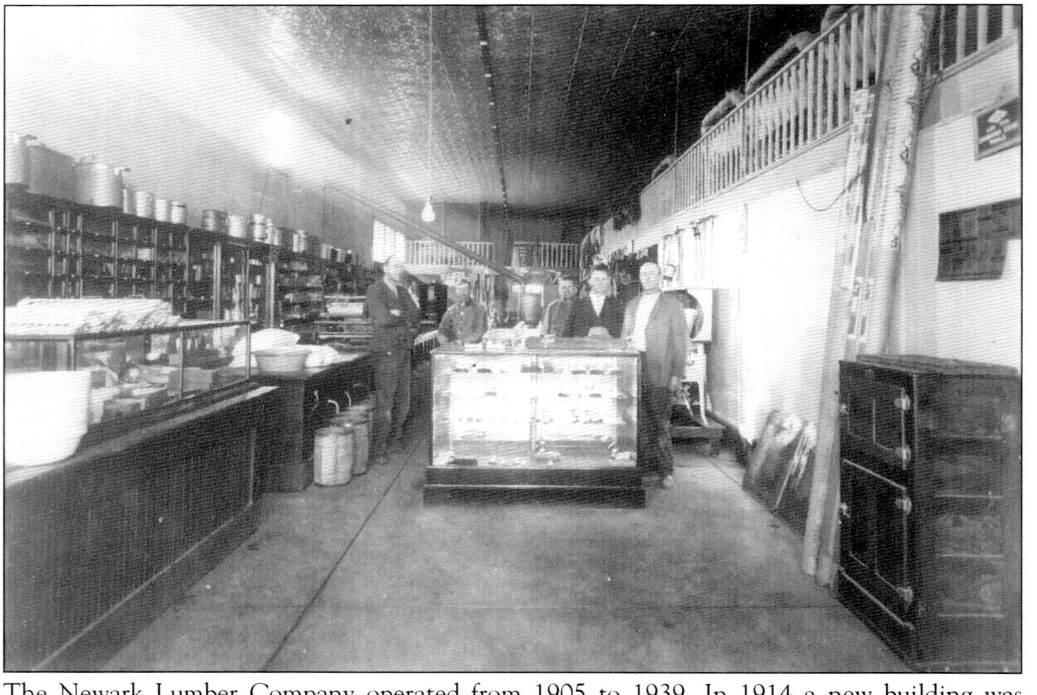

The Newark Lumber Company operated from 1905 to 1939. In 1914 a new building was constructed at the corner of Main and Front streets in downtown Newark. The company changed hands a couple of times before moving into new quarters in 1928. The building burned down in 1938. (George Ann Magness Ramey)

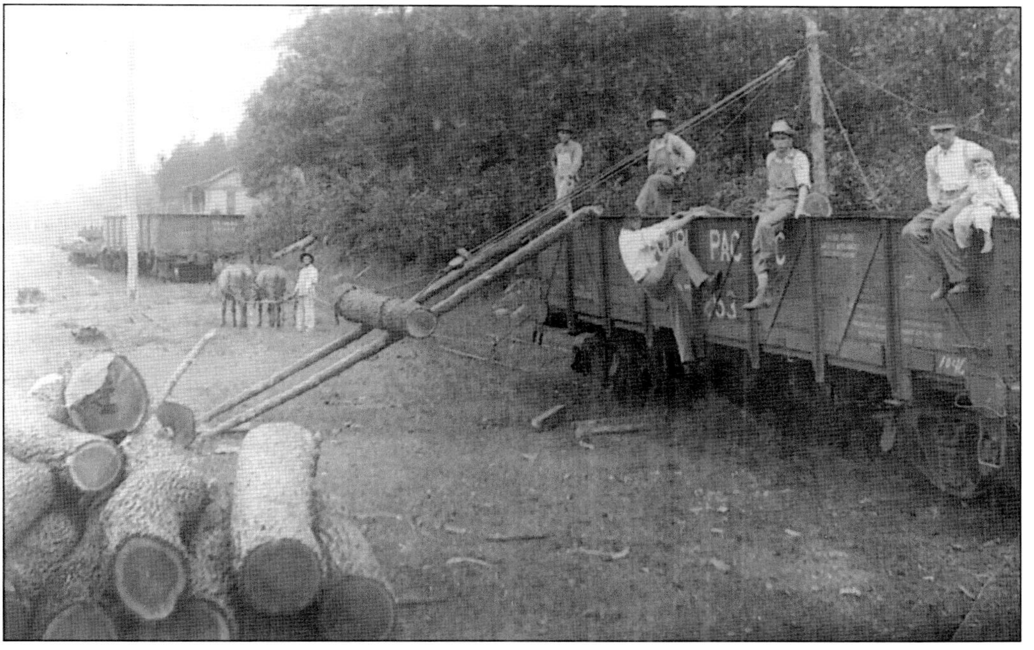

These workers in Washington Township are loading cut timber onto railcars in this early 20th century image. (Brian Robertson)

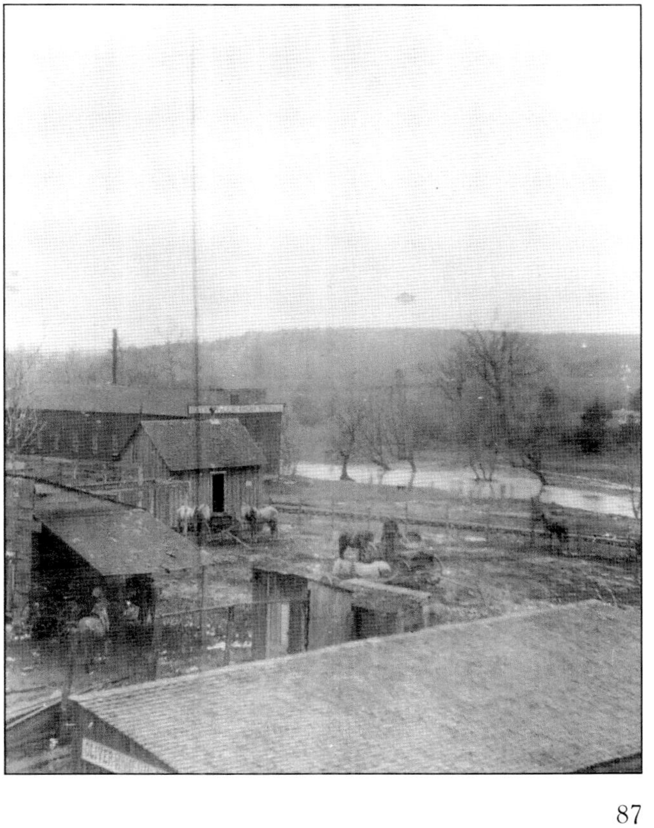

Batesville Iron Works located on Poke Bayou was owned by G.H. Kealer and began operation in 1889. It was one of the most important industries in the county and "means much to mill men and the farmers, saving them thousands of dollars each year." In the foreground of this picture is Schott's Camp Yard. (Regional Studies Center, Lyon College)

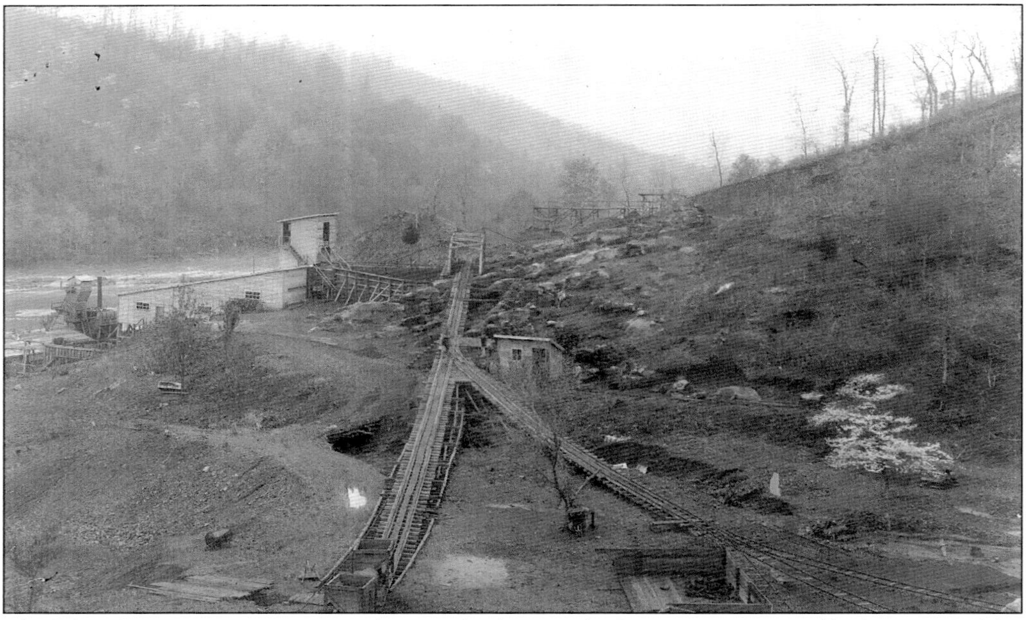

The Rhinehart manganese ore washer was built on Poke Bayou near Batesville during World War I. This photo by J.R. Lewis was taken in 1918. (Wilson Powell)

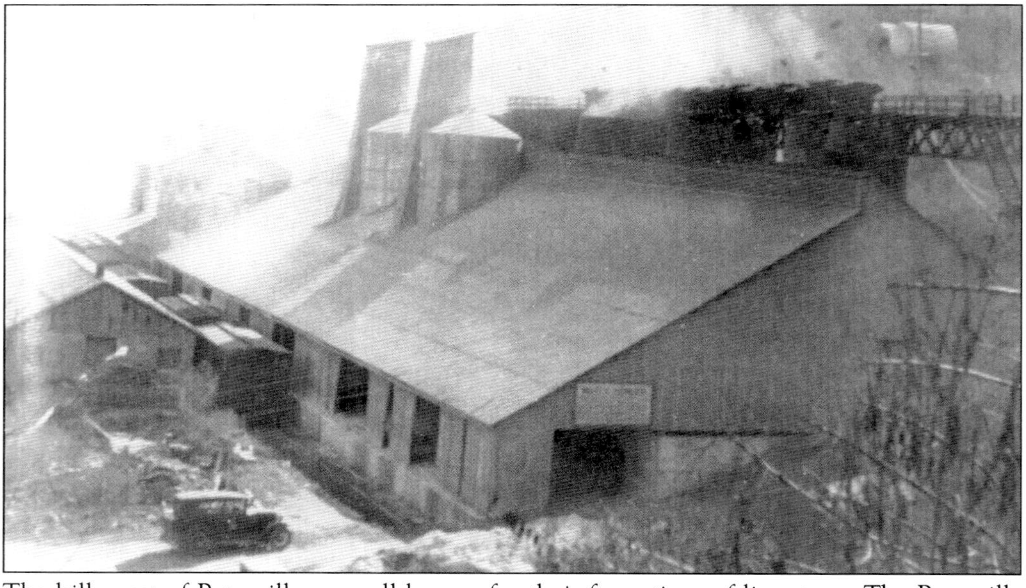

The hills west of Batesville are well known for their formations of limestone. The Batesville White Lime Company can trace its origin back to 1906 when Edgar Young established the Young Lime Company in neighboring Izard County. After a number of conversions, the corporate title was changed to the Batesville White Lime Company in 1924. By 1928, the company was producing 308,700 barrels of lime a year. The Great Depression was a difficult time for the company and it was forced to close one of its two facilities, but the company soon bounced back and the coming war would provide a much needed boost in profits. This photo shows a portion of the plant at Limedale in 1940. (Independence County Historical Society)

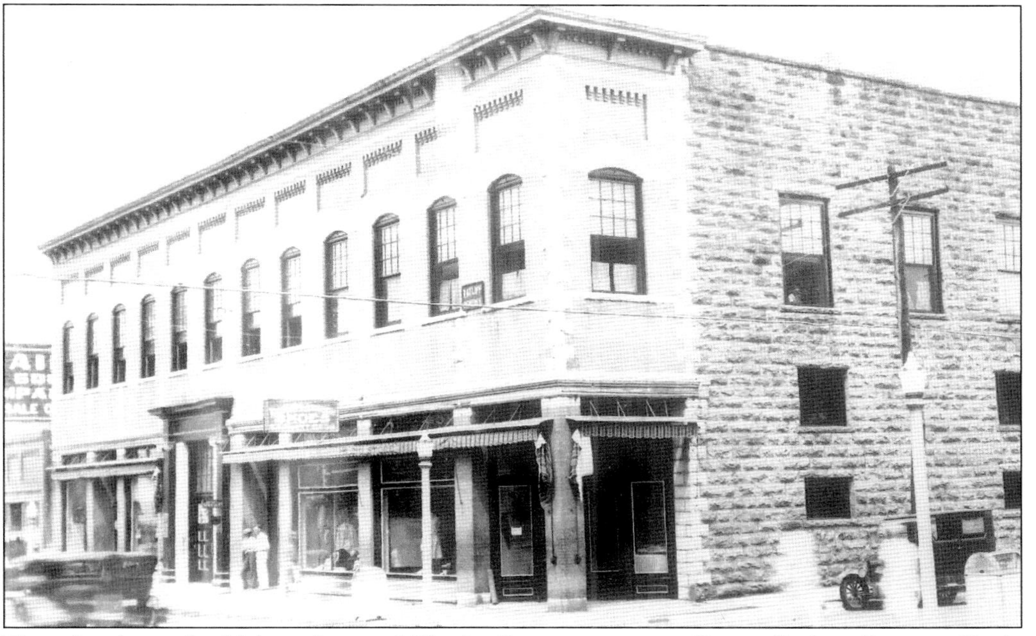

Three brothers—Ira Nelson, Jim, and Charles Barnett—came to Batesville from Evening Shade in 1885. They came to work for their uncle, R.D. Williams, in a general merchandise store and bought him out in 1890. In 1895, they established Barnett Brothers, Inc. and began to embark on a number of business enterprises. The main Barnett Brothers Store, pictured here about 1934, was built in 1903 and remained one of the anchor stores in downtown Batesville for some 85 years. The brothers also operated the Bargain Annex, wholesale grocery and dry goods businesses, a feed and seed store, an insurance and abstract company, and were among the founders of the original Citizens' Bank. They also bought and sold land in Independence County. I.N. Barnett Sr. had three sons—I.N. Jr., Jim, and Charles—and I.N. Jr. had three sons, again named Jim, Nelson, and Charles. All were involved in various aspects of the family businesses until 1988. (Regional Studies Center, Lyon College)

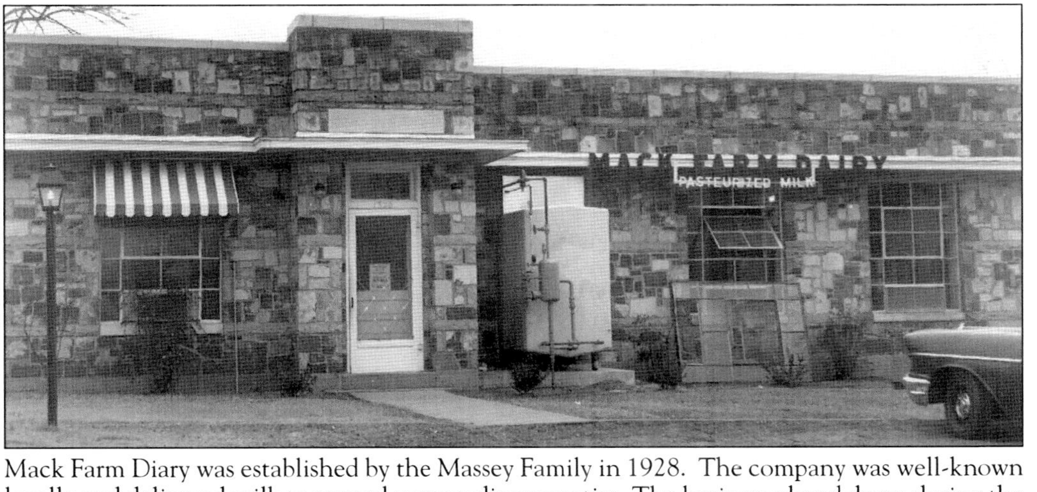

Mack Farm Diary was established by the Massey Family in 1928. The company was well-known locally and delivered milk to several surrounding counties. The business closed down during the 1970s. (Regional Studies Center, Lyon College)

HOW IS OUR MONEY USED?

This will give you some idea of the cost of equipping a modern army.

M-1 Garand Rifle	$80
Machine Guns	$500-$3,000
Demolition Bombs	$500
37MM Anti-tank Guns	$6,000
37MM Anti-aircraft Guns	$30,000
75MM Rifles	$10,000
90MM Anti-aircraft Guns	$50,000
Medium Tanks	$75,000
Heavy Bomber	$335,000

BUY WAR BONDS
EQUIP A WINNING ARMY

CITIZENS BANK & TRUST COMPANY

The strength of the homefront was a vital component to the success of our military efforts during World War II. In this 1944 ad, Citizens Bank in Batesville attempts to educate the local populace on the monetary costs of the war effort. (Regional Studies Center, Lyon College)

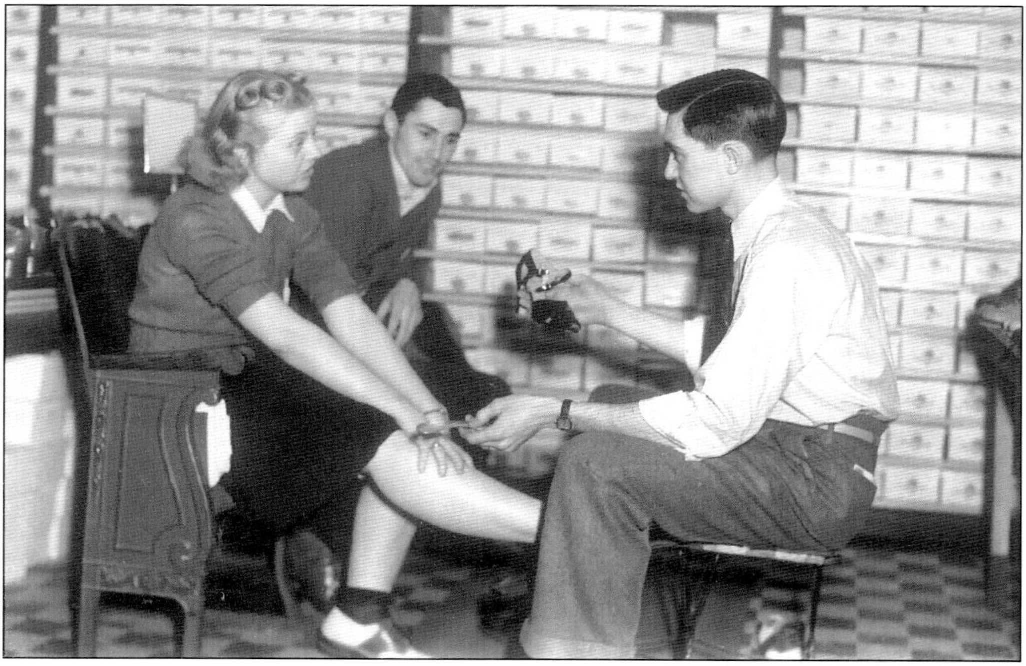

Heuer's Shoe Store has been a longtime resident on Batesville's Main Street. A salesman is assisting a young couple with a pair of shoes in this 1940 image. (Regional Studies Center, Lyon College)

Seven

Transportation

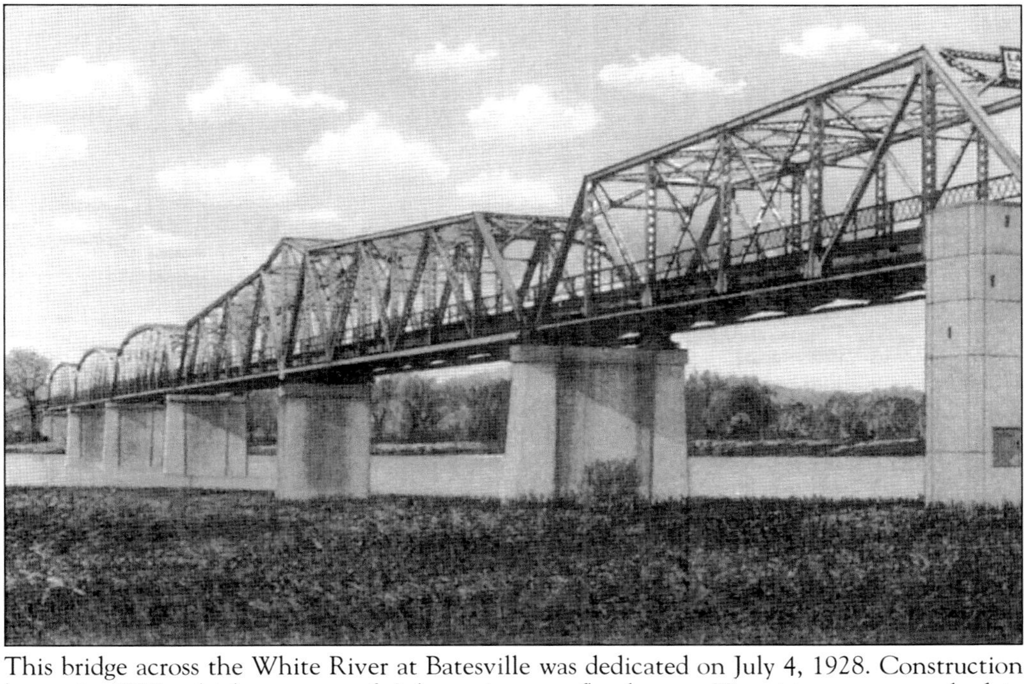

This bridge across the White River at Batesville was dedicated on July 4, 1928. Construction began in 1927, which was one of Arkansas's worst flood years. The rising water resulted in several delays and near disaster for the contractor. The newly completed bridge was the only one on the White River between Branson, Missouri, and Devall's Bluff suitable for highway traffic. (Brian Robertson)

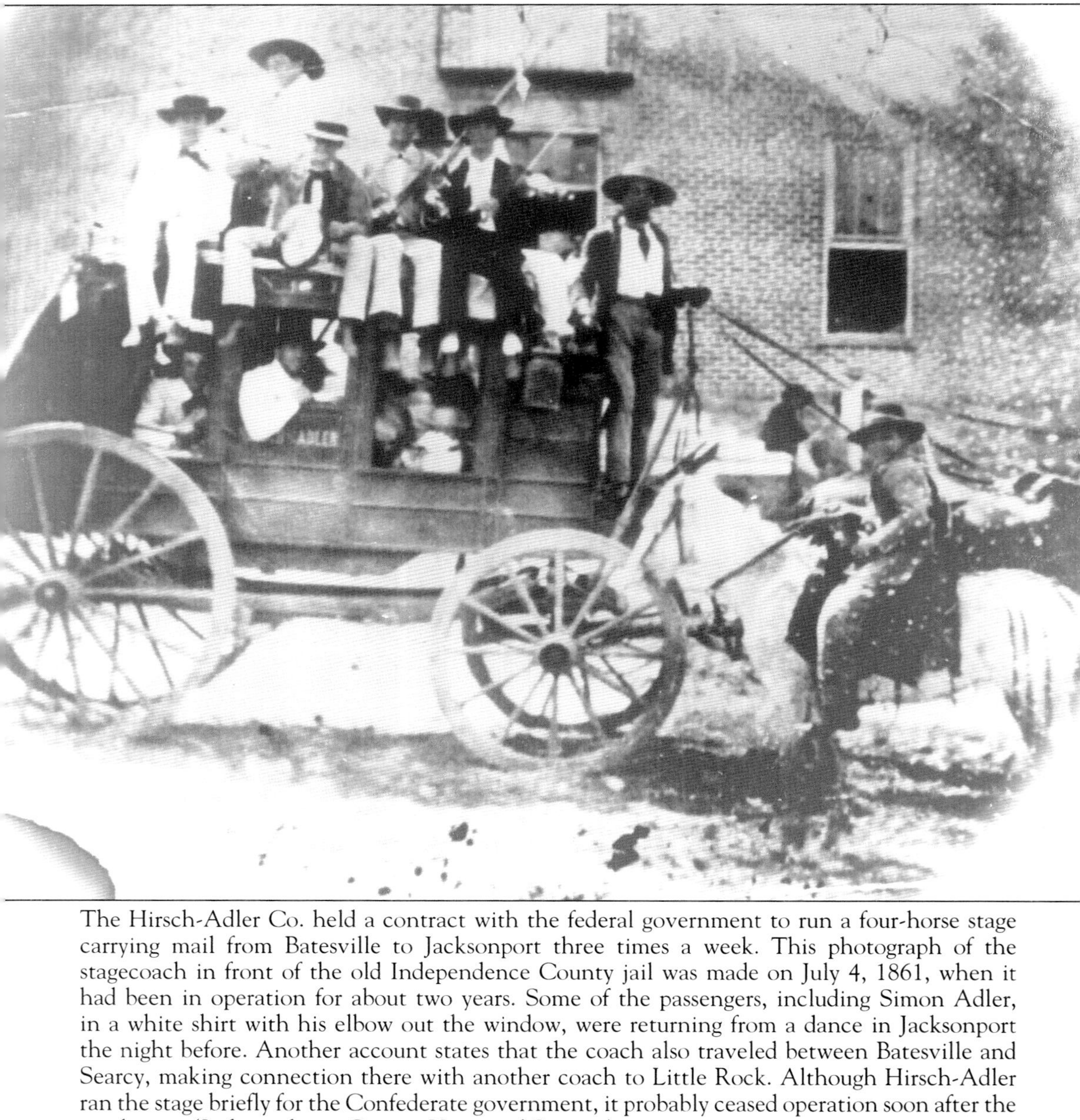

The Hirsch-Adler Co. held a contract with the federal government to run a four-horse stage carrying mail from Batesville to Jacksonport three times a week. This photograph of the stagecoach in front of the old Independence County jail was made on July 4, 1861, when it had been in operation for about two years. Some of the passengers, including Simon Adler, in a white shirt with his elbow out the window, were returning from a dance in Jacksonport the night before. Another account states that the coach also traveled between Batesville and Searcy, making connection there with another coach to Little Rock. Although Hirsch-Adler ran the stage briefly for the Confederate government, it probably ceased operation soon after the war began. (Independence County Historical Society)

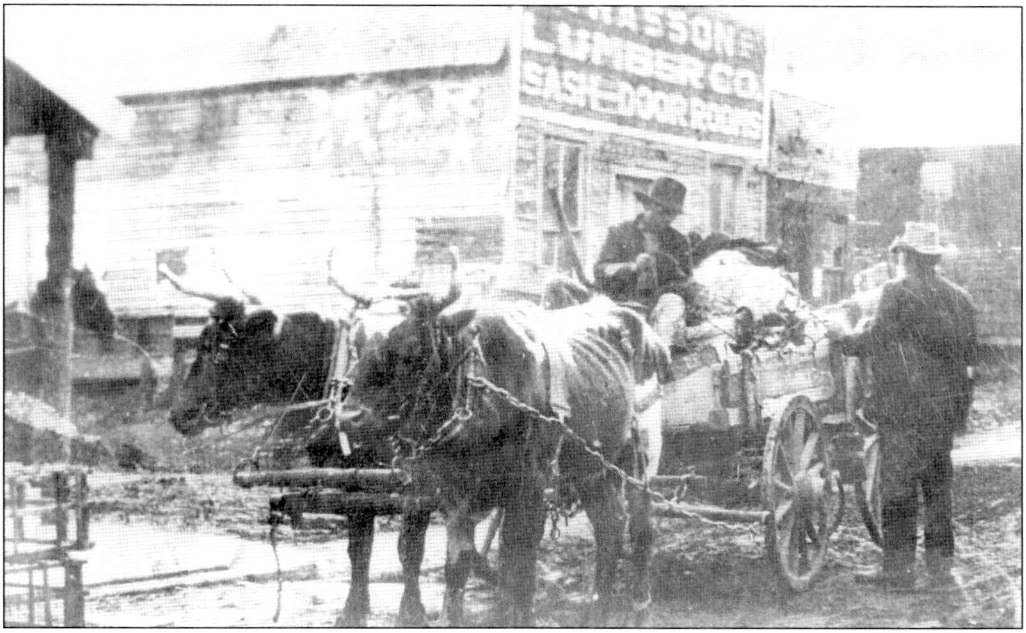

This team of oxen is traveling down Spring Street (now known as Central Avenue) in Batesville near the bayou bridge. The use of oxen declined greatly after the arrival of the automobile. Visible in the background of the picture is the Wasson Lumber Company which was established in 1912. The general lumber and building material company was reportedly one of the largest and most successful business firms in the city. (Regional Studies Center, Lyon College)

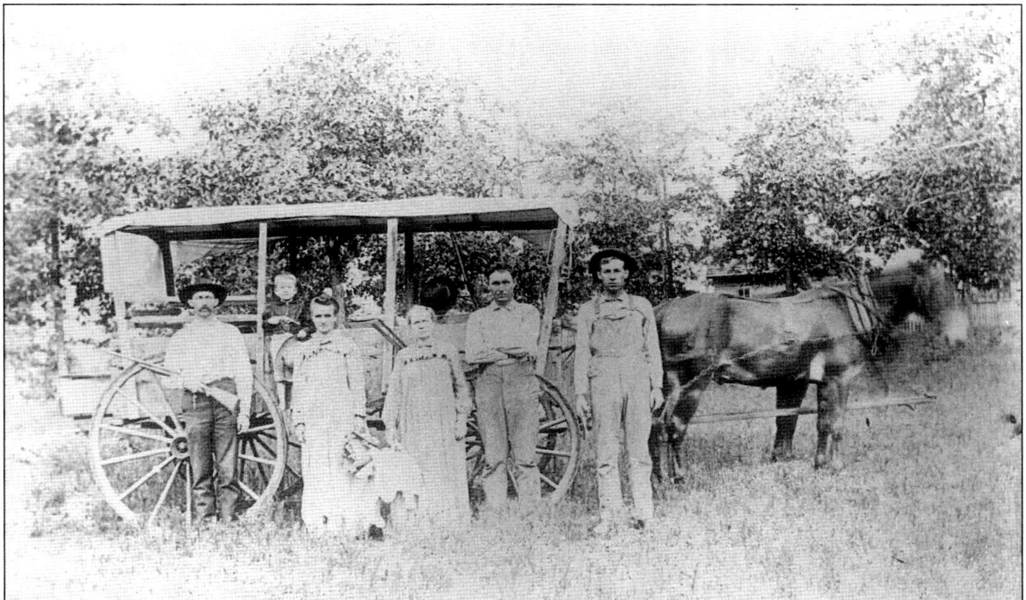

Members of the Ingram family—Willie, Paul, Beckie, Mattie, Osco, and Roland—pose beside the covered wagon which brought them from Tennessee to the Pleasant Plains area. (W.C. Blankenship/Independence County Historical Society)

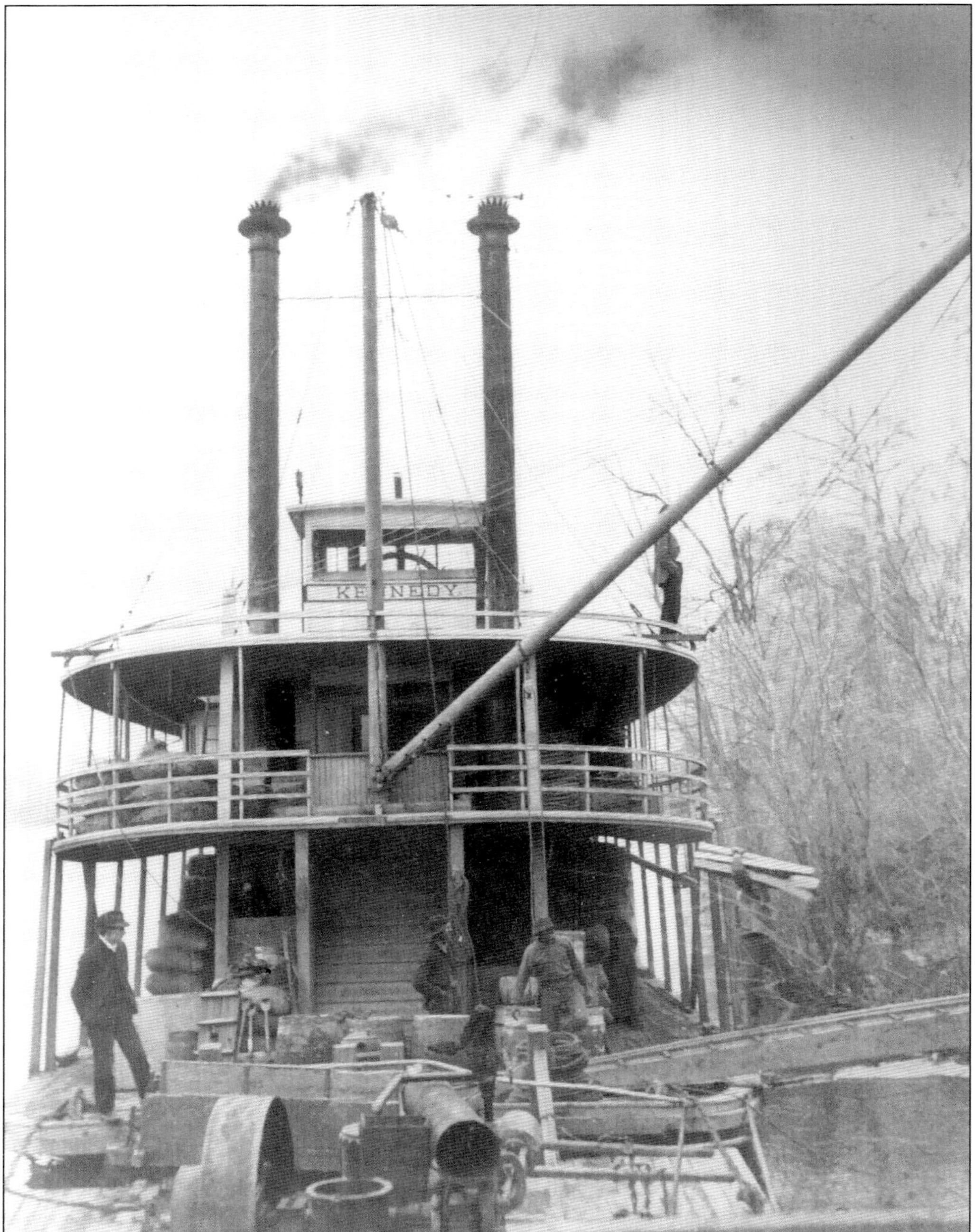

The Steamer *Kennedy* was owned by Capt. William M. Heckmann and piloted by Ed. B. Warner. Here the boat is docked to take on wood at an unknown landing on the White River. The *Kennedy* transported supplies up and down the River during the construction of the White River branch of the St. Louis Iron Mountain and Southern Railway. (Regional Studies Center, Lyon College)

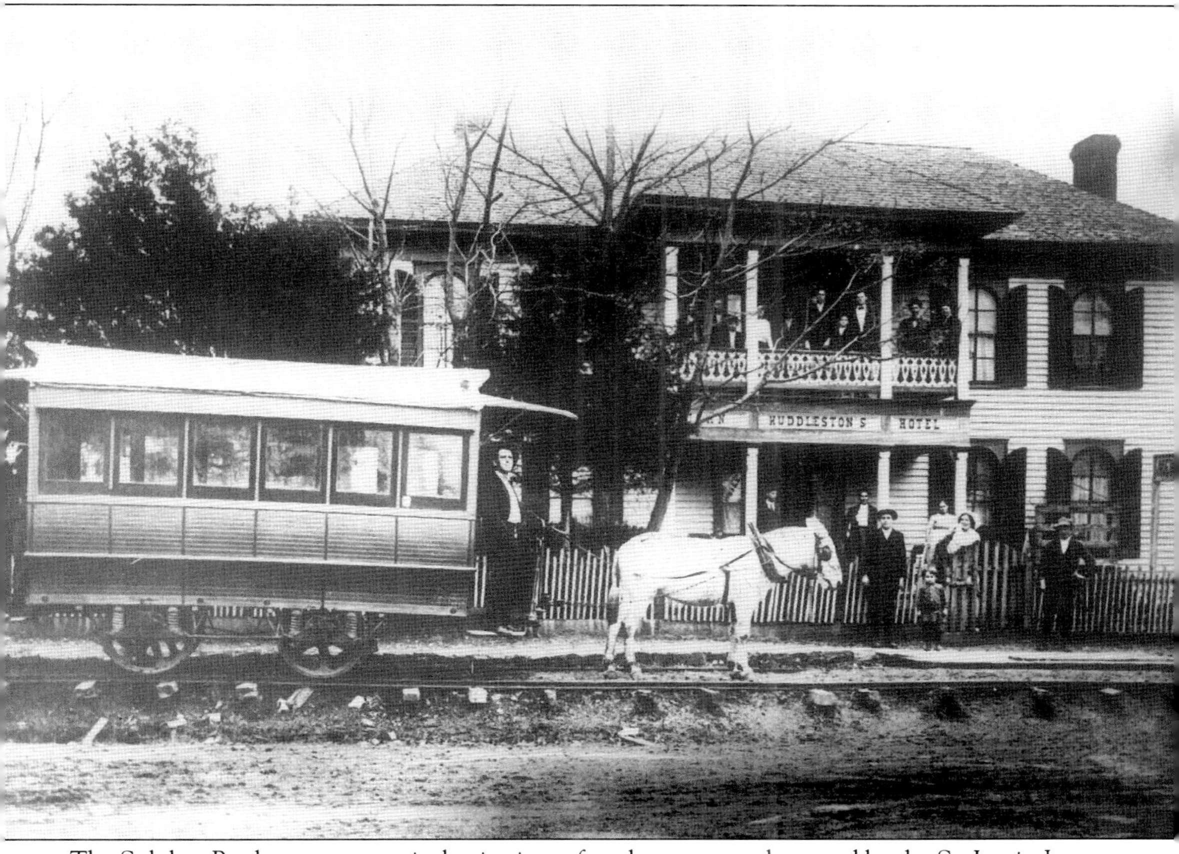

The Sulphur Rock streetcar got its beginnings after the town was bypassed by the St. Louis, Iron Mountain, and Southern Railroad in 1883. The track missed the town by one mile. Citizens were eager to use the railroad services, but were hampered by the distance between town and the tracks. They were anxious to find a solution to the problem. Thus in 1889 the right of way for the Sulphur Rock Railway Company was granted. This photo taken in 1910 shows the mule drawn streetcar in front of the Huddleston Hotel. John C. Huddleston is the car operator, his son, Carl, stands in front of the mule, "Old Dick;" another son, Clyde, stands on the extreme right. Standing at the gate is Mrs. Ed Hammer, and behind her is her mother, Margaret Susan Huddleston, and at her left is Mrs. John C. Huddleston. At the extreme right on the balcony is Sam Tuggle. The streetcar was reputedly one of the last mule driven streetcars to operate in the country. In 1983, it became the subject for a United States Postal Service stamp. (Butler Center for Arkansas Studies, Central Arkansas Library System)

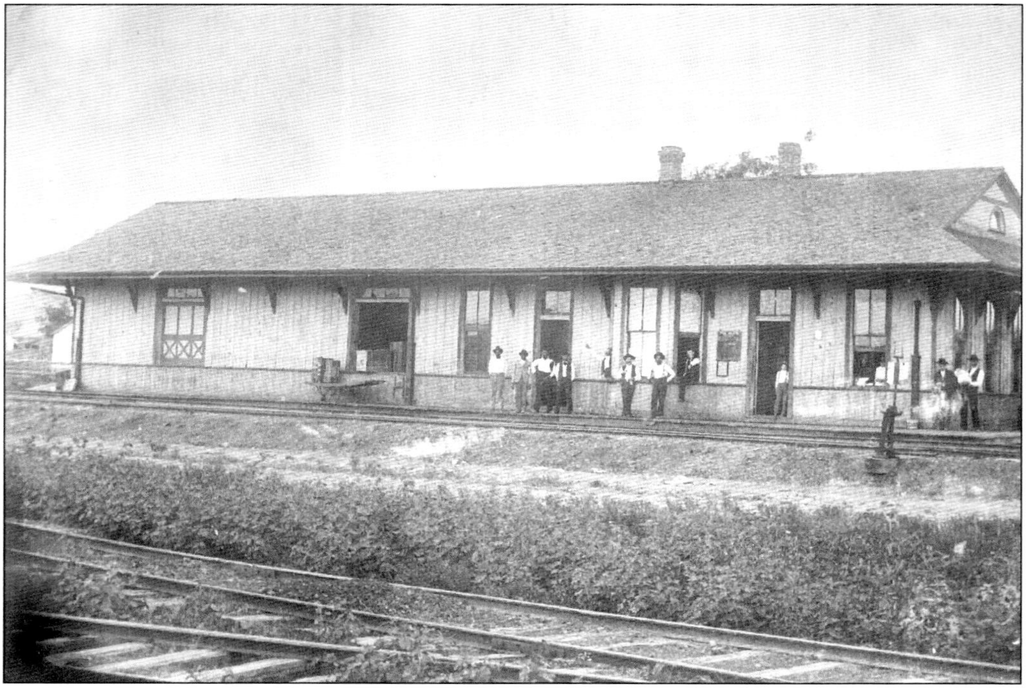

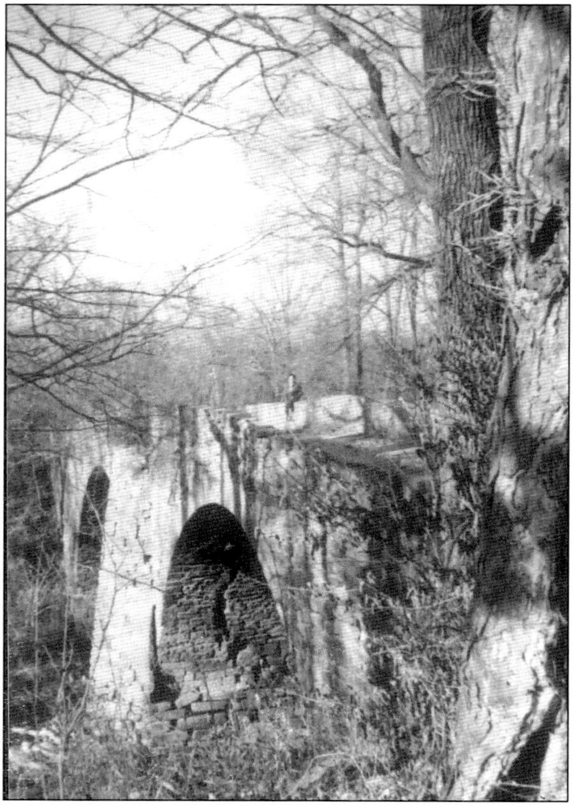

The coming of the railroad in 1883 was an important milestone for Independence County. The railroad brought significant changes to the area and increased the importance of Batesville as a trading destination. This depot located on the corner of Lawrence and State Streets is believed to be the second depot built in city. The photo was made about 1895. (Regional Studies Center, Lyon College)

The historic Salado Bridge, completed in 1870, was built by engineer John Schnable. The twin-arched stone structure received a great deal of use, but collapsed in January 1958. (Independence County Historical Society)

In 1893, the steamboat *Ralph E. Warner* landed at Batesville and reported passing 27 rafts of cedar logs en route down White River from McBee's Landing, a distance of about 100 miles. The rafts were bound for the Handford Cedar Yard, once a prosperous business located approximately where the White River Stadium is today. The logs were used for railroad crossties, fence posts, and pilings. This raft was photographed in 1903. (Regional Studies Center, Lyon College)

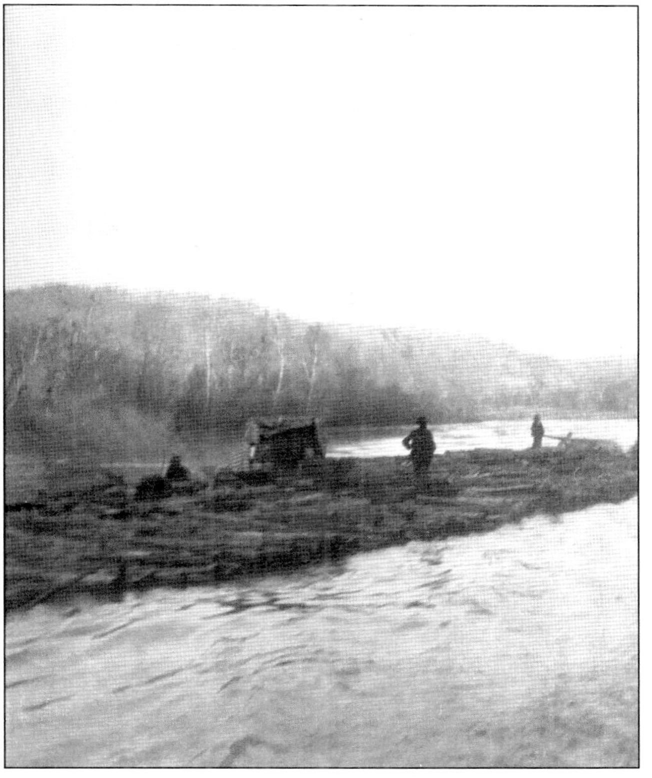

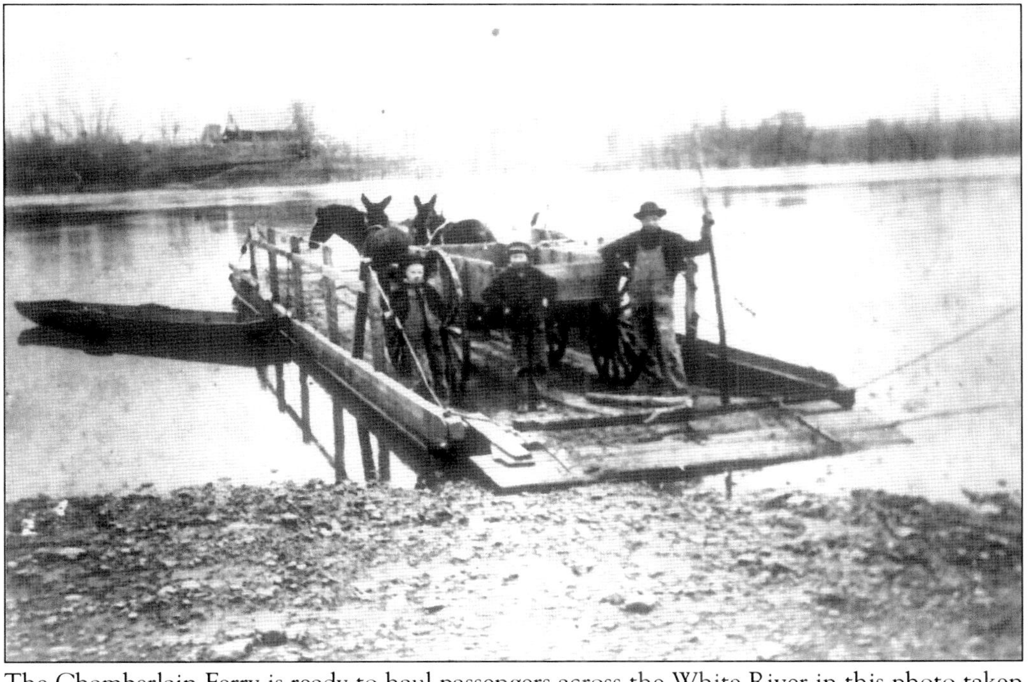

The Chamberlain Ferry is ready to haul passengers across the White River in this photo taken around the turn of the 20th century. (Marietta Postier)

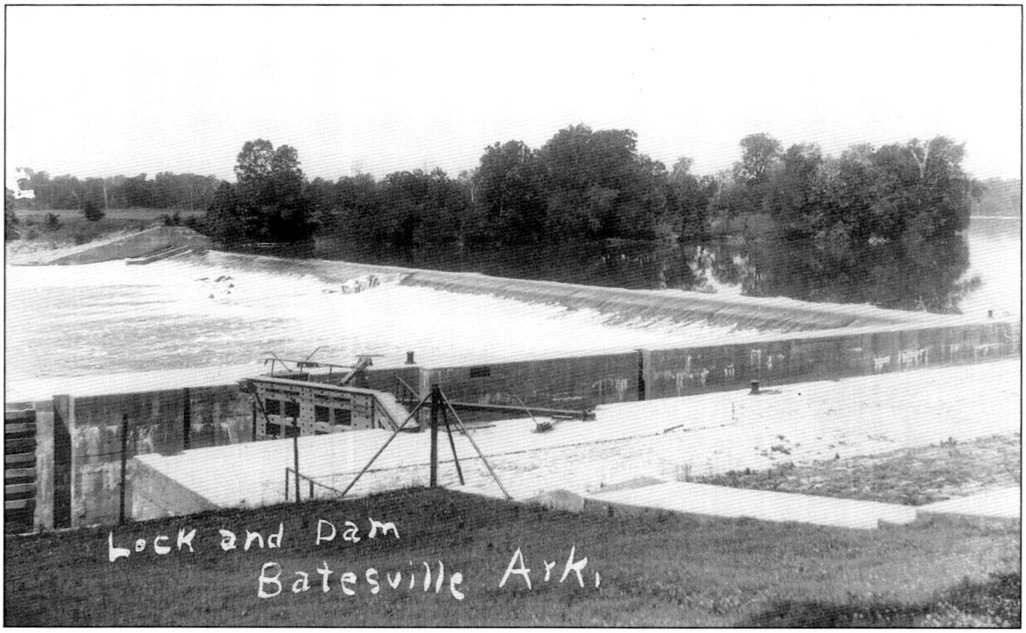

Lock and Dam No. 1 was constructed by the federal government to facilitate navigation on the White River. Once the project was completed a celebration was held on November 27, 1902, in Batesville. The occasion was marked with a large banquet and much speech-making. The construction of locks and dams on the river was a financial boon to Batesville and the surrounding areas. (Brian Robertson)

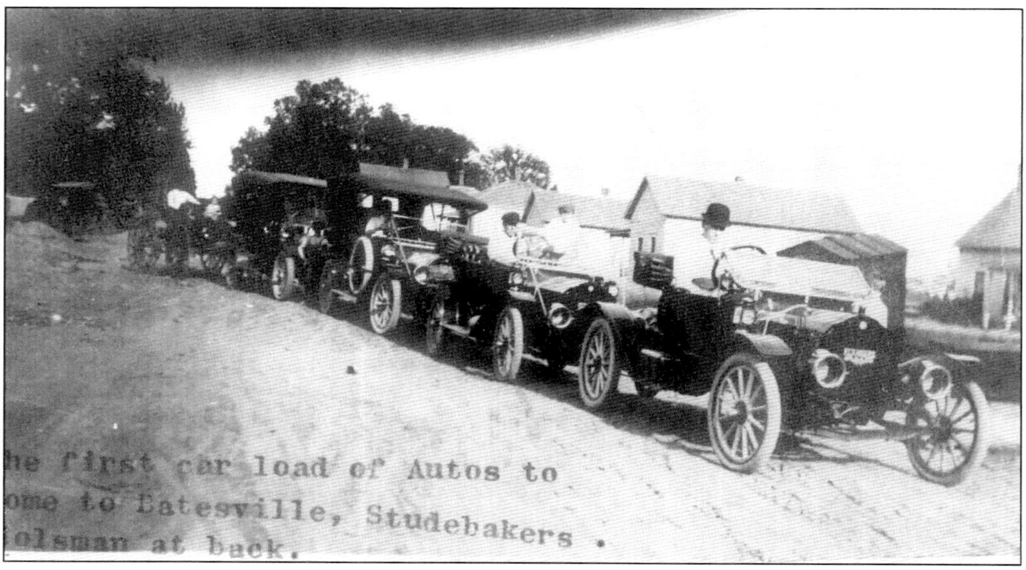

The first load of automobiles arrived in Batesville about 1910. This photo shows a row of Studebakers with a Holsom in the back. (Independence County Historical Society)

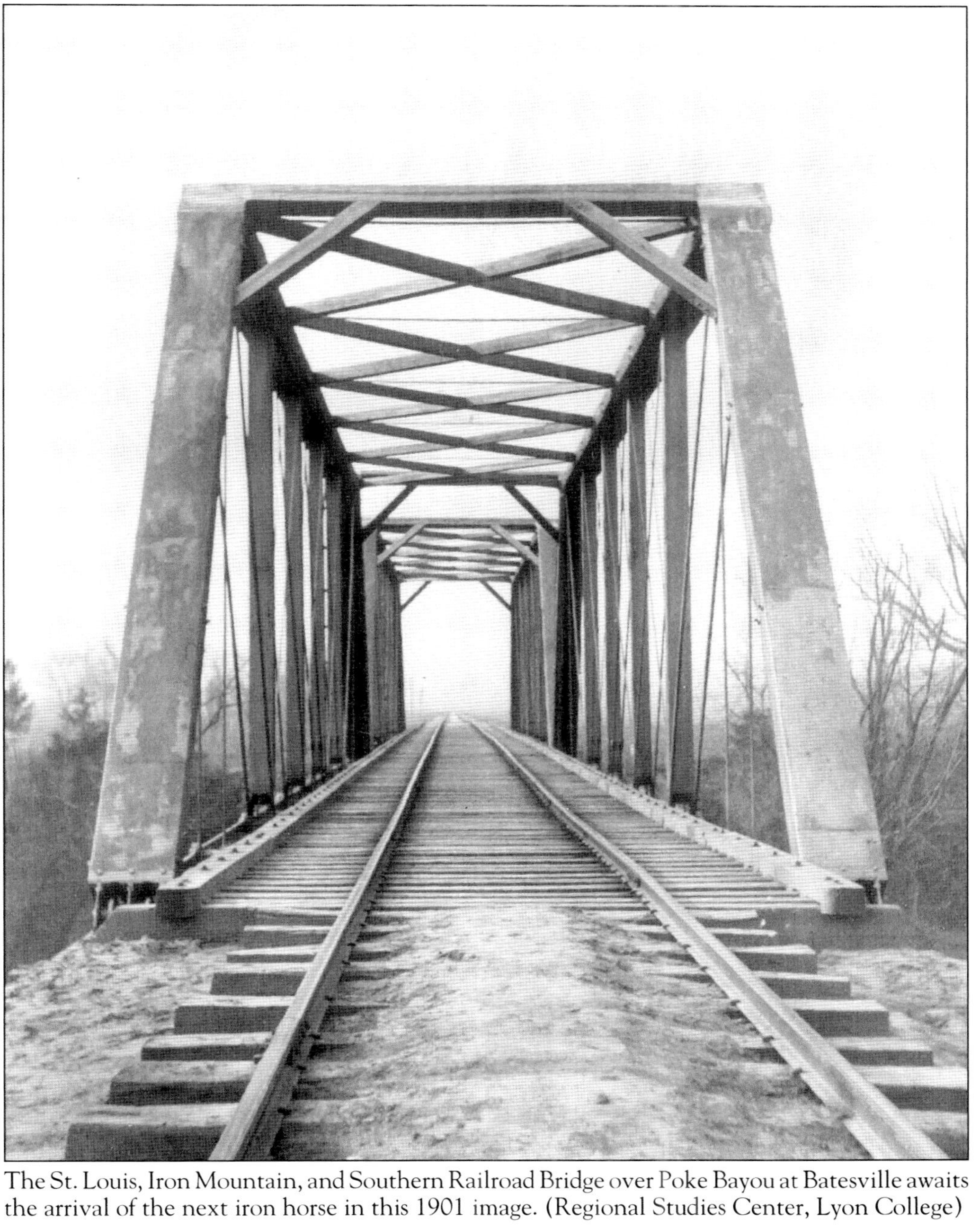

The St. Louis, Iron Mountain, and Southern Railroad Bridge over Poke Bayou at Batesville awaits the arrival of the next iron horse in this 1901 image. (Regional Studies Center, Lyon College)

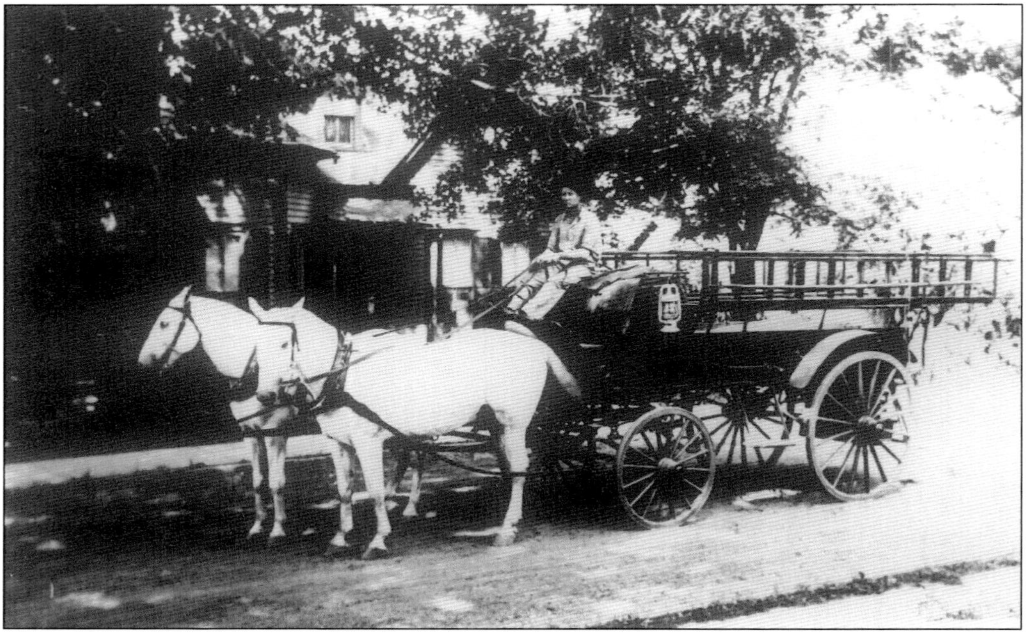

The Batesville Fire Department is ready to respond with its horse drawn truck in this early 20th century photograph. (Old Independence Regional Museum)

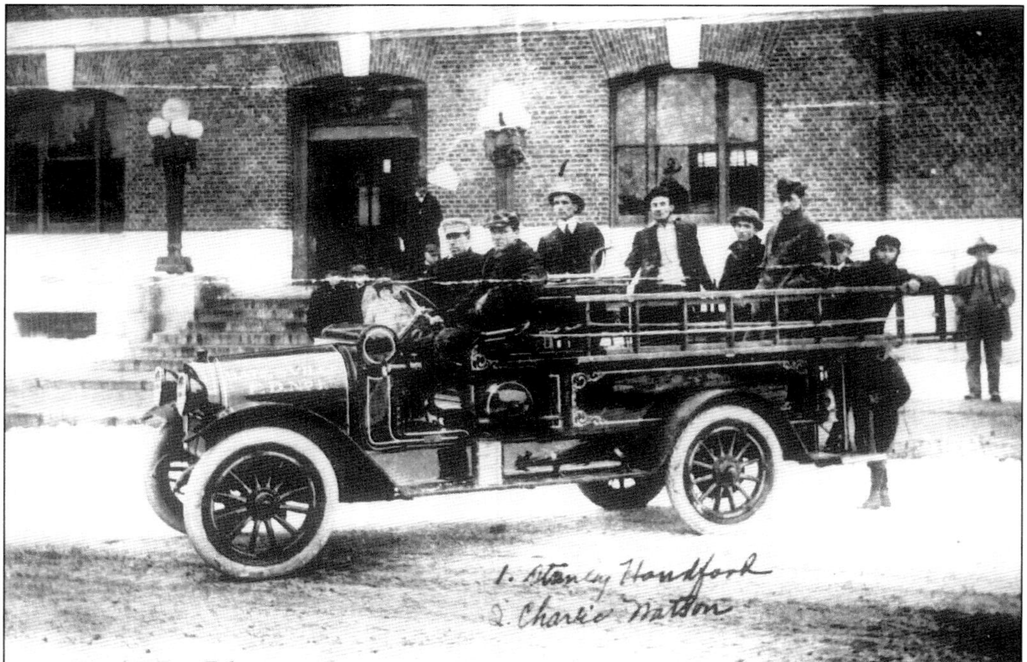

The development of the internal combustion engine led to significant improvements in the ability of the Batesville Fire Department to respond to calls. Undoubtedly these men were quite proud of their new piece of equipment. (Old Independence Regional Museum)

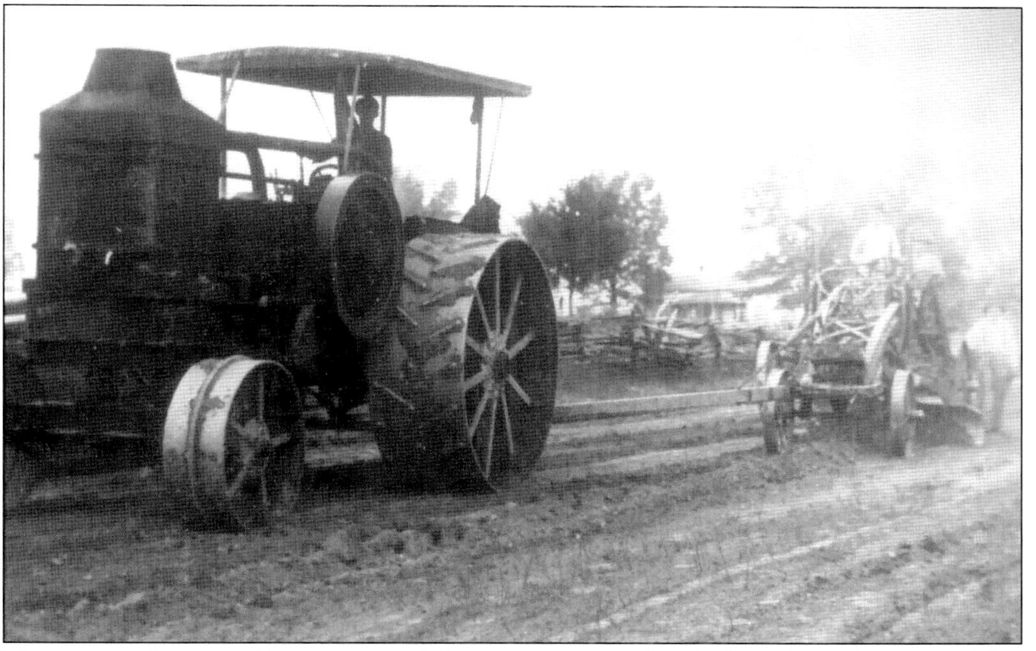

The advent of automobiles necessitated the improvement of roads throughout the county. This road construction is believed to be taking place in the Jamestown area. (Independence County Historical Society)

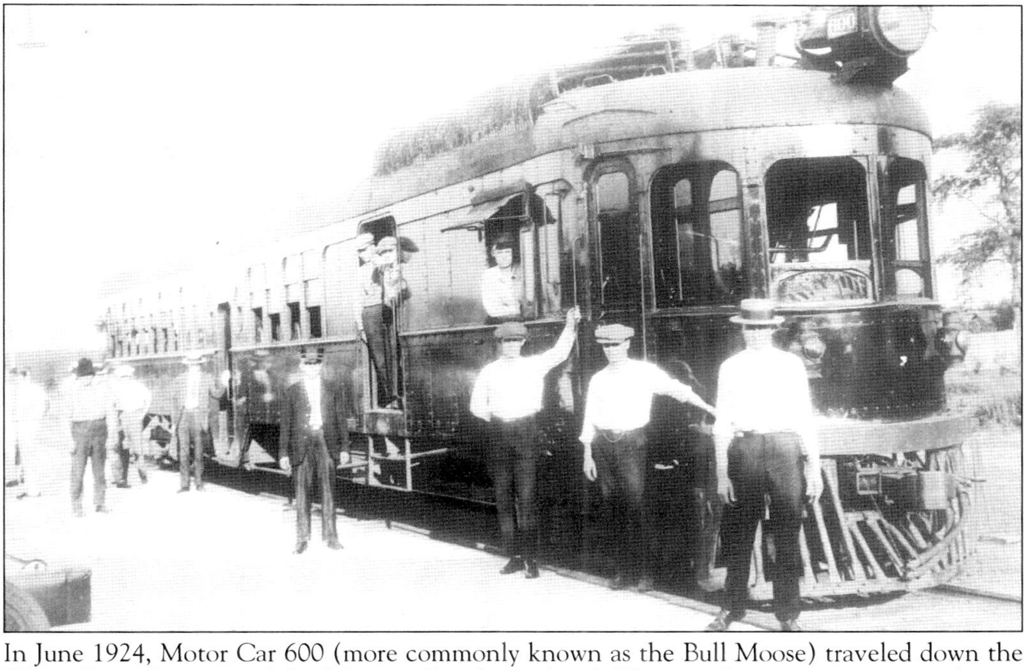

In June 1924, Motor Car 600 (more commonly known as the Bull Moose) traveled down the White River Division of the Missouri Pacific Railroad. The gas-electric motor car made two trips daily between Newport and Batesville. In November of that year, 5,815 passengers made the trip. (Ann Benson Nicholas)

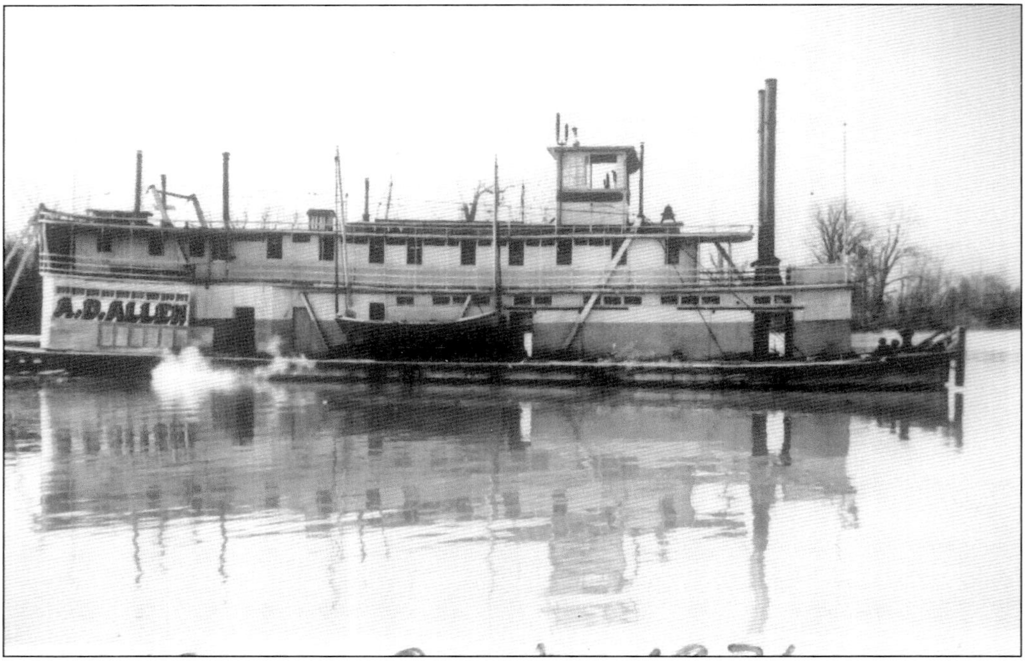

The steamboat *A.D. Allen* traveled the White River during the early 1900s carrying a variety of different types of freight, including shells from the profitable pearling industry that thrived on the River. (Independence County Historical Society)

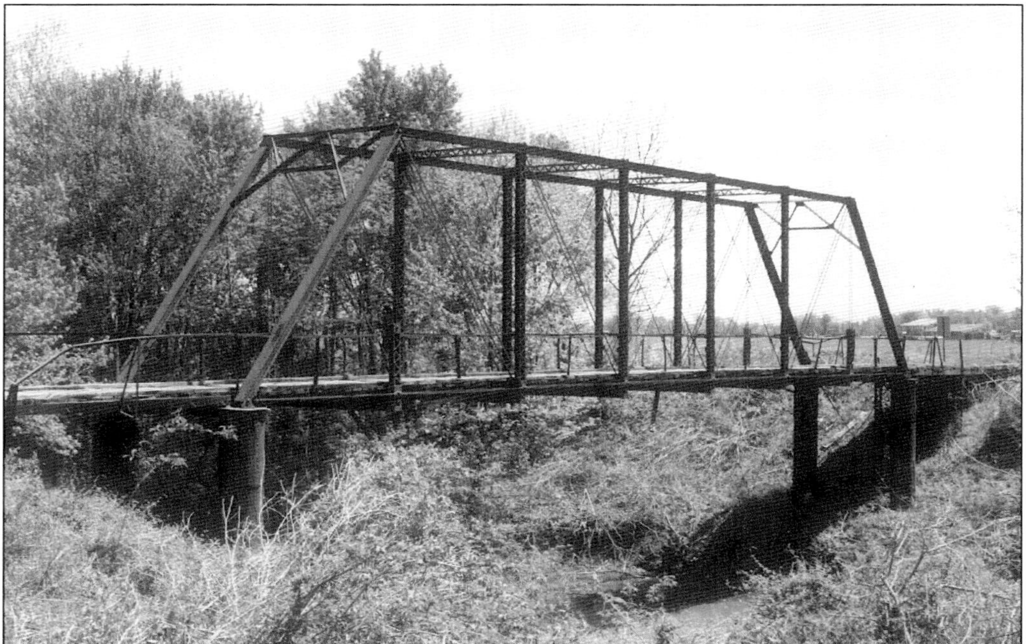

The last overhead-truss steel bridge in the county was built in 1909 and crosses Akron Slough. It is still in use today. (Robert D. Craig)

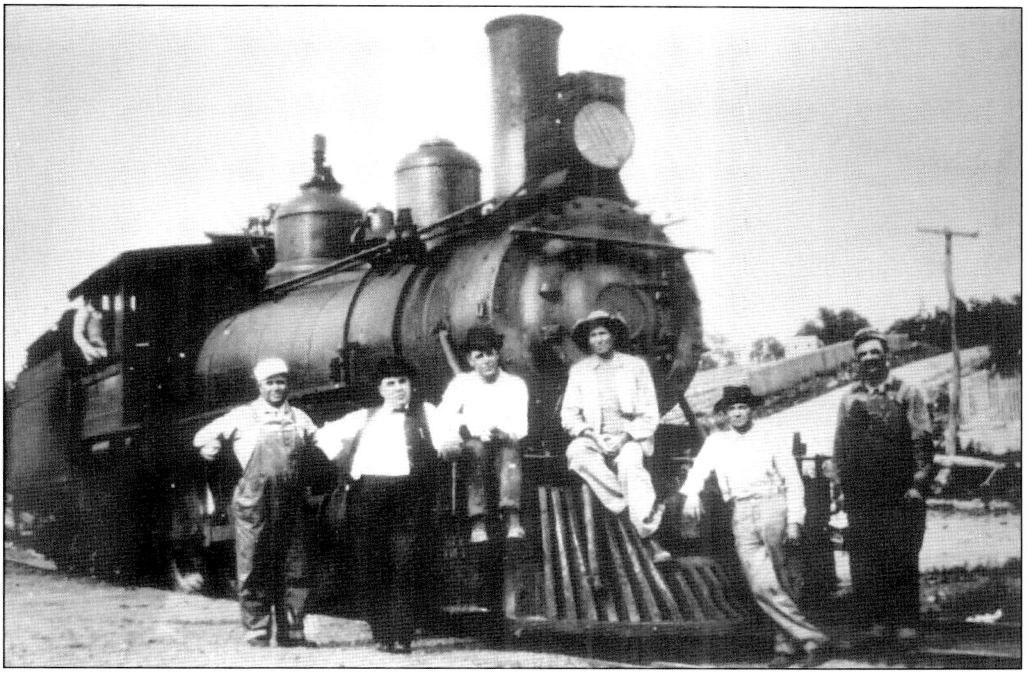

The Cushman Local carried passengers, mail, and freight between Cushman and Newport daily. Pictured in this photo is Happy Hendrickson, fireman; W.B. Young, Brakeman; Puss Adams, Brakeman; Alvis Smith, Brakeman; Pete Busshardt, Engineer; and Gene Steward, watchman in cab. (Cushman History Project)

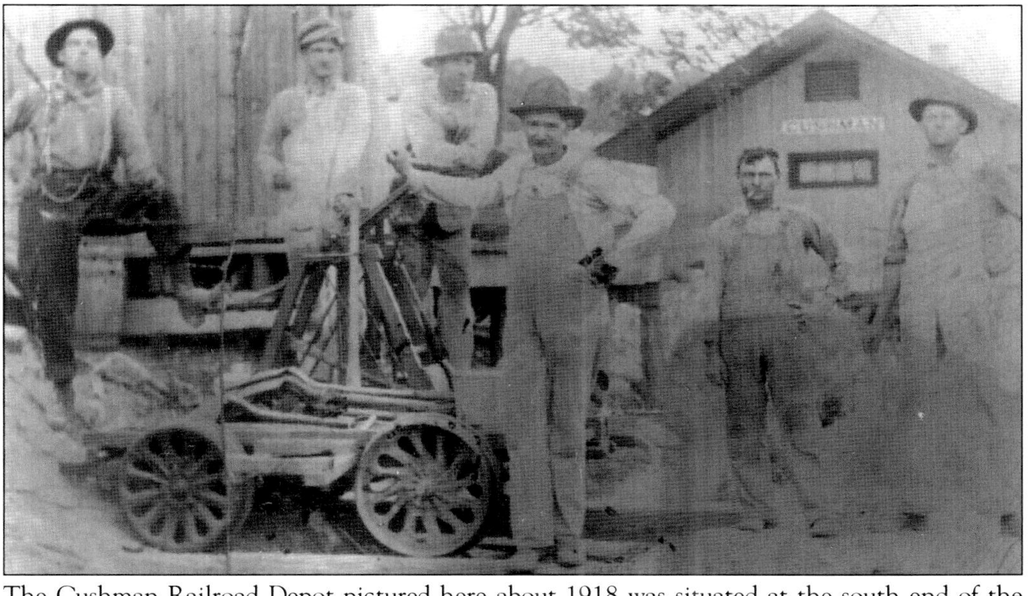

The Cushman Railroad Depot pictured here about 1918 was situated at the south end of the business district, near the spot where the railroad tracks crossed the highway. Cattle pens and lumber yards were located nearby. Shown here, from left to right, are John Brown, Bob Neeley, J.C. Crumpton, Herman Comer, Ed Hand, and unidentified. (Cushman History Project)

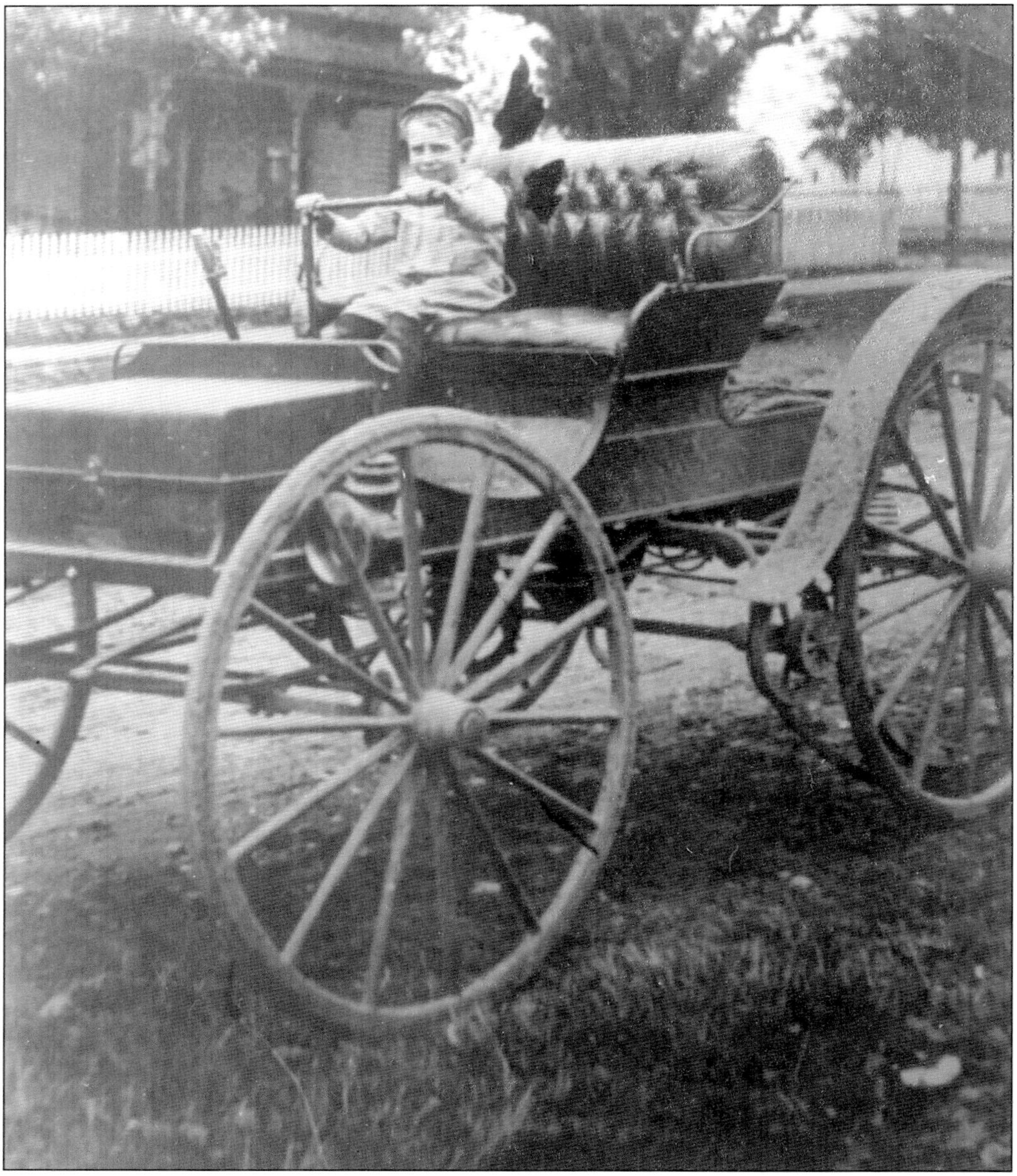

This is a photo of one of Batesville's first automobiles, a Holsman, with Harry Maxfield at the controls. (Wilson Powell)

Eight

MEDICINE

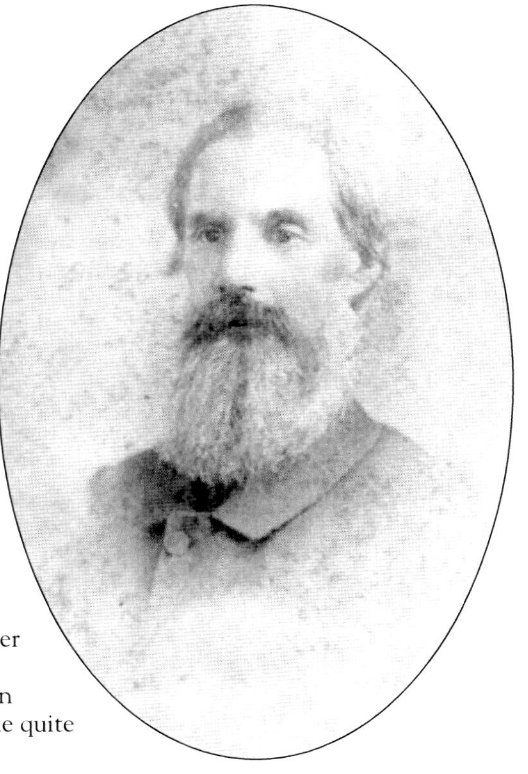

A Virginian, Dr. Philip Burton moved to Batesville in 1838. In October 1841, his son Nicholas was shot and killed in an ambush, many believed by a rival physician, Dr. Trent Aiken, who had quarreled with Burton. Another Burton son, Philip Jr., shot and killed Aiken in 1847 but was acquitted of murder. Dr. Burton moved to Little Rock in 1842, where he became quite well known. (Dora Le Ferguson)

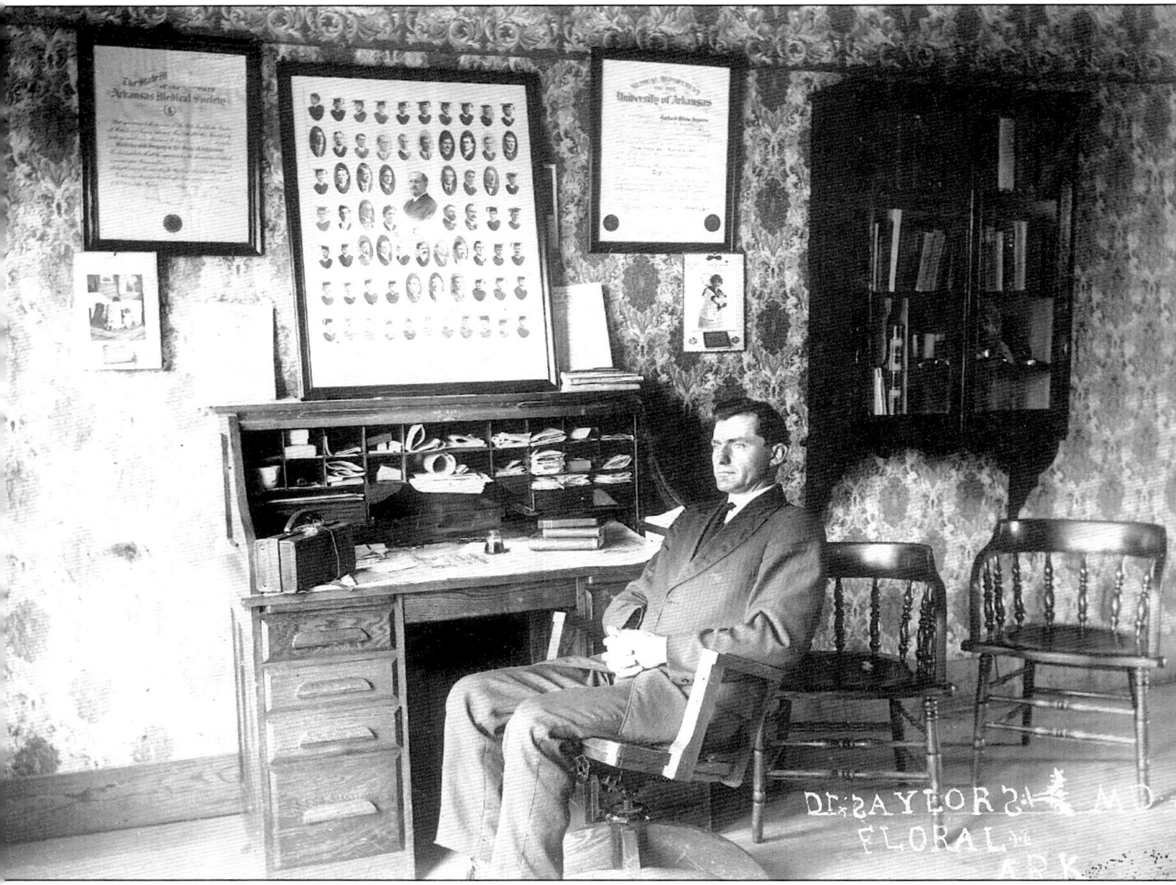

Dr. Garland Saylors in his office at Floral. Dr. Saylors died quite young in 1916, and is buried in Pleasant Hill Cemetery in Dota Township. (Sandra Cox)

Dr. John Farrell Allen received his medical degree from the University of Pennsylvania in 1847 and moved immediately to Batesville. Here he married Elizabeth Agnew, a niece of the prominent Presbyterian educator Aaron Lyon. Allen became well known in church and educational affairs, as well as medicine. He was a trustee of Arkansas (now Lyon) College and an elder of the Presbyterian Church for 34 years. (Nancy Britton)

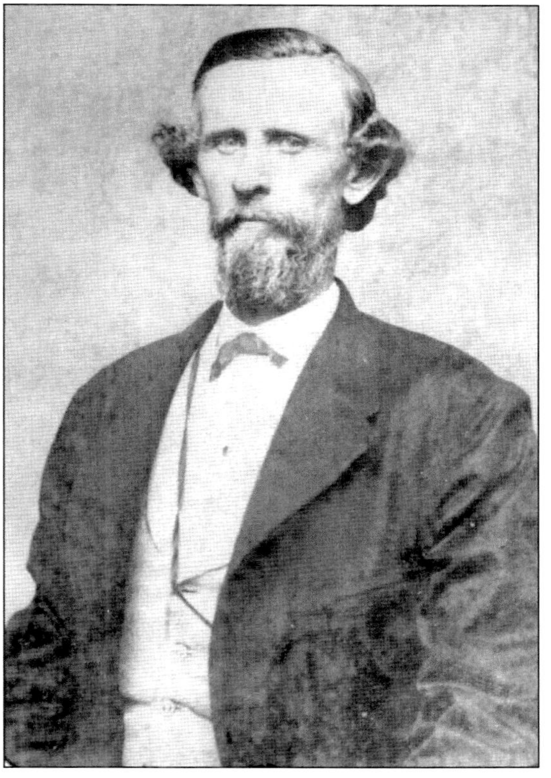

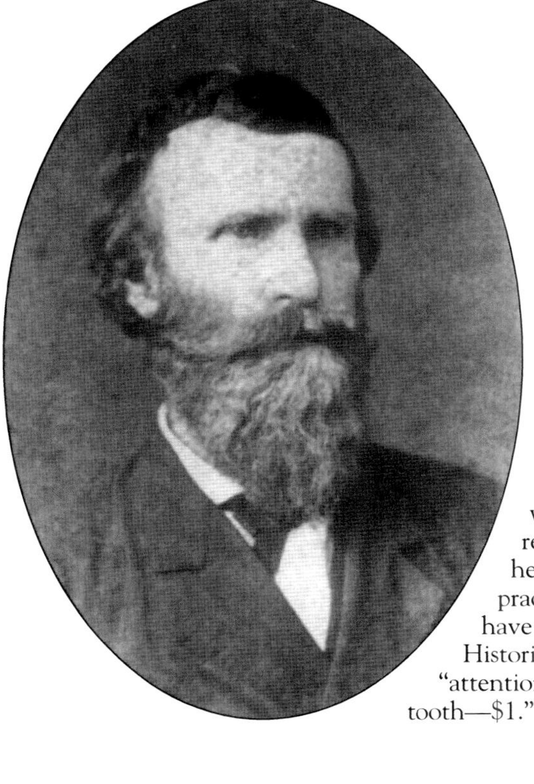

Dr. Lycurgus Adair Dickson was a graduate of Jefferson Medical School in Philadelphia. He came to Independence County from Tennessee in 1856. After serving as surgeon with the 8th Arkansas Infantry, CSA, Dickson returned to the Desha community, where he married Elizabeth Neill and continued to practice for many years. Dr. Dickson's ledgers have been preserved by the Independence County Historical Society and include entries such as "attention to wife in labor—$10" and "extracting tooth—$1." (Nancy Britton)

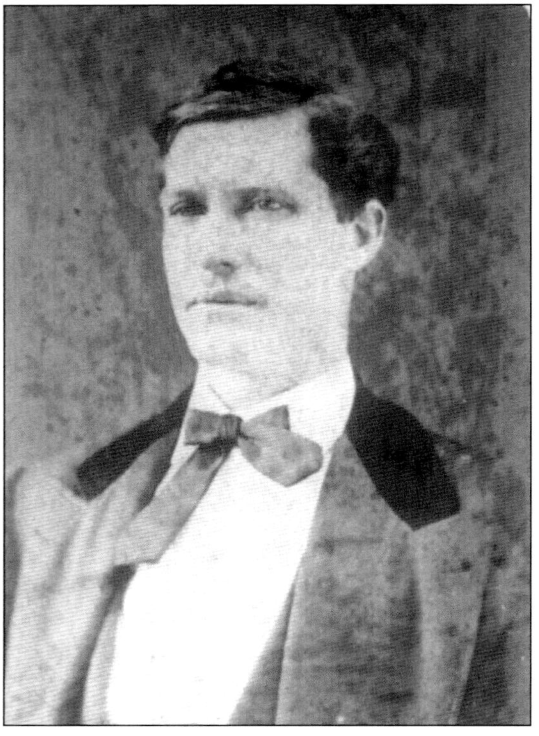

Dr. D.C. Ewing also saw Confederate service but as a regular soldier under Nathan Bedford Forrest. After the war he began medical studies and graduated from the University of Louisville. He moved to Batesville in 1871 and became associated in practice with Drs. William M. and William B. Lawrence. In 1874, he married Mrs. Laura Erwin Cox. They resided in the magnificent 1845 brick mansion known as the Ewing House (razed in 1956). Dr. Ewing was killed in 1898, when loose bricks fell on him from the roof of his office building during a windstorm. (Nancy Britton)

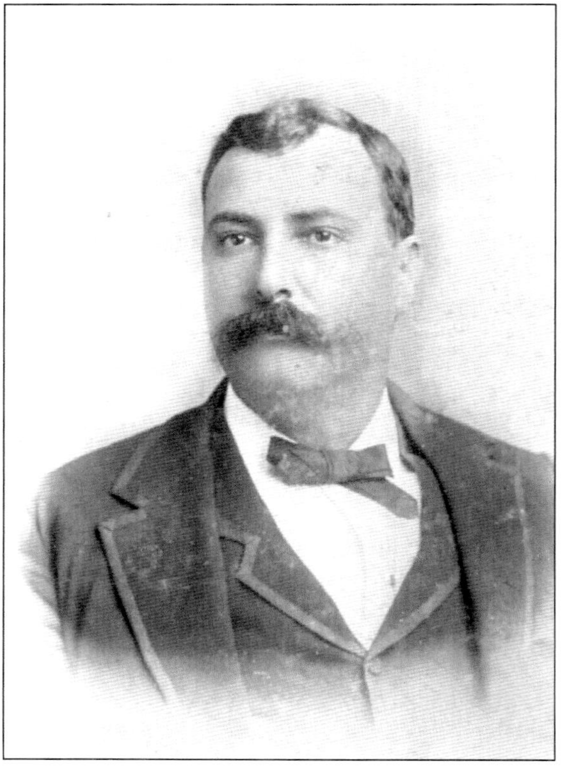

Dr. James P. Dorr was one of the five doctor sons of Dr. Francis Dorr, a German immigrant who came to America as a boy in 1832. Dr. Jim Dorr studied medicine under his father, then graduated as a "licensed physician" in 1881 from what is now Washington University in St. Louis. He purchased land from his father in the Dota Creek neighborhood between Sulphur Rock and the Black River in 1889, and practiced in that area for over 40 years. He also operated a general store on the property, which included one room for the sale of caskets. (Independence County Historical Society)

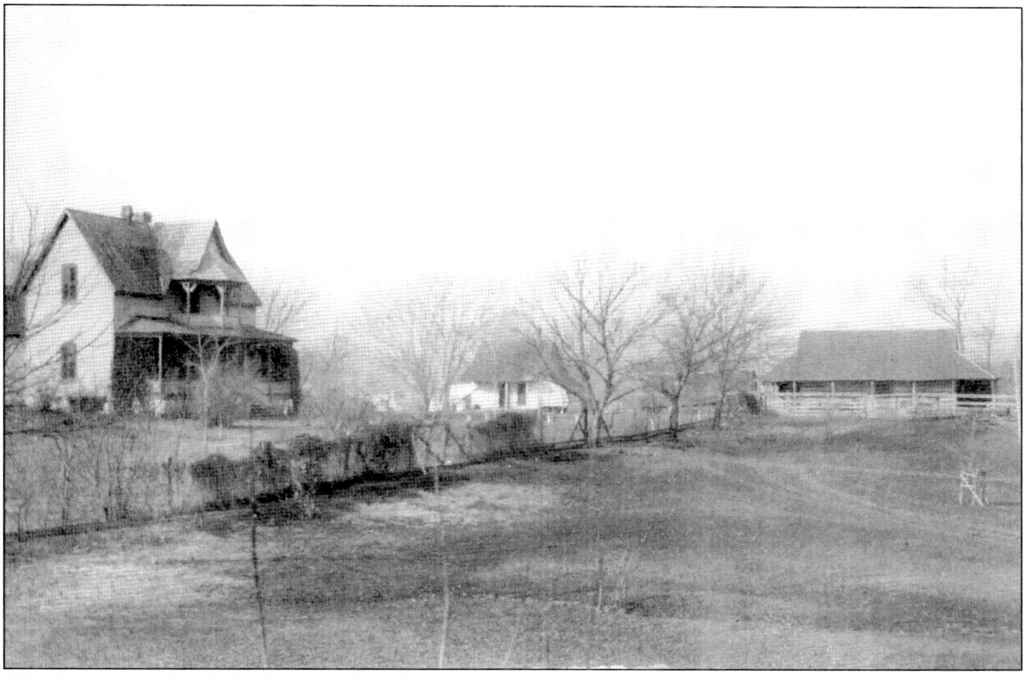

This home was built by Dr. Mosby Clayton Weaver near Jamestown. Dr. Weaver (1885–1928) practiced medicine in the Jamestown area for many years. He eventually moved to Batesville where he was a partner in a dry goods business, Weaver and Dowdy, and operated a cotton broker. The house later became the home of the Burks family. (Independence County Historical Society)

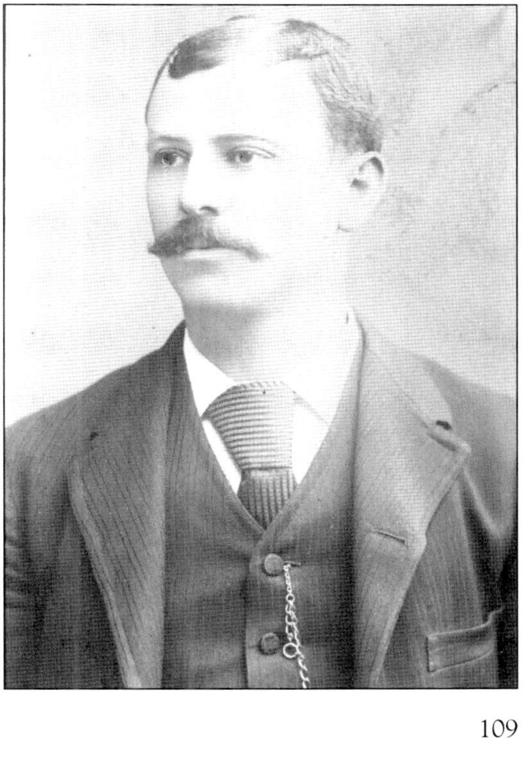

Dr. R.C. "Rob" Dorr was a brother of Dr. Jim Dorr. Rob Dorr also attended Missouri Medical College, later Washington University, and graduated in 1883. He practiced medicine in the Charlotte and Sulphur Rock communities before moving to Batesville, where he opened a clinic on Main Street with Dr. J.H. Kennerly. He served as president of the Independence County Medical Society in 1888 and 1893, and as president of the Arkansas Medical Society in 1910–11. (Independence County Historical Society)

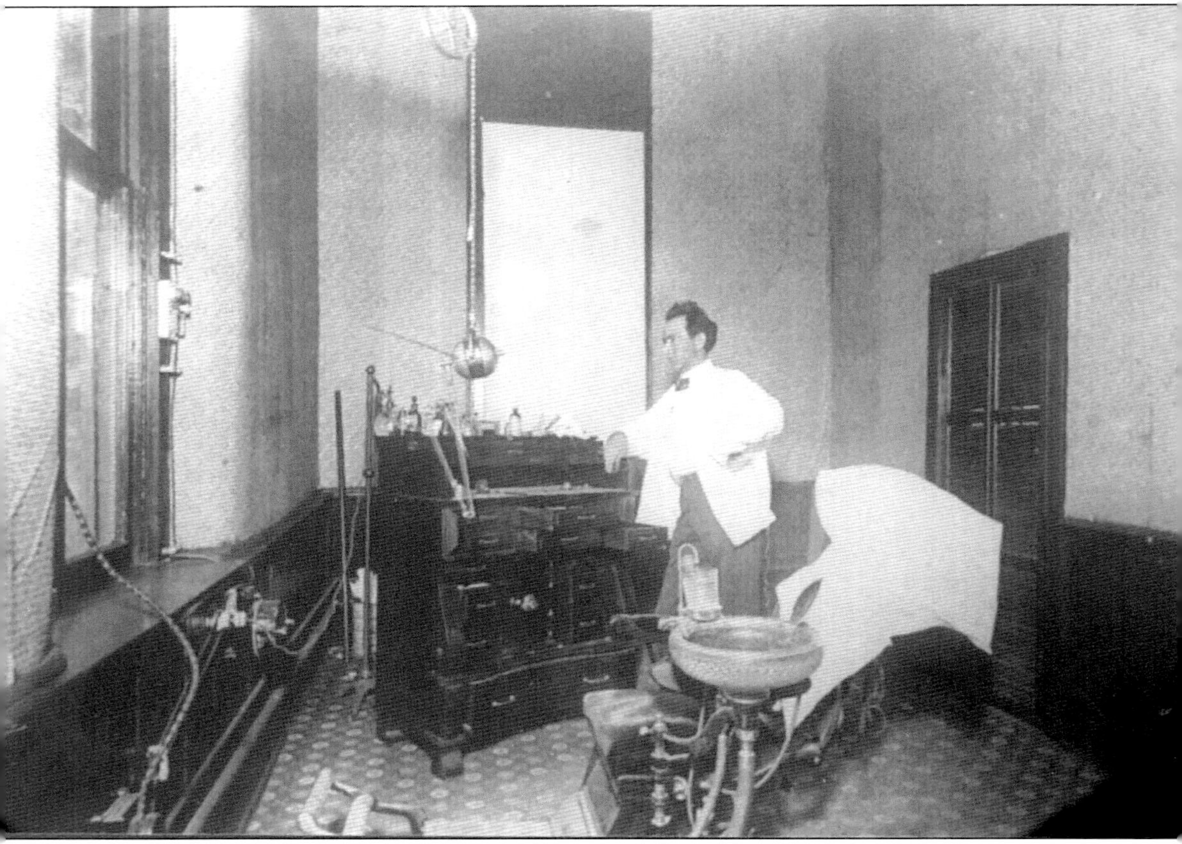

This unidentified dentist's office is believed to have been located in Batesville. (Wilson Powell)

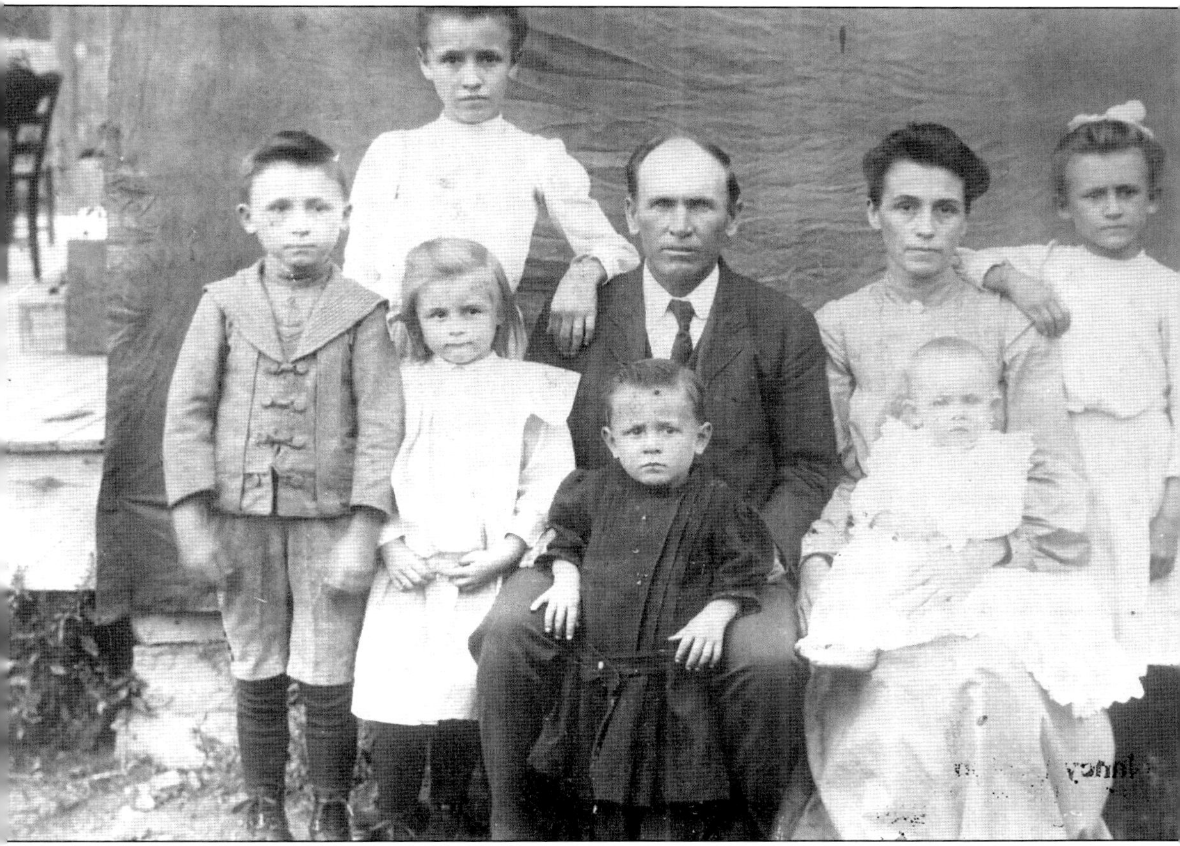

Dr. Columbus Gray practiced medicine for 40 years in the Curia Creek area. He is pictured here with his wife, Harriet Montgomery Gray, and six of their eight children who grew to adulthood. (Independence County Historical Society)

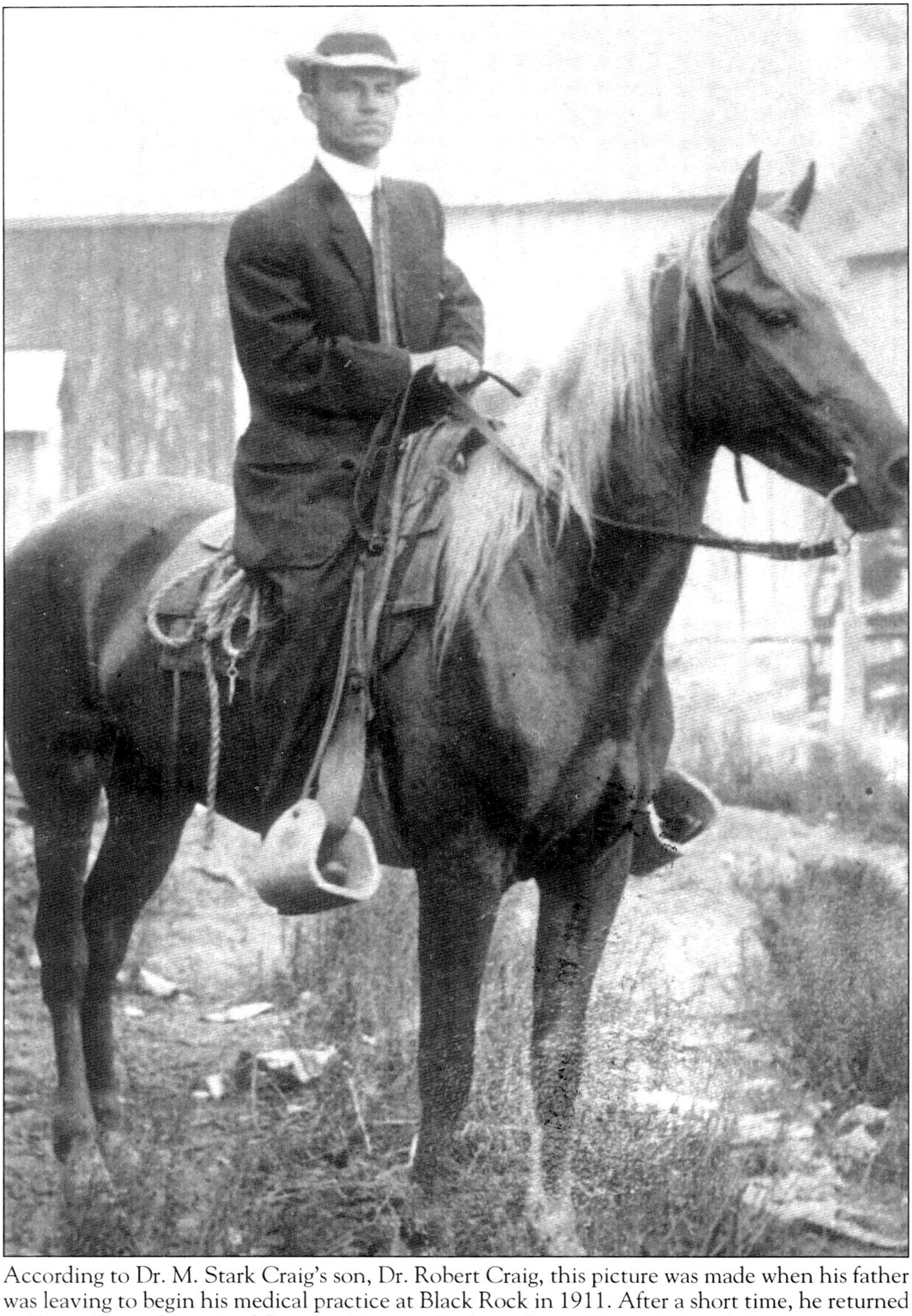

According to Dr. M. Stark Craig's son, Dr. Robert Craig, this picture was made when his father was leaving to begin his medical practice at Black Rock in 1911. After a short time, he returned to Batesville and practiced for over 40 years. (Independence County Historical Society)

Dr. William M. Lawrence was in Batesville by 1848 when he married Sophia Hynson, a niece of merchant John Ringgold. After Ringgold's death, the Lawrences lived in his handsome home on lower Main Street for many years. Dr. Lawrence served as a surgeon in the Confederate Army, then returned to his practice in Batesville, first in partnership with Dr. D.C. Ewing, then with his son Dr. W.B. Lawrence. In 1881 he was appointed surgeon-general of the state of Arkansas by Governor Churchill. (Nancy Britton)

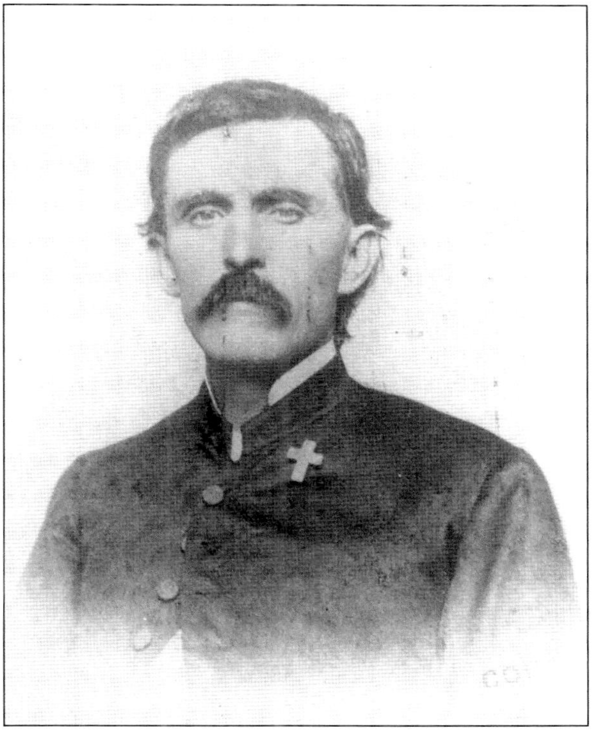

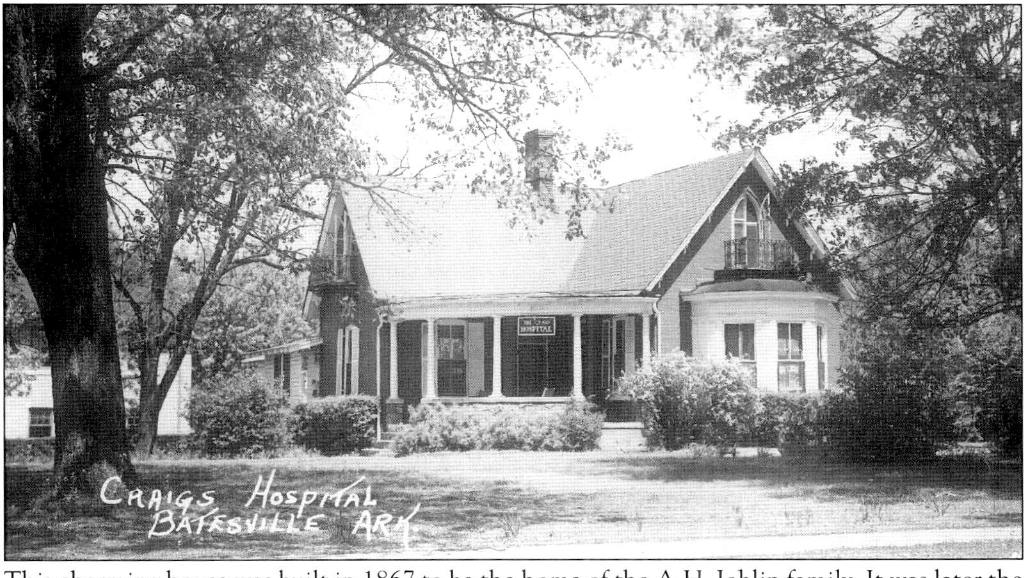

This charming house was built in 1867 to be the home of the A.H. Joblin family. It was later the home of Judge D.D. Adams, then was converted by Drs. M.S. Craig and O.J.T. Johnston into a small hospital. In 1959, the property was acquired by Mr. and Mrs. Allie Crouch who tore down the house, carefully preserving the fine old bricks. Since the bricks had been painted dark red at some point, a new house was constructed with the bricks placed painted side in. Now the home of Mr. and Mrs. Jim Crouch, the house still boasts the small wrought-iron balcony rail, also from the original structure. (Brian Robertson)

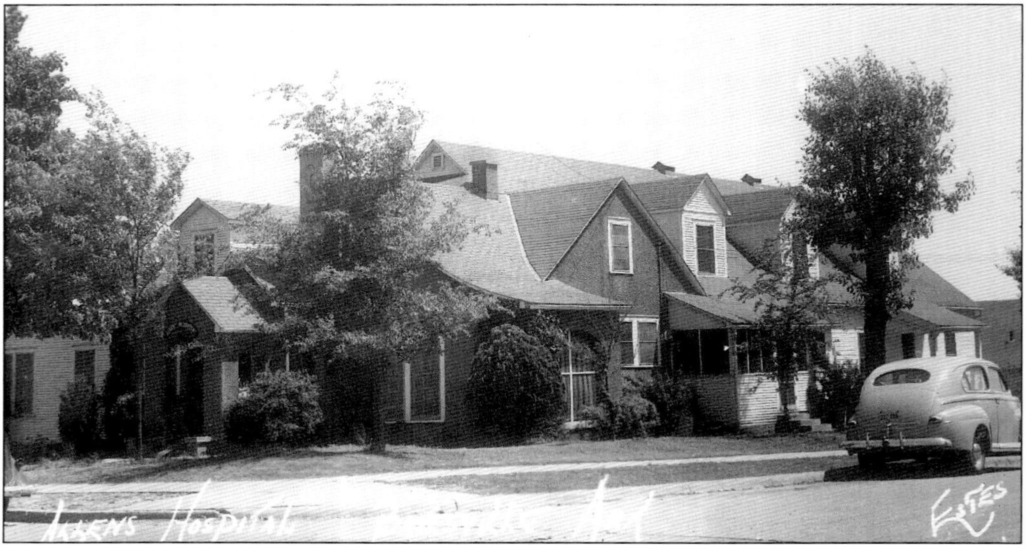

Allen's Hospital, which stood on the corner of Sidney and Harrison Streets, was first established in the home of Mr. and Mrs. Walter Allen. Mrs. Allen was the hospital director according to Dr. Wesley J. Ketz, one of the earliest physicians to care for patients there. By 1957, Allen's had become a nursing home for Independence County residents. It was eventually replaced by Woodlawn Nursing Home, and the building was razed in the 1970s. (Brian Robertson)

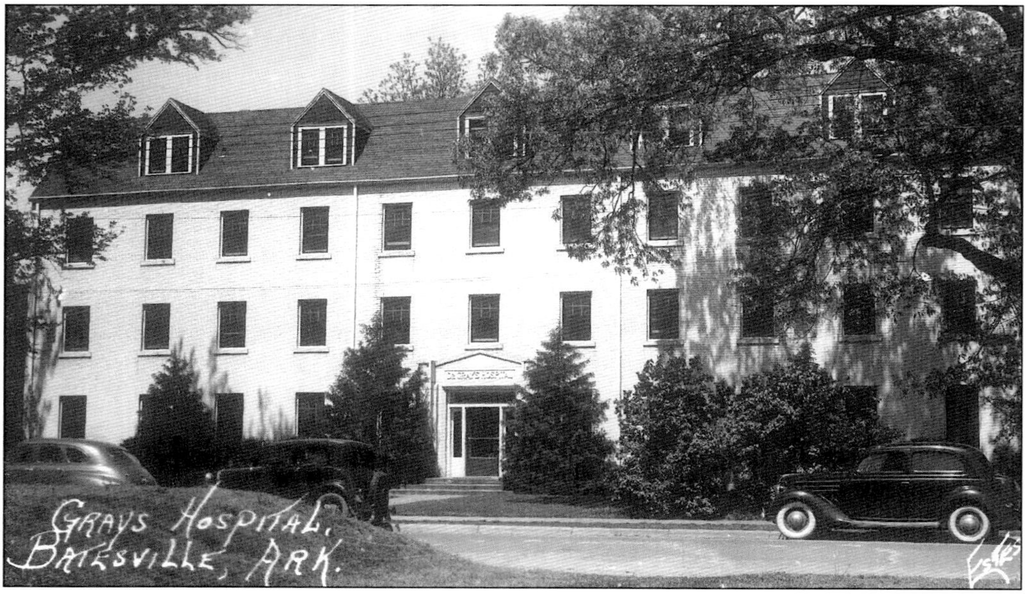

Dr. F.A. Gray bought this property from the Thomas B. Padgett family in 1937. The old family home was torn down, and this hospital building erected on the site (northwest corner of Fourth and Main Streets). Dr. Gray had earlier operated a hospital in the old Presbyterian Church sanctuary on the northeast corner. He also used what was later known as the Cooper Boarding House just west of this building. This hospital, later directed by F.A. Gray's son, Dr. Paul Gray, ceased operation in the 1980s when it was purchased by the White River Medical Center. It currently houses the Independence County Sheriff's Office. (Brian Robertson)

Nine

Activities and Events

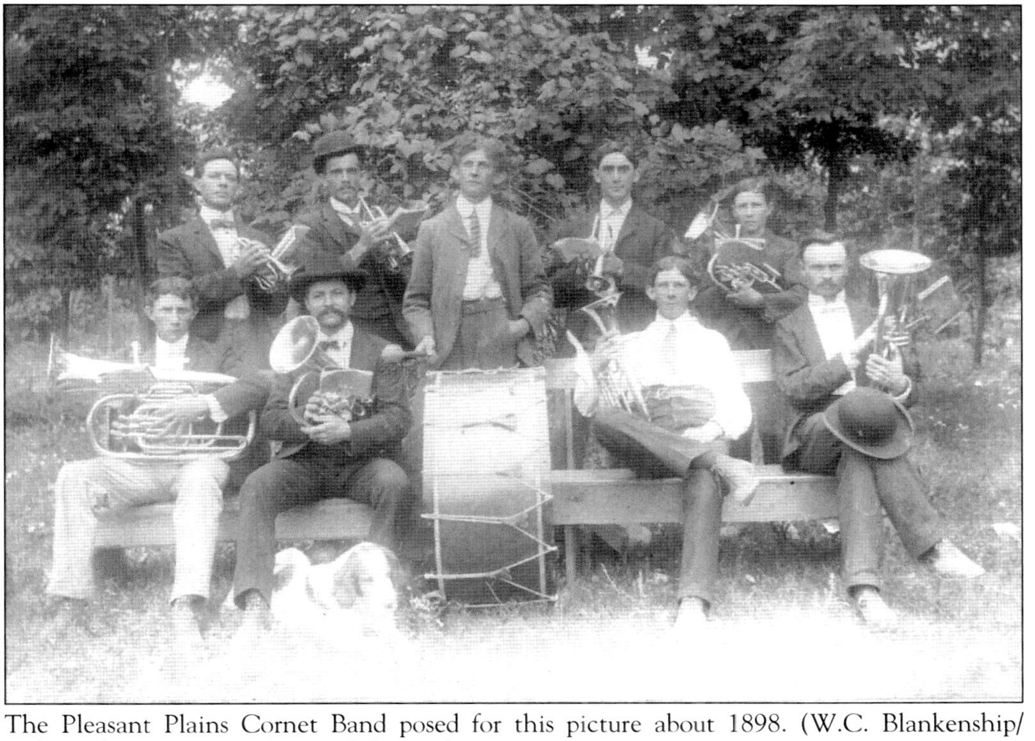

The Pleasant Plains Cornet Band posed for this picture about 1898. (W.C. Blankenship/ Independence County Historical Society)

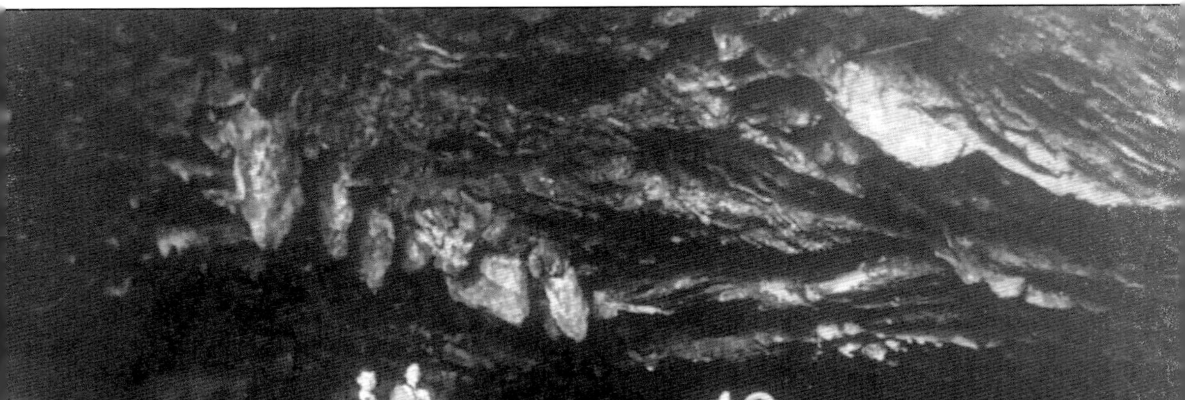

Limestone caves are common in Independence County. Excursions to explore them and enjoy picnics in the cool environs are still popular today. One young woman recorded such an outing in her journal in August 1861: "The entrance to [Bell] cave for about 20 yards is large, then we had to climb a ladder about 12 feet high up through a small hole in solid rock. Then we came to a very large room covered with large rocks lying in the greatest confusion . . ." The cave pictured here is not identified, nor are the young people posed at its entrance. (Independence County Historical Society)

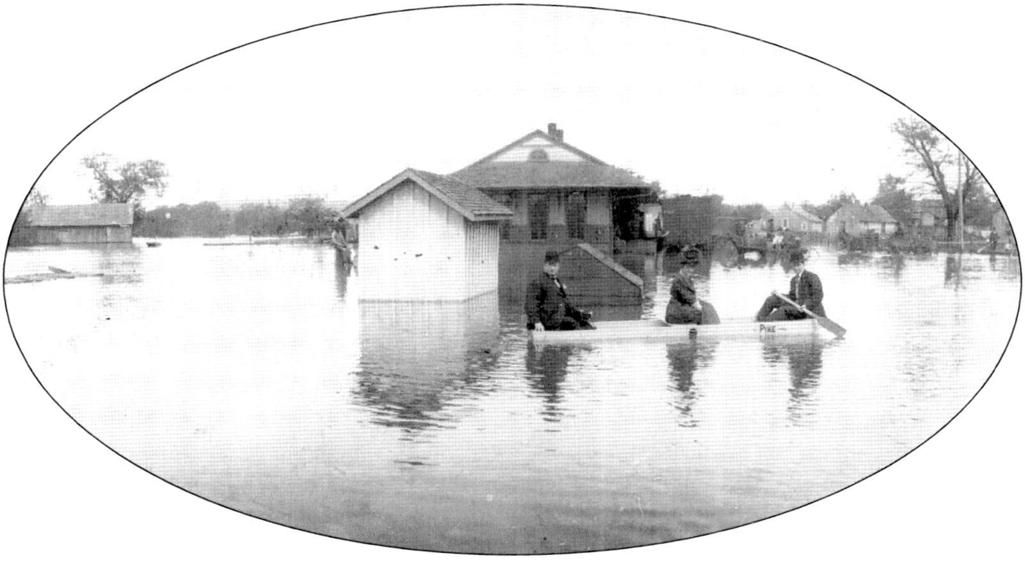

The Batesville Railroad Depot during the 1907 White River flood. The people in the boat were identified, from left to right, as an unknown photographer, Mrs. John W. Glenn, and her son, E.H. Glenn. (Wilson Powell)

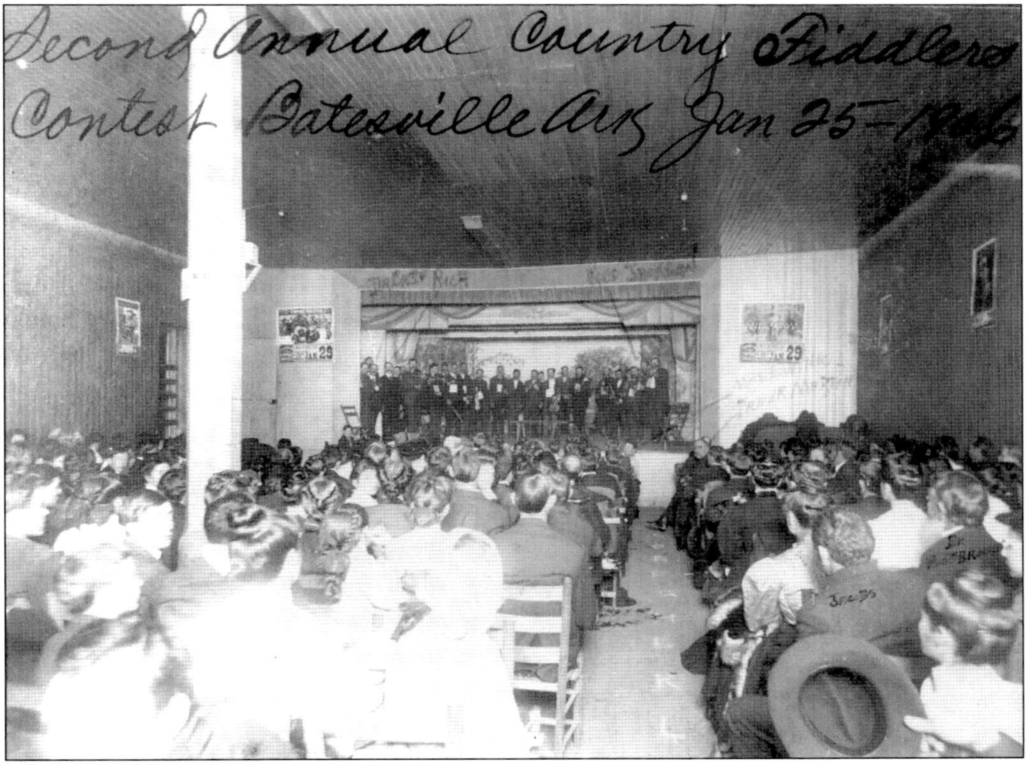

The Second Annual Country Fiddler's Contest was held in Batesville on January 25, 1906. (Regional Studies Center, Lyon College)

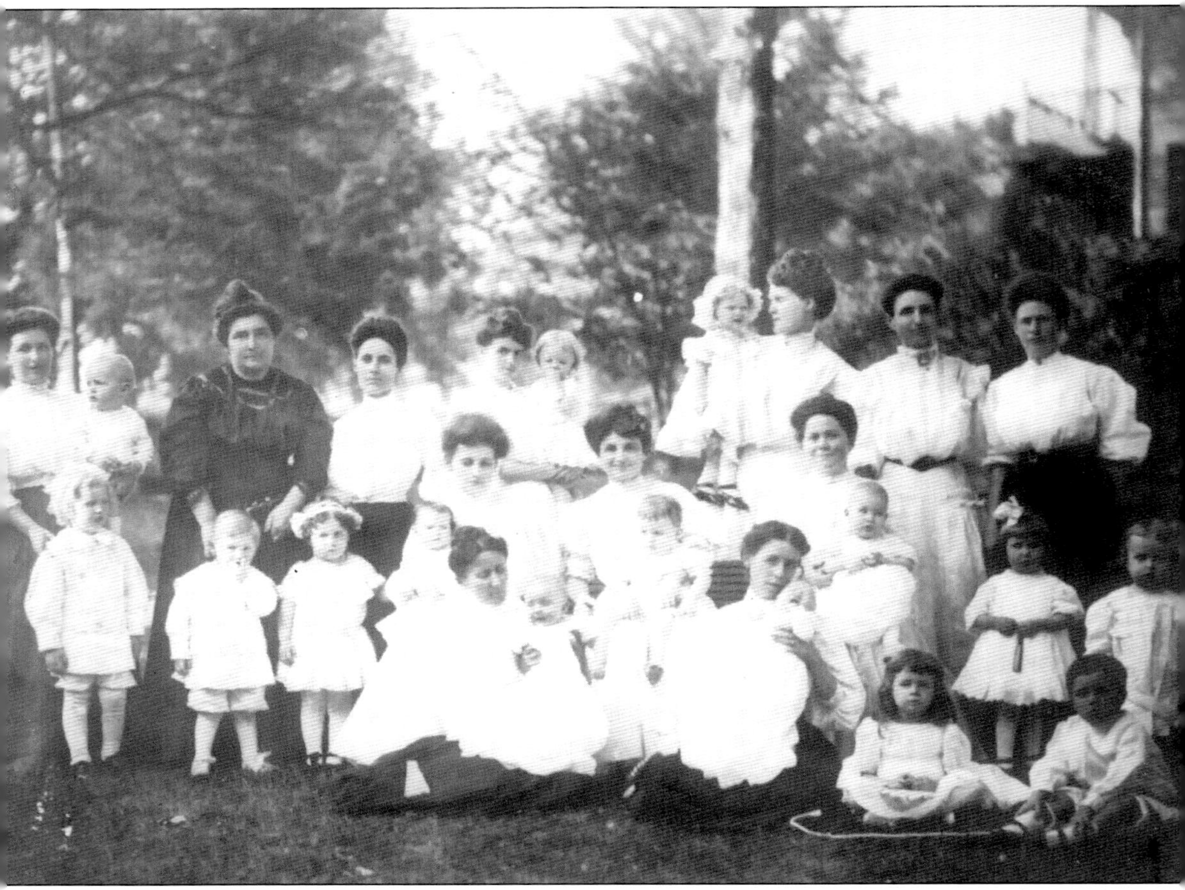

This Prize Baby Contest was held in Batesville on July 25, 1907. Only a few of these mothers and children have been identified. Standing at left is Mrs. W.P. Jones holding her son W.P. Jones Jr. In front of her is her daughter, Evelyn. Standing second from right is Mrs. I.N. Barnett; her little son Nels is seated right, front. Standing to Mrs. Barnett's right is believed to be Mrs. R.C. Dorr, holding her little daughter Dorothy. Also written on the back of the picture was largest child for age—Raymond Grant. (Roberta Dorr Brown)

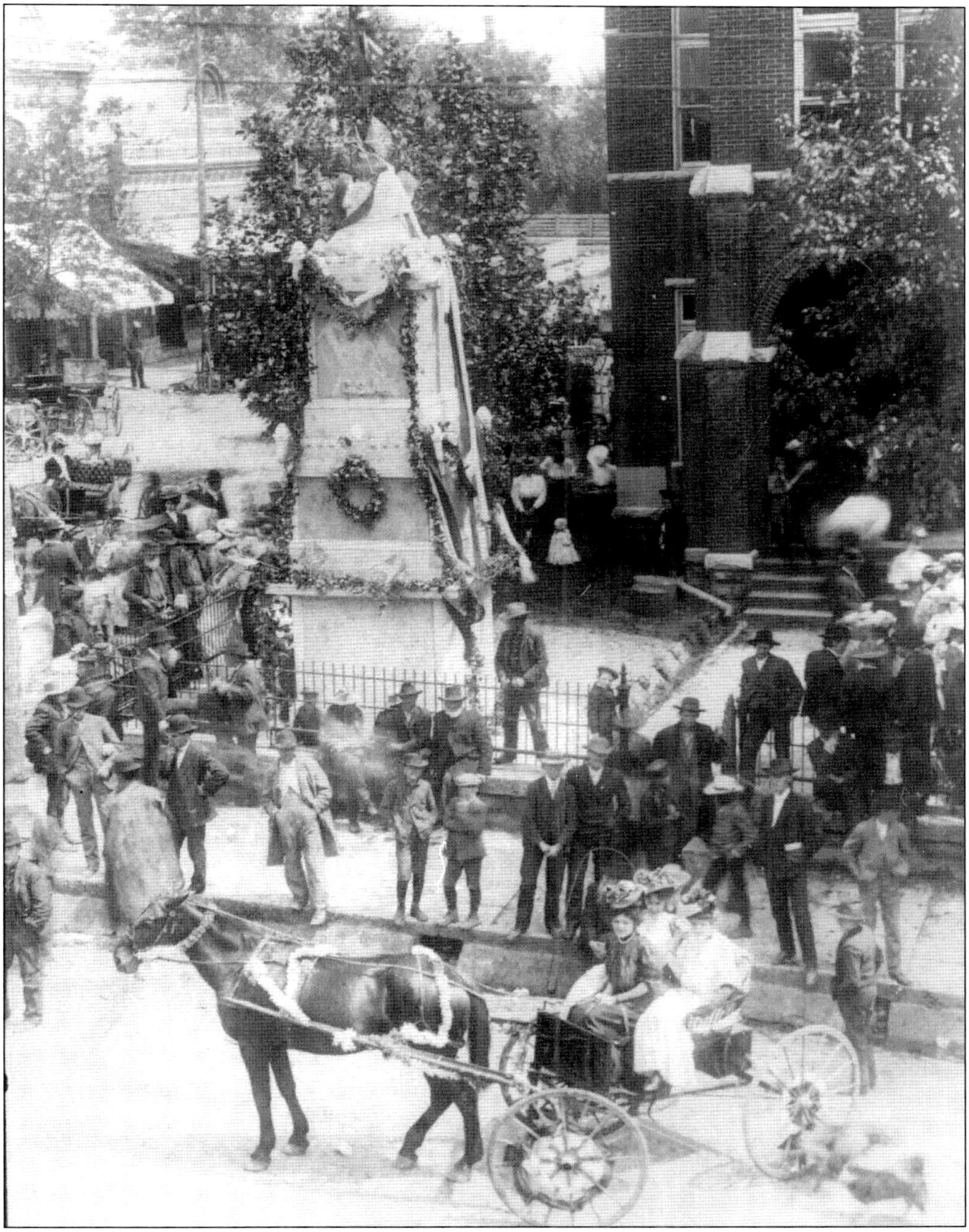

The turn of the century in the southern states saw a renewed interest in the Lost Cause of the Confederacy. As the participants of the War Between the States grew older and began to pass away, citizens of various locales throughout the South decided it was time to honor the sacrifices of the their soldiers. This monument was dedicated in 1907 on the courthouse lawn in Batesville. Inscribed on the monument are the names of 19 Confederate captains who were responsible for raising 23 companies of men from Independence County. Riding in the buggy to celebrate this occasion were Carrie Martin, Estelle Handford, and Nell Glenn. (Dora Le Ferguson)

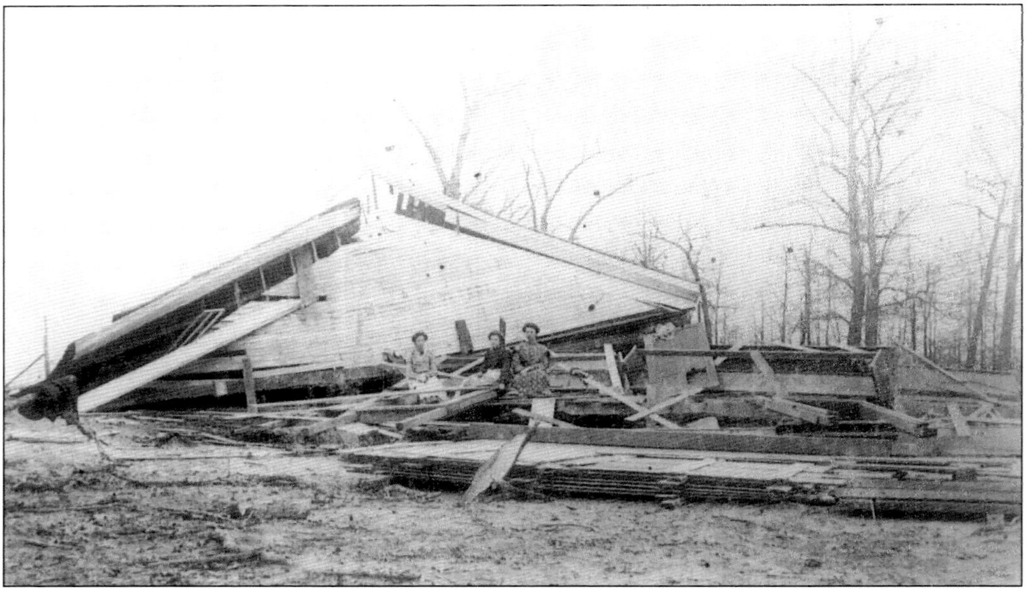

This is all that remained of the Hopewell Cumberland Presbyterian Church near Cord following a tornado on March 4, 1904. (Old Independence Regional Museum)

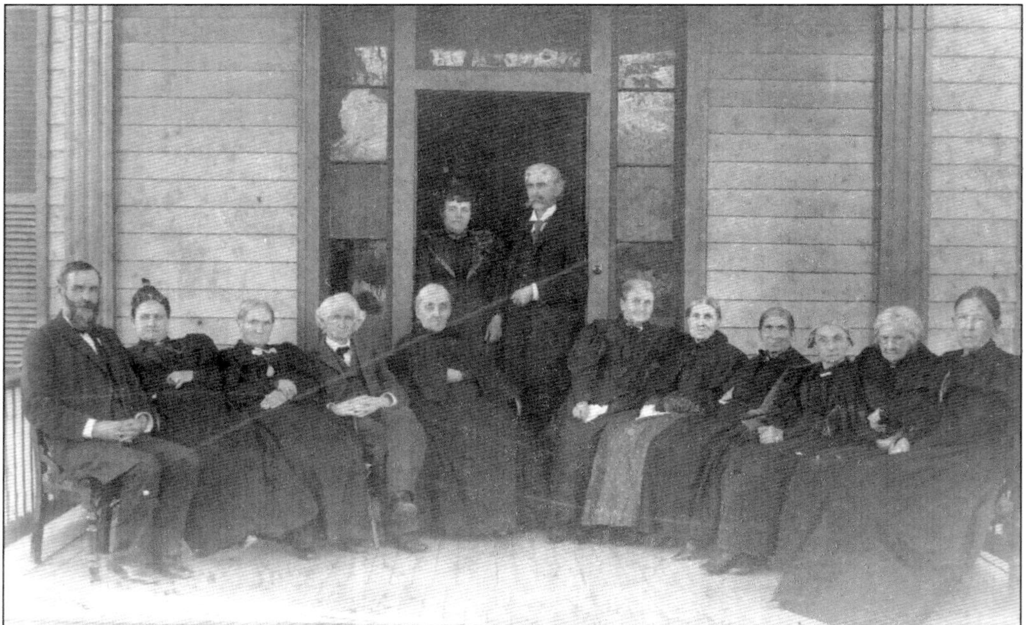

This picture was made at a tea given by Sarah Maxfield Glenn for a group of early Independence County settlers. Mrs. Glenn is standing in the doorway with her husband, J.W. Glenn. Shown from left to right are (seated) Rev. and Mrs. Sidney H. Babcock, Mrs. Judge Beaufort Neely, Mr. and Mrs. W.W. Glenn, Mrs. G.A. Baker, Mrs. Sarah Case, Mrs. Eleanor Spitler, Mrs. Narcissa Handford, Mrs. Mary Green, and Mrs. Sophia Lawrence. (Independence County Historical Society)

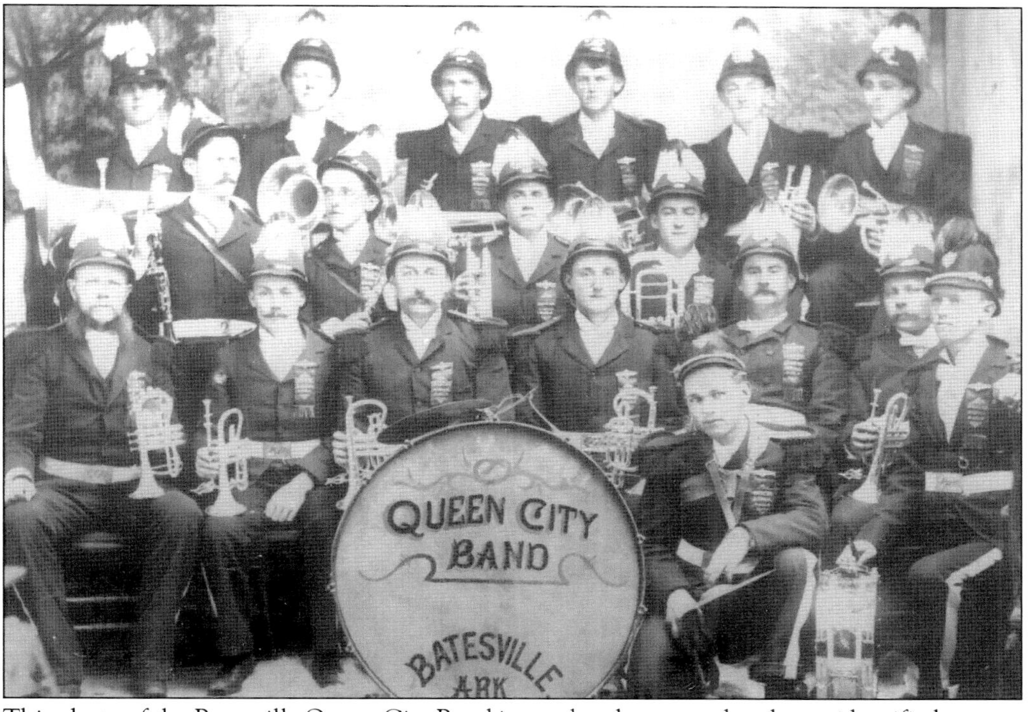

This photo of the Batesville Queen City Band is not dated, nor are the players identified, except for the young man at the extreme right of the top row. He is Walter Baker, father of the donor of the picture, Dora Le Ferguson.

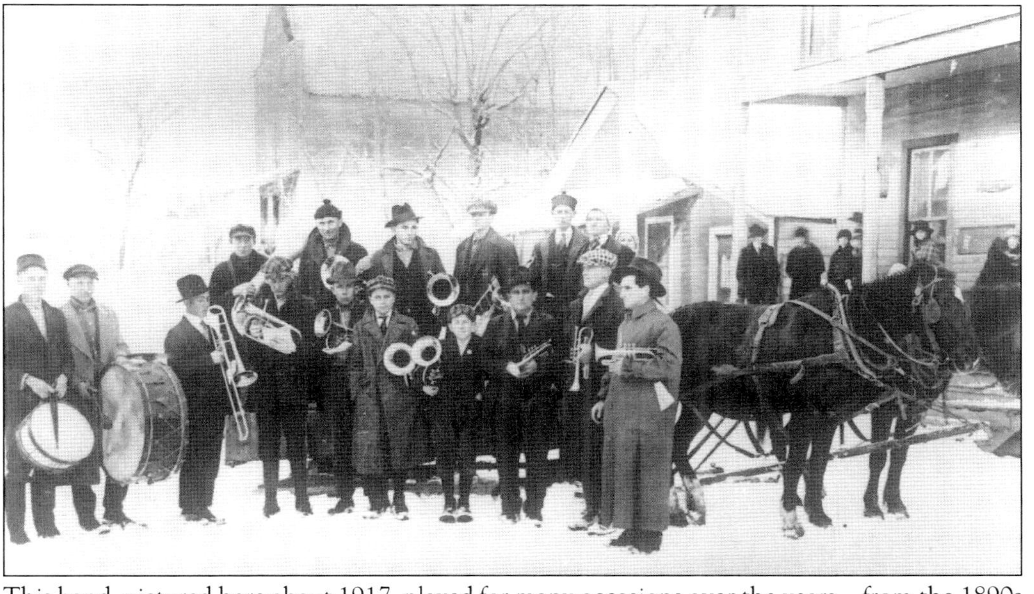

This band, pictured here about 1917, played for many occasions over the years—from the 1890s to 1921. They posed here in front of the Long Building, the major building in Jamestown before the big fire of 1921. Practice sessions were held in the building, and the band instruments and Band Wagon were stored in it. (Bubba Burks)

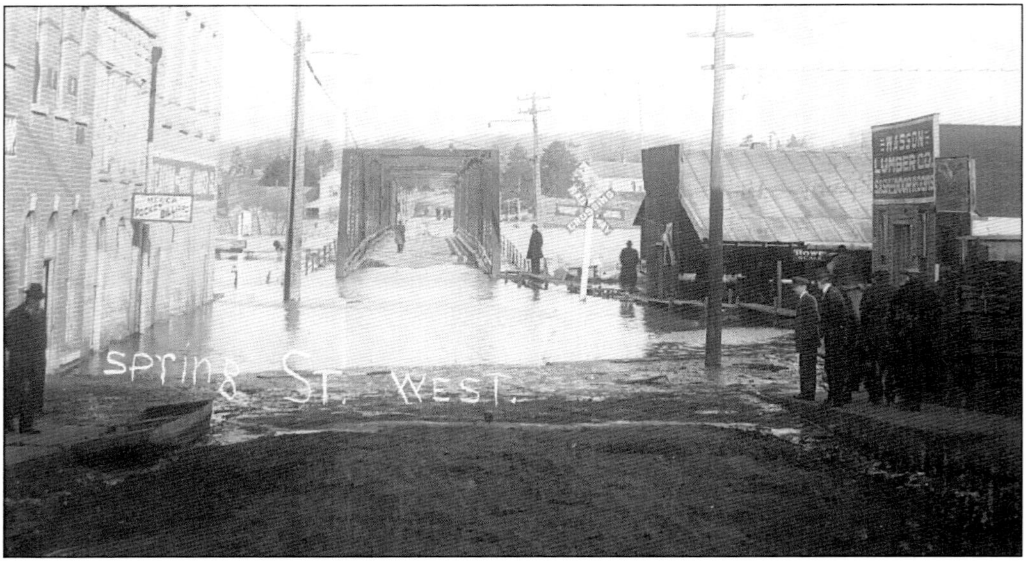

In years past it was not uncommon for Poke Bayou to flood out of its banks as in this 1916 photo. The view is looking west from Spring Street, now Central Avenue in Batesville. (Wilson Powell)

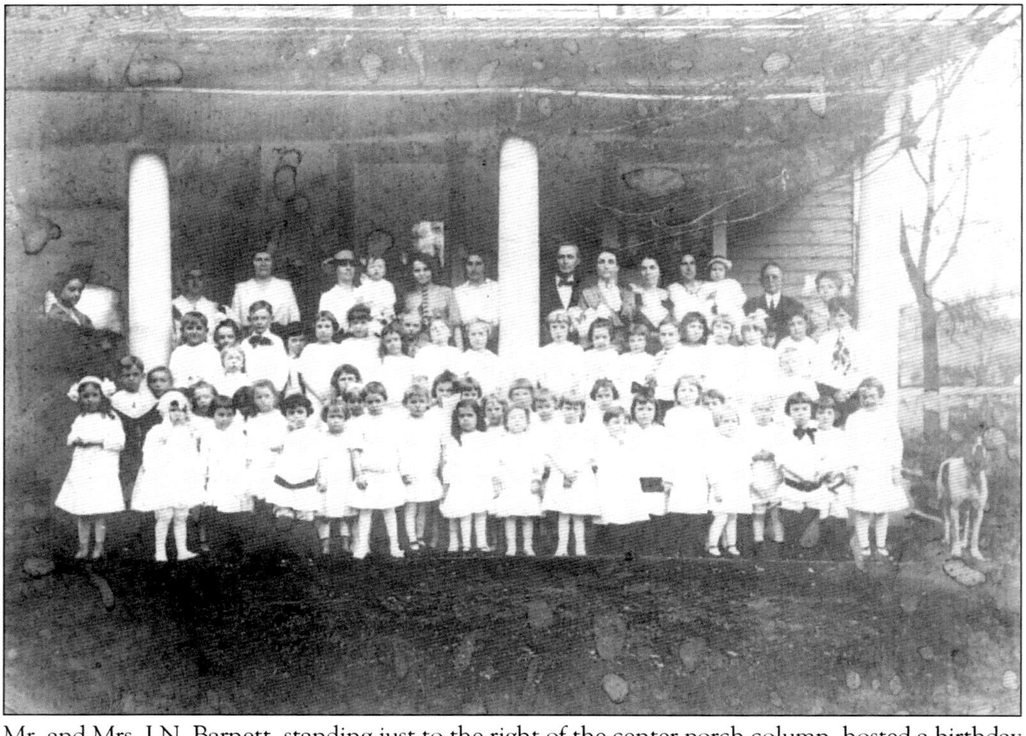

Mr. and Mrs. I.N. Barnett, standing just to the right of the center porch column, hosted a birthday party for their daughter, Mary Louise, about 1912. The group is posed on the front porch of the family's home on Main Street. Mary Louise, later Mrs. A.H. Hathcock, is the little girl with the big bow in her hair standing in front of her parents. (Independence County Historical Society)

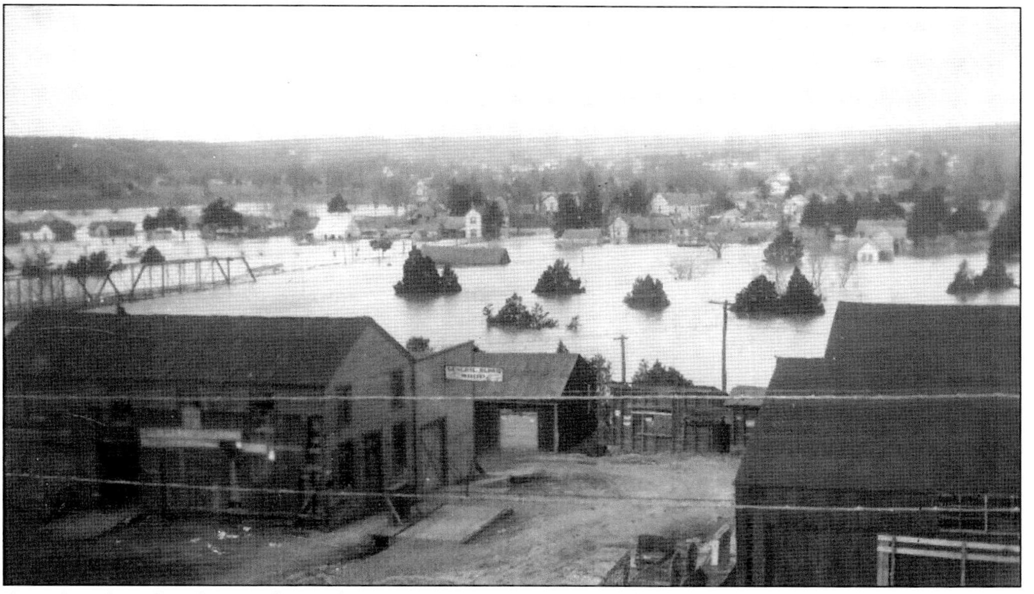

Another big flood year for Arkansas was 1927. During this flood 6,000 square miles, or 13 percent of the state, was underwater. This view of Poke Bayou was taken from Broad Street in Batesville. (Independence County Historical Society)

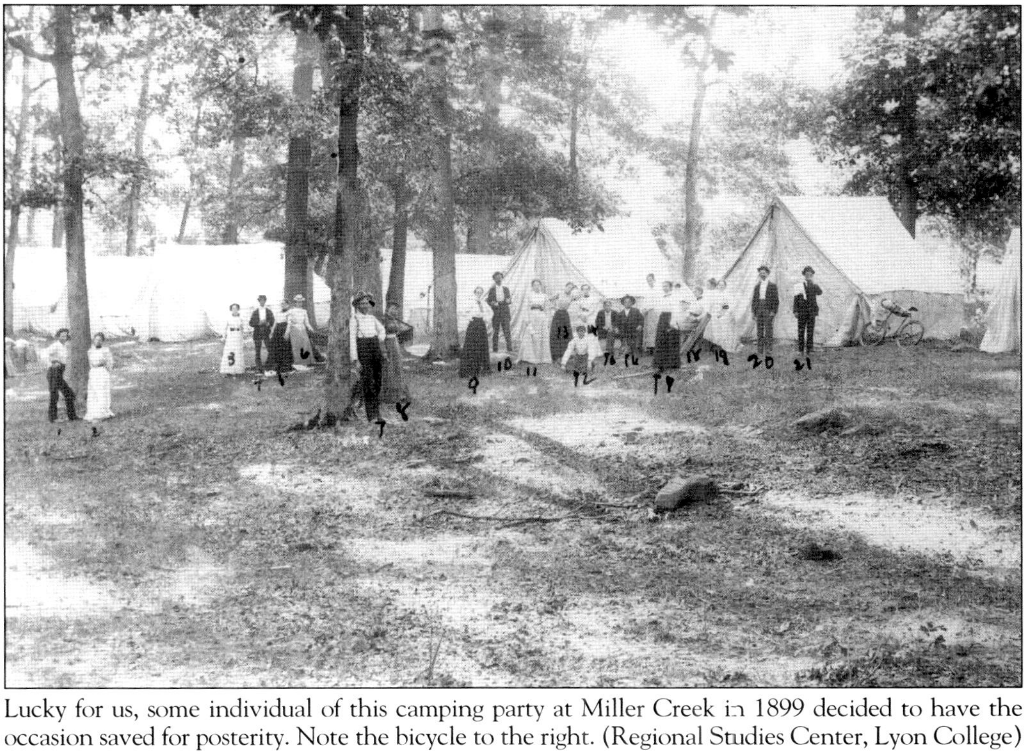

Lucky for us, some individual of this camping party at Miller Creek in 1899 decided to have the occasion saved for posterity. Note the bicycle to the right. (Regional Studies Center, Lyon College)

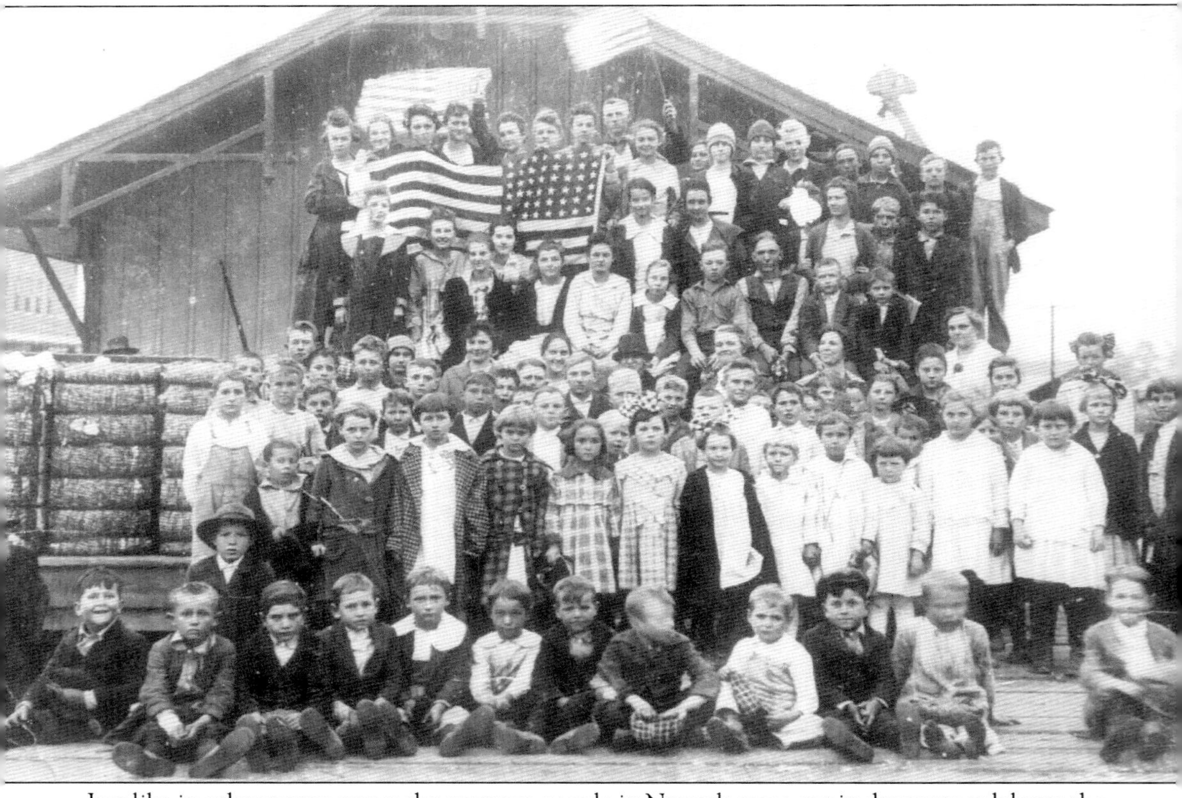

Just like in other towns across the country, people in Newark came out in droves to celebrate the end of World War I in November 1918. This group of children is posing in front of the Newark depot. (Craig-Lester-Stroud Collection)

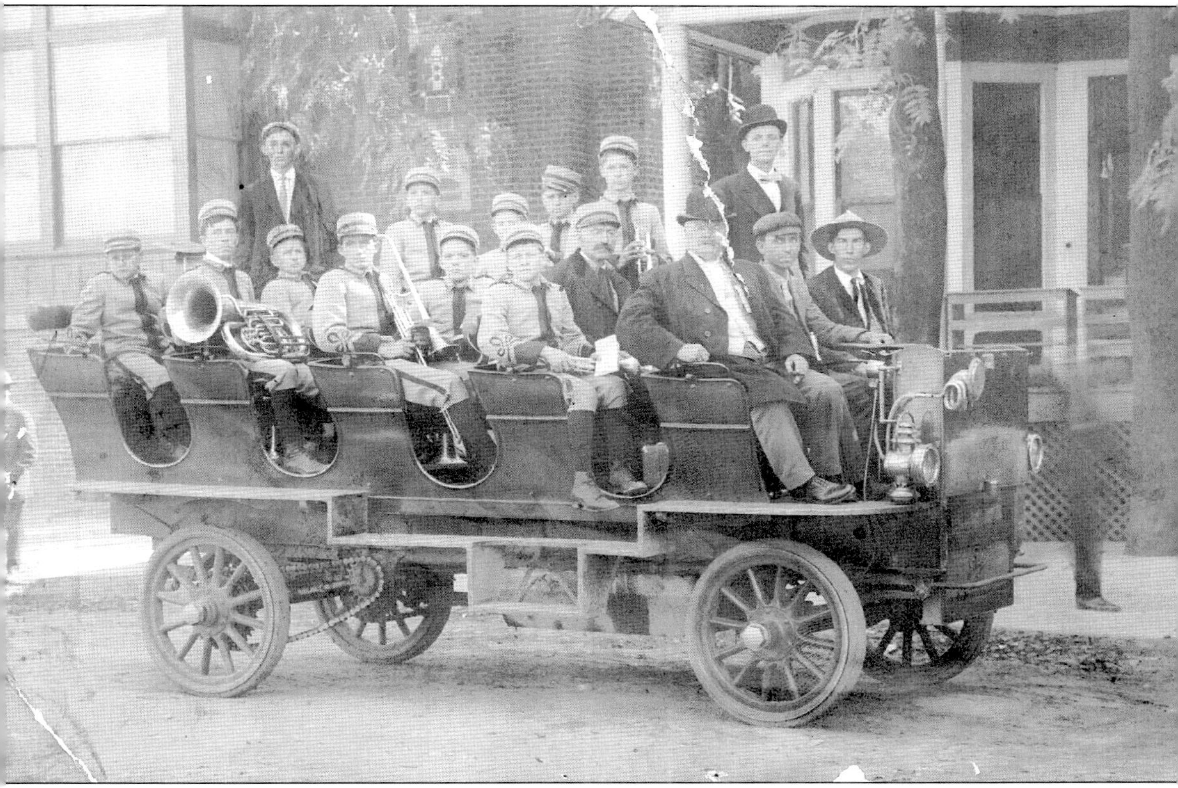

The Batesville Masonic Home Boys Band is ready to take off to their next big event in this early 20th century image. (Robert D. Craig)

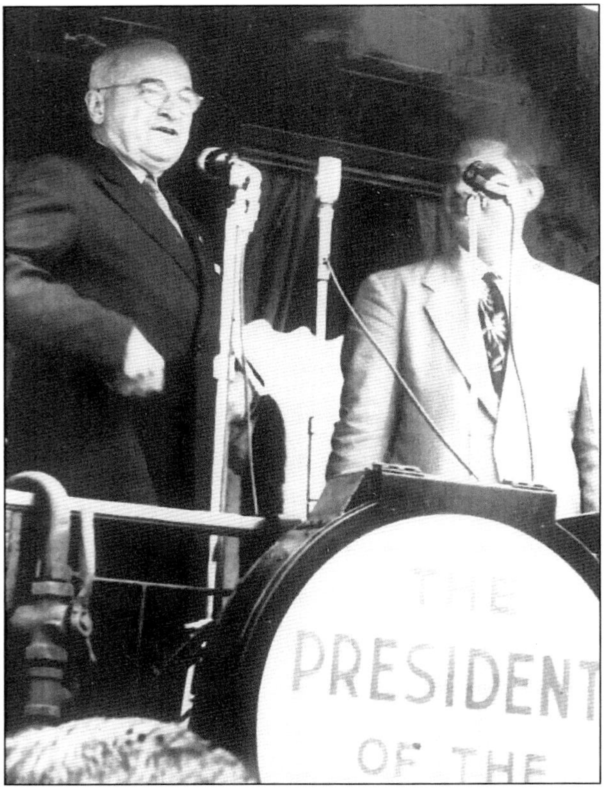

President Harry S. Truman barnstorming in Batesville with Representative Wilbur Mills during the election of 1948. (Independence County Historical Society)

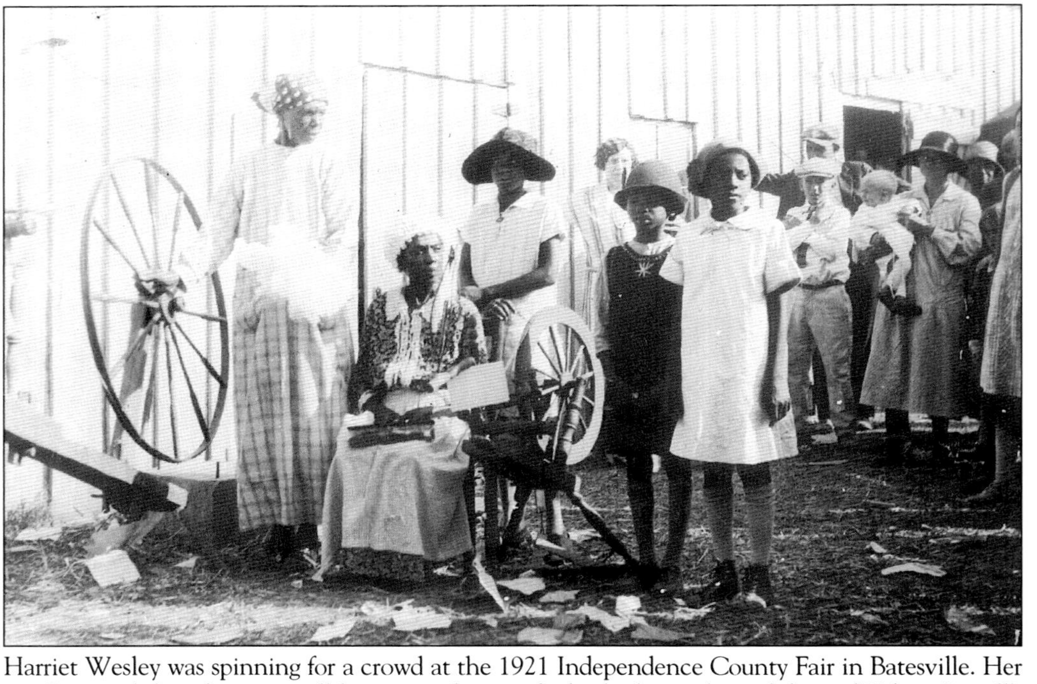

Harriet Wesley was spinning for a crowd at the 1921 Independence County Fair in Batesville. Her son Roosevelt later became well-known in the area for his basket making abilities. (Wilson Powell)

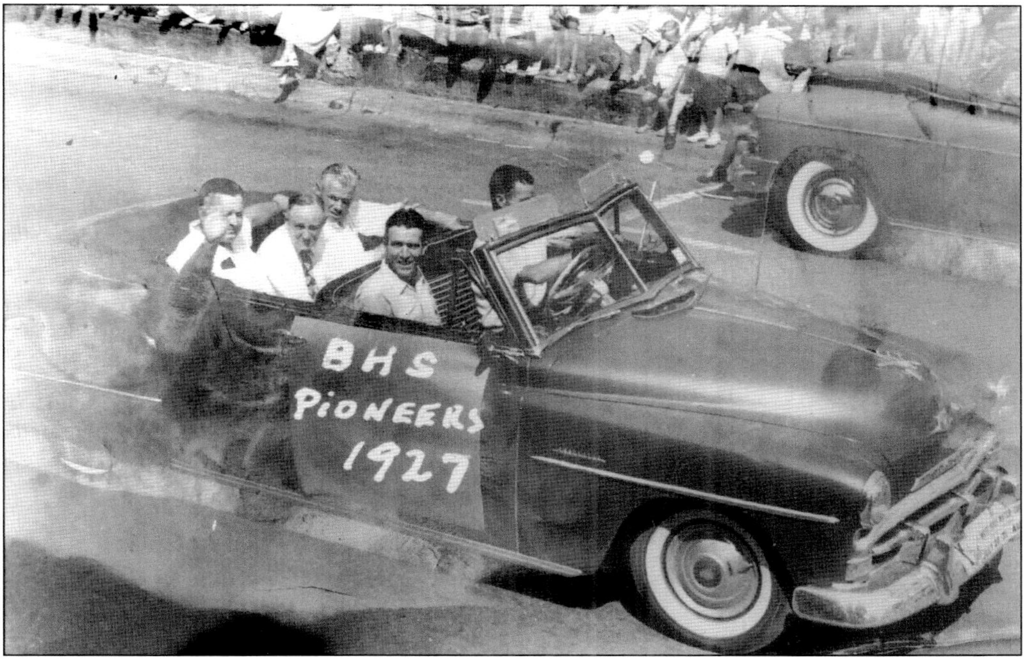

Members of the 1927 Batesville Pioneer basketball team came together years later for a reunion in the White River Carnival parade. The team made it to the national championships, but lost in the final round to Cicero, Illinois. Their coach, Duke Ward, is seated in the middle of the back seat. (Independence County Historical Society)

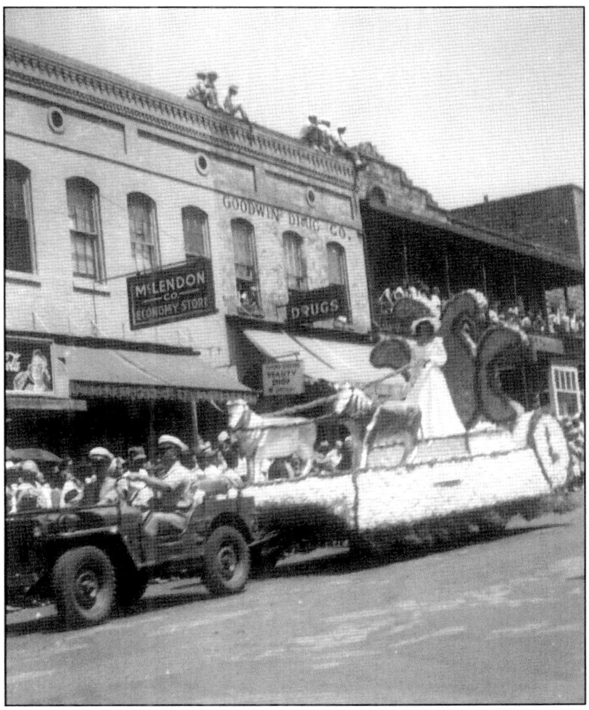

The White River Carnival is large event drawing in thousands of people every year during the dog days of summer. In this image one of the floats of the 1948 Water Carnival parade is traveling down Main Street in Batesville much to the enjoyment of the crowd. (Nancy Britton)

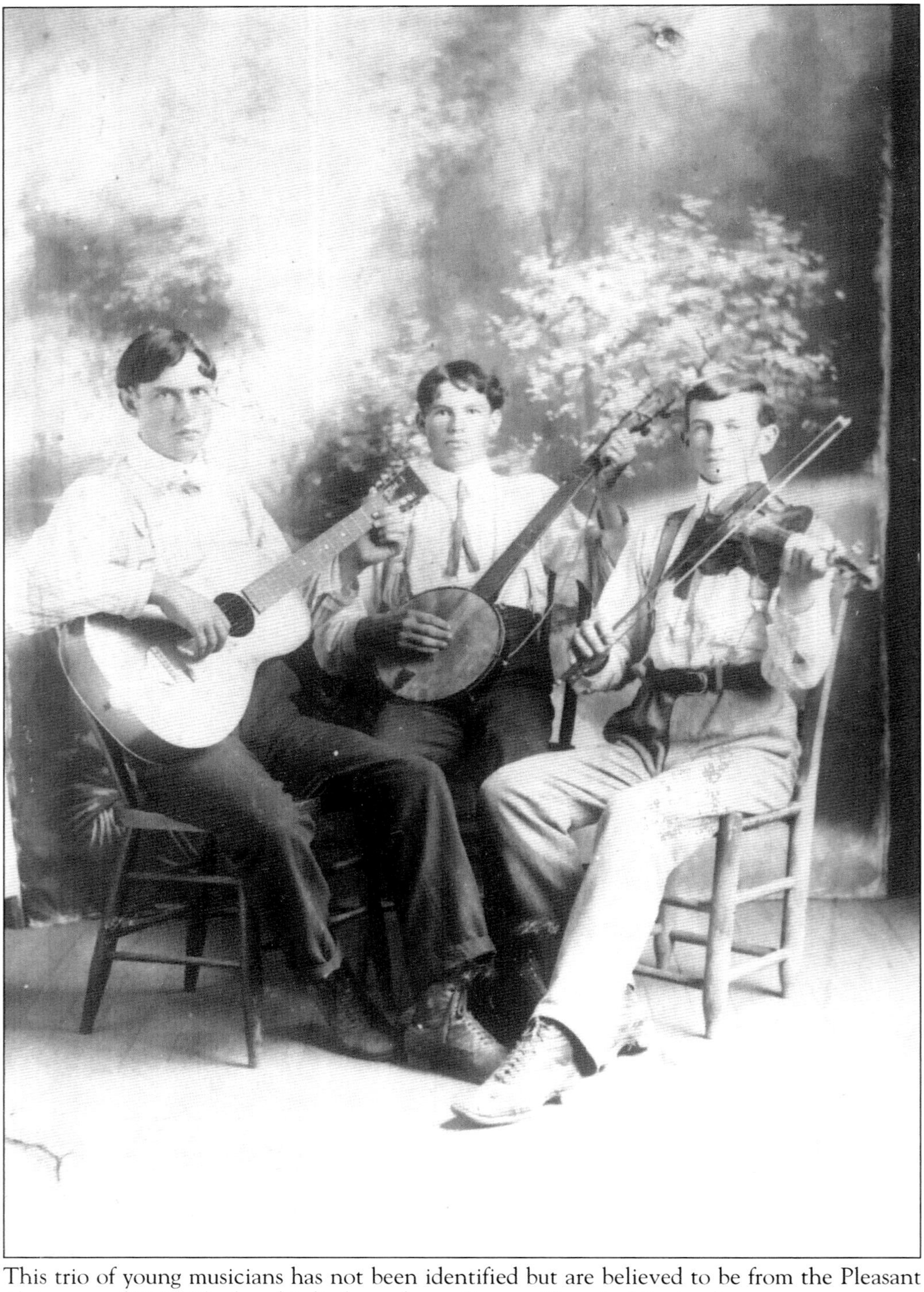

This trio of young musicians has not been identified but are believed to be from the Pleasant Plains area. (W.C. Blankenship/Independence County Historical Society)